Anna May Mangan has been shortlisted for the London Fringe Short Fiction Award, the RTE Radio/Frank MacManus Short Story Competition and was placed second in the 2008 Seán O'F____n Short Story Competition.

ME AND MINE

A warm-hearted memoir of a
London Irish Family

ANNA MAY MANGAN

virago

VIRAGO

First published in Great Britain in 2011 by Virago Press
Reprinted 2011

A CIP catalogue record for this book
is available from the British Library.

ISBN 978-1-84408-672-6

Typeset in Bembo by M Rules
Printed and bound in Great Britain by
Clays Ltd, St Ives plc

Papers used by Virago are from well-managed forests
and other responsible sources.

MIX
Paper from
responsible sources
FSC® C104740

Virago Press
An imprint of
Little, Brown Book Group
100 Victoria Embankment
London EC4Y 0DY

An Hachette UK Company
www.hachette.co.uk

www.virago.co.uk

For gentleman George, always

Prologue

The golden-haired bride was a symphony in cream chiffon. Floppy-hatted, soft-eyed and long-limbed she leant in, on tip-toes, to kiss her husband in celebration of their ten-minute anniversary. Wide-shouldered and straight-backed the groom adored her with his hands, circling the small of her back, cupping her elbows, and first softly blowing and then smoothing an escaped curl behind her ear. Silk on silk, her dress fused to his shirt as the cameras clicked. Friends gathered around, laughing in high notes and casting confetti.

Delicious, all of them. But theirs wasn't the wedding I'd been invited to. My lot were on their way. I could feel the ground shake as they made their way through the building and headed towards the exit.

The doors of the register office were shunted open by a nine-months-pregnant stomach deployed as a battering ram. It was encased in a frills with frills topped with frills dress. My cousin Aednat, a ruched blind on swollen ankles, moved like a tank to clear her space. With a hike of one of Aednat's heavily black-pencilled eyebrows, the elegant pair immediately understood their instruction. Too wise or too polite to argue, the beautiful people fluttered off and a satisfied Aednat shouted to her guests to gather round. 'Come on! It's our turn now.' Then she turned to kiss her new husband on his nose. This was flattened to the left side of his face and still blue and yellow from the recent bar brawl that had put it there. Both his hands were on his bride's backside as he steered her into position in the centre of the steps for a photo.

The wedding photographer had a full set of gold teeth and a large toy rifle that he used to marshal people into position for the group photographs. 'Get a move on for Chrissake! I need a bloody beer!' he growled, impatiently prodding stragglers into place. They obediently stood in line – men's hair smoothed, women's backcombed, dentures taken out of pockets, jammed into mouths (quick-licked to remove any fluff) and bared.

That afternoon was the last time my mum and her family were pictured together, six sisters and two brothers – the survivors into adulthood from a family of thirteen. I would love to have those wedding photographs in my family album, but they no longer exist. Less than a year later, Aednat burnt them on the command of her new love, the woman who had been the monumentally bored matron of honour at her first wedding.

Fuelled by passion, Aednat and her Spanish amour, a spiral-haired woman with a name that sounded like a heavy smoker clearing their throat, lit a bonfire to purge their past. They constructed a pyramid of memories and then razed it: those precious extended-family photos included, in the communal gardens of their council flat home. Some of the clothes they were wearing made it onto the bonfire, which sparked the following headline in the local paper, 'Drunken Irishwoman flouts UK decency laws'. Aednat read it with glee and was hugely disappointed they didn't include her photograph. Aednat bear-wrestled with life and when she saw illness ravage the women dearest to her she became even more outrageous. 'Cancer might get me young, too,' said Aednat, 'and if I'm not living long, I may as well live wide!'

What started as a fling led to a commitment ceremony two years after conducted by a female bus driver who had done a US-based correspondence training course to qualify as a lay minister. My mum and I were on the guest list, but the invitation stated that the wearing of fascinators was compulsory so she refused to go, uttering one word by way of explanation, 'Pagans!' Followed after a long thoughtful pause by, 'Go and buy a wedding card for them les-beans.' She said the word with an undeniable spark of curiosity in her eyes.

Those precious photographs and an entire generation – all ashes now.

1

Shoes, Suitcase and a Suit

It was like they ran a relay race to the cemetery, and cancer was the baton. I became the reluctant family matriarch before I reached forty. My predecessors were two Irish families who built new lives for themselves in London, and pretended, with great cheer, not to notice that they were despised by the locals. One by one, they arrived in 1950s England to nothing but a huge welcome from each other. My dad described Londoners as 'miserable feckers' because no one ever greeted him in the street. When he first arrived the man was kept busy tipping his hat and offering a cheery 'Howaya?', 'Good morning!' or 'Good afternoon!' to everyone he met, just like at home. There it would be unthinkable not to acknowledge a passer-by on the road. His elder brother Jem warned him to stop being so nice. 'You're looking simple, so you are. Someone'll give you a puck in the snot if you don't pack that in. Get it into your thick skull, Andy, they hate you.'

One of my dad's first cousins, Lizzine, arrived at Euston

Station at dawn on a train connection from the Holyhead ferry. Unable to read or write, she had memorised her brother's instructions about how to get to his address in Baker Street where he had a live-in job in a pub. For a subsistence wage, he worked all hours and hadn't dared to ask for time off to collect his sister. The very important Getting To London instructions were repeated in Lizzine's head and under her breath a few hundred times on her eighteen-hour journey. She had recalled the train, boat, train ones but came a cropper on the last leg, Lizzine's first trip on a London bus. Her brother had drummed into her, 'Be sure to get off the bus at the big building with columns and steps flanked by lions. Count eight bus stops from the train station and then you'll see it.' Lizzine was barely five feet tall and had a suit-case almost as high as herself. A storm of freckles, she was clutching a St Christopher medal tight in her left hand that she had not put down since she left Ireland fourteen hours before. Swaying on the open platform of the fast-moving bus she was perplexed as to why it pulled in at some stops and not others. She was unsure about whether to count the ones that flew by, or only the ones where it stopped. Her brother had warned her not to speak to anyone because if she did she would surely be abducted – a daily occurrence in London, he told her – which is why she didn't dare ask for help. In her whirling up, up and away when-to-get-off-the-bus panic, Lizzine didn't make a con-nection between the bell ringing and the bus stopping. Craning her neck she searched for pillars and steps and lions and to her horror saw them flash by and recede into the distance. And now she was hurtling into the dark heart of a big city where she would surely be lost and never found. Lizzine picked up her suitcase, kissed her St Christopher medal and threw herself off the plat-form of the moving bus in the hopeful direction of the pavement.

St Mary's Hospital, Praed Street was Lizzine's first London address. As an in-patient, there for two weeks with head injuries and a broken left arm. Always a half-glass-full sort of girl, Lizzine regularly told staff and other patients that it was St Christopher who had protected her from death overseas and in thanks and praise she held her medal of the Saint aloft using her unbroken right arm during all her waking hours. St Christopher, Patron Saint of Travellers, hadn't been working alone. She believed it was he and St Drogo, Patron Saint of Broken Bones, who had teamed up to arrange her recovery, under the directorship of St Anthony, Patron Saint of Miracles.

My relatives arrived in London with hopeful hearts – all teenagers, barely literate, dangerously naive and shot through with a heavyweight work ethic. One job wasn't enough; each of them had two or three unskilled jobs apiece, and after the bills were paid, there still wasn't a penny to show for their efforts. Whatever the Latin is for 'We didn't have a pot to piss in' should be my family motto, I heard it said so many times, and it was just as true in London as it had been in Ireland.

Leaving home was a simple 'sail or starve' choice. There was no work in rural Ireland, nor any prospect of it for my aunts and uncles. My nan's expression 'It's easy to half the potato where there's love' was drowned out by the rumbling of hungry bellies. Letters home from friends and neighbours already working in London told proudly of flushing toilets, electricity, hot running water and dances seven nights a week and in the afternoons, too. 'The bands over here are out of this world,' wrote Auntie Peggy, after a few nights stepping the boards in the Irish dance halls. 'They do send us home sweating!' Hearing that was my mother's tipping point; she ached to dance herself sweaty too. She was the next in line to set sail.

They would have loved to travel to England in twos and threes, but had to wait and save up for the three 'S's' – shoes, suitcase and a suit – before departure. My grandma said, 'The arse of the trousers in them suits was as thin as a spider's web by the time they all got work in London.' The suitcase containing the suit and shoes (or replacements bought in England) would be posted or brought back on a visit for the next brother or sister to use. One by one, according to who was older or had most common sense, they set off for London. In a state of high excitement they sailed, envied by the brothers and sisters they left behind, who were all counting the hours until it would be their turn to leave. Their mother taught herself to offer a bright, brave smile, a kiss and a 'get going' kind of hug to each of her departing sons and daughters. And no matter what they earnestly promised her as they set off, she knew there would be no coming back.

Some didn't have the patience to save up for the fare. Uncle Tom, one of Dad's six brothers, stole a cow from a neighbour and sold it for £10 to pay his passage to England. Every penny he earned when he first arrived in London was saved to repay the neighbour, and within three months he had enough to post back the price of the stolen cow with generous interest. A note of sincere apology was included along with the banknotes. He dictated this to a friend because he wasn't at all good at writing himself, and when he signed and posted the letter he said he enjoyed the feeling of a clear conscience for the first time since he'd left Ireland. It was a feeling that didn't last long, because the money came back by return post from the neighbour. He enclosed a letter in which he called my uncle Tom a 'scut' and a 'blaggard' and described the money as soiled and unlucky. The neighbour cursed him inside out for breaking the eighth commandment, 'Thou shall not steal', and warned that no good luck would ever come his way in England after what he had done. My uncle got someone to read the long letter aloud to him and listened intently, nodding along. Afterwards, his eyes watery with tears, he said, 'Didn't God himself say we were to forgive one another?' Years later he said, 'That fecking cow walked through every dream I've ever had. I wish I'd never laid a hand on it.'

Another of Dad's brothers, Patrick, took two years to save enough money to travel to England. He kept his precious getaway stash in a tea caddy that was well hidden from his brothers and sisters. For sure, if they'd known where Patrick's savings were, they would have been dipping in and cheerfully spending his money as fast as he could save it. The hidey-hole for his stash was a ledge in the small barn that ran alongside their cottage. It lay up there in a bed of straw tucked out of sight, and a ladder was needed to get to it. But Patrick had a problem that would separate him from his precious money, and he didn't even know it. He was a sleepwalker. In the dead of night and fast asleep he would regularly climb out of the communal bed, clambering over the prone bodies of his brothers, and head out for the barn. One night he was followed out there by the five lanky and curly-haired lads whose sleep he had disturbed. Patrick was in the land of dreams, and that night he took his brothers to the land of their dreams, too, when he led them out into the moonlight to the barn, up the ladder and straight to his money pile. Patrick felt with his fingers for his tin, gave it a reassuring shake and headed back to bed. Even the sound of his five delighted brothers, all bent double with laughter, didn't wake Patrick up.

That money was used to buy a sailing ticket to England, but not by the person who had saved it up. Uncle Joseph, a year younger than prudent Patrick, helped himself and took off ahead of his older brother. As soon as he had made enough in England, Joseph paid his brother back. He sent over the fare money for Patrick to join him, which he did. Joseph met his brother from the boat train at Euston Station and got knocked out cold onto the platform floor with a single punch. 'Now I'm paying *you* back,' said Patrick, as his fist met his brother's face.

They owned nothing between them, no houses, no cars, no valuables of any kind. Funerals were their biggest spend. They were a generation without engagement rings, best china or even a firsthand coat.

You need to get up close to see that Mum and Dad's wedding photograph is of their special day because there are no flowers, no bridal dress and my dad's black curls are slicked back with margarine because he couldn't afford Brylcreem. His bride, too skint for stockings, browned her Celtic egg-white legs with tea for the ceremony. It was a no razzle-dazzle affair that took place over sixty years ago, my parents captured on film in their Sunday best, pure beaming at the camera.

To celebrate, the newlyweds took themselves off to Lyons Tea House in the Strand for a pot of tea and some scones. They clinked cups to the following toast: 'May more than a fence run around our garden.' That was a wish for children, dogs, cats, a house and a little bit of lawn. A tall order for two penniless, unskilled Irish immigrants. Their hope had no boundaries.

Unfashionably poor, a long way from his Irish home and barely educated, my dad managed to misspell his surname on their wedding certificate. He did this even though he had been practising the all-important signature for weeks beforehand under the tutelage of his elder brother Thomas. Thomas was considered the family scholar because he was working as a bus conductor in south London.

In that illiterate moment, Dad acquired a family surname that was different to all twelve of his brothers and sisters and all of his forefathers. My mum, who couldn't read very well herself, didn't even notice what he had signed, and didn't care either. 'I was too busy gazing into his eyes,' she said, laughing, when she explained our surname shift to us years later.

The newlyweds shared a birthplace, a birthday and twelve siblings apiece, and a simple belief that everything in their lives was, and would continue to be, quite wonderful. Born not into cribs but wooden boxes in cottages ten miles apart and reared in a crowd, they were natural sharers. Clothes, beds, boots – nothing was theirs alone, and this shaped their sweet and generous sensibilities. My mum said that even a single small orange would be shared thirteen ways in her home. She called sharing their way of loving one another, and it was dubbed 'the nature'. This was something you had if you were very lucky, like she and her family had been. It was there in the way they made a big pile of themselves when they were together, squashing up and moulding together in preparation for a chat. And in how the notes of their conversation overlapped and yet harmonised – even though there might be four or five of them talking at once. And it was definitely in their gaze. They didn't look at one another, they looked into one another. When my brother and sister and I quarrelled as children, she would observe us and lament, 'You haven't got the nature.' This was a worse correction for me than any slap. It made my young head hurt working out that 'the nature', whilst it was apparently all about sharing, couldn't be shared out. You either had it or you didn't.

My dad got punched in his freckled, sixteen-year-old face on the September day in 1950 he arrived in London for the first time. The big-fisted policeman who stopped him on a street in Cricklewood was brusque. Open notebook at the ready, he demanded Dad's name and to know what business he had in the area. 'I'm Andy Mannion, sir,' my dad answered with his blinding smile, 'and I've just come from Hollywood.'

He had momentarily confused Holyhead in North Wales, where his ferry from Dublin had docked, with Hollywood USA. An easy mistake to make when you've only been to places in your dreams. But the policeman was convinced he was being made fun of, and within moments Dad was laid out on the pavement seeing stars, and not of the Sunset Boulevard variety. The officer then leant over, took aim and spat down onto Dad's face, warning him to learn fast never to take the piss, and then went away to do more good work elsewhere. Dad stood up, wiped the spit and blood from his face and carried on walking the streets, looking for a house that might offer him cheap lodging.

Cricklewood was a great place for the Irish, so the Jamaican toilet cleaner at Euston Station had told him – three bus rides and a lot of walking earlier. That cleaner was the first black man my dad had ever seen in the flesh, and he was blissfully unaware that in London the black man was considered to be his brother.

Many of the properties in the street where he was hoping to find a room had signs prominently displayed in their front windows that read 'NO BLACKS, NO DOGS, NO IRISH', but because Dad couldn't read or write, he went ahead and knocked anyway.

Years later, when I was in primary school, Dad took my brother and sister and me on a mystery tour. It began with a visit to see that room in Cricklewood, his first London home, and ended, as all of our outings with him always did, behind a pyramid of whipped cream in a Tennessee Pancake House. Pancakes, gateaux, éclairs, fudge or nougat – my dad was a hard-line sugar addict and my brother and sister and I were his devotees. But no matter how hard we tried, he would out-eat the three of us combined every time we went out together.

We got off the bus and the house was right there in front of us. Tall, mean, thin, his old lodging house leant sharply to the left and was long overdue for demolition. Health and safety laws were decades away, and the front door simply swung loose on its broken hinges. A rubbish skip in the front garden was piled high with original panelled doors and Victorian fireplaces.

As he crossed its threshold that day, Dad suddenly choked up. He disguised this punch of emotion as a cough and waved at the air in front of his face with his big, hard hands. But I saw his features shift in a way he couldn't control, and my knees went soft with a mix of love and fear that he might somehow break and what would happen if he did. 'Sweat and boiled cabbage, can you smell it?' he asked us, claiming that the same air from fifteen years before still hung sour in the air.

A flight of giggly seesaw stairs took us to his former 'room', a cupboard which housed a single bed that extended out into the landing so his door could never close. Dad claimed the other lodgers would tickle his huge bare feet, which jutted out into the hallway when he slept, on Thursday nights as they passed his room. We children wanted to know why they only got tickled on a Thursday. 'Because Thursday was Paddy's pay day and we'd been to the pubs,' he answered. My brother asked him who

Paddy was, and Dad touched his face and said, 'He's you, son, and be proud of him.' We didn't understand what he meant; my brother was called Michael, but we could see that Dad's eyes were shining and heard the emotional rat-tat-tat wobble in his voice, so we decided this Paddy must be a good guy.

He told us the landlord's rules were: No Food, No Visitors, No Music or Singing and No Flushing after 9.30pm, and that all lodgers had to get out and stay out of the house between the hours of 8am and 8pm.

The single communal bathroom was on the floor above and the toilet itself was on a raised platform of wobbly planks and topped with a square wooden seat with a vast overhang. Dad said it had been the most comfortable place in London to have a sit-down. The overhead cast-iron cistern was wall-mounted and when Dad flushed it to scare us there was a metal and water explosion. Next to the toilet, in a dome of dusty dead spiders, was a small box of what I thought was greaseproof paper – I'd seen my nan use it when she baked – but my dad explained it was actually toilet paper that 'sliced not wiped'.

That toilet was shared by fourteen men, and he told us how it blocked and overflowed every day. There was a claw-footed bath in there, too; in good condition when I saw it. Dad said that was because it was barely used – for bathing anyway. 'Can you keep a secret from your mother?' Dad asked, and we all nodded nervously knowing full well we were making a false promise. She would stare any secrets out of us as soon as we got home. But he seemed convinced by our pathetic pledge and confided that on many a morning as one lodger sat on the 'throne', others would be chatting and laughing about the day ahead and doing what was urgent and necessary down into the huge cast-iron bath.

14

If anyone said the word 'bath' within earshot of me, I heard 'torture trap'. At the time we visited Dad's old lodgings, we were living in a council house in north-west London with bath-room facilities that involved a lot of heave-ho. There was an outside loo, just about bum-bearable in summer but that would administer ice burns like savage dog bites in winter. For wash-ing, bodies, clothes, dogs and anything else that wouldn't fit in the kitchen sink, we used a tin bath.

This steely receptacle spent all week chilling to perfection on a hook in the garden until Saturday nights. That was when all five of us would get a dousing and de-lousing and a hairwash in preparation for Mass on Sunday morning. My mum would make the sign of the cross and claim that the Pope himself had decreed that every Catholic should bathe on a Saturday night, and that we would go immediately to hell if we didn't strip off and submit to a soaping. There were definitely some fine folk of the parish who ignored the Pope's 'washing for Mass' dictate. Easy enough to spot, they stood in the pews in front of us and we could see busy lice rushing all over the men's shirt collars and red shaved necks. The women were probably crawling with lice as well, but their hair curls provided big loopy hiding places for them.

My dad's get-knocked-down, get-up-again-and-try-one-more-time spirit was his glow-in-the-dark quality. It got him a room in a house where he wasn't wanted and it got him a job. Most significantly of all it got him a date, eventually, with the grey-eyed, black-haired girl who worked alongside him there, bagging and weighing sweets. That girl was my mum, Annie. The couple met on the Pick 'n' Mix counter in Woolworths on the Edgware Road in London, even though they had lived less than ten miles apart in their native land.

Dad was exactly one year older than Annie. For every birthday they shared after they met, all gifts were refused. They insisted, year after year, that each was the other's birthday present and that that was plenty. What clinched their love deal was a very special bond – from the Woolworths Pick 'n' Mix counter they both ranked Rhubarb-and-Custards and Jazz Drops as their equal favourites. It was a match made in heaven.

It took Mum almost a year to agree to go on a date with Dad, all because of boozy, brassy Bridie Scanlon. She ruled the chip fryer in Woolworths cafeteria and slyly appointed herself as Mum's confidante and adviser in all matters romantic.

Bridie insisted that playing hard to get would pay dividends for my inexperienced Mum where Dad was concerned. Bridie fancied Dad rotten and was convinced that if Mum refused him often enough, he'd eventually get around to asking her out on a date instead. She always managed to take her breaks when Dad took his and would sit opposite, blinding him with her high-shine ketchup-red lips. Bridie would then set about cutting up, spearing and feeding him his sausages – steaming chunk after hot steaming chunk. All the while Bridie assured my mum that these lunchtime sessions were essential so that she could properly establish and examine his suitor potential. 'Annie, I'm making sure he's good enough for you,' claimed Bridie.

Mum witnessed this spectacle day in day out for months, waiting for Dad to get savvy and cut up his own sausages. She could see very well that he was flattered and terrified by Bridie in equal parts, and feared that he might be marooned in the Woolworths staff canteen eating chopped-up sausage until they were both old and grey. So she made a decision. Two, actually. The first was that Bridie was a malevolent banger-bearing man-hunter – and the second was that it was way past time to claim

16

Dad as her own. So after almost a year, and a stack of hot sausages, my mum finally agreed to go on a date with him.

Bridie Scanlon was enraged by this development. She'd worked hard to get Dad's attention and wanted revenge on the pretty worm that had turned. Alight with humiliation and indignation, Bridie stamped back to her chip fryer but not before she announced over the store's tannoy system, 'Andy Mannion's got the biggest ears I've ever seen and if you make it up the aisle with him, you little fecking bitch, you'll surely be tripping over them!'

She was right. And wrong. My dad was drop-dead gorgeous in a just-can't-help-it kind of way – dark-haired and six foot two with the sort of natural teeth that looked like they slept in a jar by the bed. His ears were big and hilarious and that was fine by him, and Mum, too.

Mum had black hair and pale skin and when I first saw pictures of Snow White in my story books, I thought she and my mum were one and the same person. With oval grey eyes, a straight nose and full red lips, Mum was much more than just the sum of her fine features. Her face was a study in good grace and kindness and when she was in a room it was hard to look away from her. People at bus stops and in shops and doctors' waiting rooms would often remark on her face. I've heard it called 'lovely' and 'kindly' and 'soft', by complete strangers. She would blush a little, always say thank you and smile her sweet eye-sucking smile that made people stare even more.

In later years her face was slashed with long, deep worry lines, at least one for every person she cared about. But on their wedding day Mum and Dad were living testimony to the power of love and optimism. They had found one another and couldn't believe their luck, and that sense of wonder never left them during almost forty years of marriage.

On their thirty-ninth wedding anniversary, the immediate family had a small tea party to celebrate the occasion. It was a low-key affair because by then Mum and Dad were both ravaged by illness. But that afternoon the two of them managed to dance together. It was the last time they ever would. Cardigan to cardigan, Dad's chin rested on Mum's white curls and they leant into one another for support. The pair swayed a lot and shuffled a little in their slippers to 'The Wonder of You' by The Platters.

Over the decades their bodies may have become frail and the precious spark of good health may have dimmed, but their love and devotion grew brighter with each hour they shared. They locked eyes. Dad's were yellowed with disease and Mum's were hooded and so tired, but long after the music was finished they held on and on with arms and hearts that *never* wanted to let go.

2
Ceilis and Curls

Their first married home in London was a rented bedsit in a house in Bayswater with a shared bathroom and toilet. A dump, but nevertheless a step-up of sorts from where they were raised in Ireland. My first memory of the cottage where my dad was born is of thinking it was their garden shed. And that was from my perspective at the time – a ten-year-old girl who lived in a two-up two-down council house without a bathroom or toilet and thought that was lovely and roomy.

Fifteen of them, my grandfather, grandmother, dad and his twelve siblings, all called a cottage with one room downstairs and two bedrooms upstairs, home. The space downstairs was big enough for a dresser that held crockery and cutlery, a wooden table with two benches either side and a pair of hard straight-backed chairs by the fireside, but not big enough for them all to sit down and eat at once. An oversized black cast-iron kettle hung on a chain above the open turf fire that burnt all year round for cooking. A minimum of two hands were needed to lift the dead-weight black kettle up onto the solid fuel range that had two top burners and an oven below the size of a shoebox.

I can testify to the powerful heat of those old-style cookers. One summer when I was about six years old, and staying at my mum's childhood home, I stamped indoors after playing outside, all complaints that my brother had yanked my bunched and be-ribboned hair. I leant on the range, the better to tell my sorry tale and dob him in to my mum, and heard a hissing noise. One that was even louder than my whingy voice. The sound was the skin on my arm sizzling as it fried on the red-hot surface below. My mother picked me up under her arm and started to run. My nan followed. We lolloped a few houses down the street to a neighbour I'd never seen before. The woman, Agnes O'Connor, was in her eighties and wearing a tightly tied floral crossover bib. It was difficult to tell where her skin ended and her white hair-line started because she was so deathly pale. She'd seen us approach through her open window and as we stepped from the street into her front room, Agnes backed into a fireside chair and spread her legs, the better to lay me across them. I caught sight of how her tan stockings were tied in a knot the size of a bread roll just above each knee and her legs beneath were the colour and temperature of fresh snow.

This icy-skinned Agnes lifted my afflicted arm close to her face and inspected my burn with pale eyes before momentarily shocking me out of my pain. She bent in to lick my red and rip-pled skin with her hot red tongue. From top to bottom and from right to left. Slowly and methodically, eyes partially closed, she lapped, long and thorough, like a cat – and all accompanied by murmurs of approval from my mum and my nan. I was silent. Every lick was a salve. I have no physical scars from that terrible burn, and my mum attributes this to Mrs O'Connor's lick. 'That auld one has the cure in her tongue, thank God!' she told me as we walked home. Two bottles of porter, hidden behind her fireside chair, were Mrs O'Connor's fee.

My poor sister caught the whooping cough when we were in Ireland the summer after I'd had my burn from the range. After several disturbed nights, I asked, 'Mummy, will Mrs O'Connor lick Julie's whoop better like she did my arm?', and I was very curious about what part of the body was the keeper of the whoop. The bark came out of her mouth but originated somewhere deep within. My sister's remedy was administered by another neighbour, Mrs Murphy, who had a face like a bull-dog, and it was a lot more terrifying than mine had been. We were taken to Mrs Murphy's house, which was a short walk through the village. Her front garden was filled with tall, floppy wild flowers. A white plaster statue of the Virgin Mary, four feet high, stood sentry by her front door. 'A sup of tay and biscuits' was the reason Mum gave us for this sudden visit. Julie was lifted from her sick bed to go and Auntie Theresa arrived to come with us 'for the walk'. When we got there, the cottage door was propped open and we let ourselves in. Mrs Murphy wasn't home but no one seemed surprised. As we waited for her, the four of us studied what was on the woman's dresser and in the big stockpot simmering on her stove. Auntie Theresa was stay-ing close by Julie and I thought that was because she was ill, but it was to best position herself to grab the poor child when she was least expecting it.

Mrs Murphy appeared in the doorway of her cottage, and was not alone. She was wrestling with a huge goose, struggling to keep it prisoner in her arms. The goose's neck was an undu-lating muscle of fury and the bird in protest peed and pooped down the front of Mrs Murphy's chrysanthemum-print apron.

Auntie Theresa got hold of Julie and my anxious mum sidled into place alongside. She tried to make reassuring noises that sounded to me like groans. Knowing that something unpleasant was about to happen, I dipped in beneath Mum's skirts.

I could barely believe my eyes when I saw Auntie Theresa tighten her grip on my sister and cue my mum to lean in and clamp her little girl's mouth open with the help of a wooden spoon she'd been hiding behind her back. 'It'll be alright, my little dote, don't be frightened ... The goose is going to make you better.' Poor Julie's last screamed-out words as the goose came in closer were: 'No! I won't eat it! You can't make me!'

The plan wasn't for her to eat the bird. It was to allow the bird to hiss into my sister's open mouth and thus exterminate the whooping cough. Apparently Mrs Murphy and the goose together had the cure for whooping cough. And Julie got a triple dose of hiss – because that goose was so cross it almost blew her tonsils out. As Julie didn't die, Mum's assessment was that the 'cure' had worked.

My sister and I got chickenpox together when we were on holiday in Ireland. Medical textbooks – the ones that say chickenpox is a mild childhood illness – need burning. Immersion in calamine lotion and binding our hands in cotton so we couldn't scratch and scar ourselves for life – like the 'poor crater' Maureen – was our treatment. Any complaints about itching or pain were met by my mother and my nan with grim warnings about poor Maureen. 'What happened to Maureen?' I was almost afraid to ask. 'She was so scarred after picking her chickenpox spots that she had to stay indoors and never married! Her face fell in, so it did.' There was a lot of chat amongst Mum and her sisters when Julie and I were in full chickenpox bloom about what a pity it was that no one in the village knew any longer of a girl with the maiden name

Clarke who had married a fellow whose surname was Clarke. 'The pair of them sailed to Boston in Amerikay,' said my nan unhelpfully. According to my nan, just five minutes in their company would have provided my sister and me with an instant cure for our chickenpox. 'Did they just stare it better?' I asked. 'You don't need to know,' was her mystery-laden reply.

My nan looked into my brother's eyes when he was around four years old and believed she saw a tinge of yellow there. 'That boy is liverish,' she declared. 'Liverish' was an all-purpose description of anything out of the ordinary from the top of the head to the tip of the toenails. The cure for liverishness was free, and always to hand in Ireland. A mouse. If you could manage to catch one alive. Michael remembers the fun of chasing down the mouse – not realising it was 'his' mouse – and managing to cup it under a bowl in the corner of the cottage kitchen. He soon stopped smiling when Nan dropped the live mouse into a saucepan of milk which she then boiled. Michael was forced to drink the milk mouse soup.

The three of us learnt from a very early age to answer, 'Very well, thank you' to the question 'And howaya?' when it was asked by an adult. We'd take the ailment over the cure every time.

Thirteen babies were made and raised in Dad's house and the ten survivors turned out to be straight-backed, clear-skinned and morally sound six-footers. Their toilet was the great outdoors and the bathroom was in your dreams and first on the left. Dad's homestead was in a village in the middle of nowhere and their family vehicle was a bicycle with a basket on the front. My mum's family seat was of similar proportions – though more of a three-legged stool than a seat, actually – and based in what she called 'a one-horse town'.

Another thing they had in common was a busy bed. Until they left home they shared a big iron bedstead with at least seven or eight siblings. Their mattresses were a patchwork of fabric remnants stuffed with straw and their sheets were sackcloths sewn together. 'Standing up was more comfortable,' was my dad's opinion of his mattress. He said that when the mattress was full up with bodies, whoever was left standing joined their parents in their bed next door. If that was full too, they bedded down on the floor with a blanket and pillow dragged off the others. Babies kept on turning up and the new arrivals slept in cupboard drawers, until they grew too lanky and more of their body was out of the drawer than in it. Then they progressed to the communal bed. 'It was always a short auld night,' my mother would lament, because the cock crowing before dawn was the wake-up call for the entire household.

Mum described how she and all her sisters would dress for bed in the coldest weather wearing coats, hats and gloves and huddle up for warmth by getting as close as possible to whoever was lying next to them. 'By having no objections to no one!' she would laugh and say when my sister and I asked her to tell us again and again how they all managed to share such a small space. Our favourite story was Auntie Peggy's asthma attack that wasn't. She woke up one night struggling to breathe and found her sister Katsie's slender big toe stuck up her nostril. There had been six of them in the bed that night.

My dad used to tell us tales about how rural households would often hide the Irish republican soldiers who were being pursued at the time by the Black and Tan soldiers sent in by the English. The soldiers always arrived in the dead of night and were given food and hot drinks before joining the family in their beds to sleep. Unwashed and infested with insects, the soldiers left a calling card – a rash known as 'the Republican Itch'. 'Very proud we were to have it too!' claimed my dad. His Republican Itch was once so bad he was frogmarched, twisting all the way, several miles to a neighbour who had the cure for skin complaints. A brown bottle with a stopper was dispensed to his mother for a fee and she marched her son back down the road, him dancing every step because of the constant snapping in his skin. She stripped him naked and stood him in front of the fire and started to apply the golden liquid in long wipes up and down all over his body. 'I wanted to jump in the fire with the pain of it,' Dad recalled, but his mother pressed him to the spot where he stood. By the time the bottle was empty, Dad said he was crying and complaining that the lotion smelt like wee. 'That's because it is wee,' his mother replied. 'And dear enough it was, too,' she said, referring to the price.

My sister and I had a bed apiece when we were growing up, but when visitors stayed over we were ordered to double up and we bellyached all night instead of sleeping. The pair of us would sit up grim-faced into the early hours, negotiating imaginary borders and no-go zones on the mattress and describing in gruesome detail what we would do to one another should our personal territory be breached by the hand or knee or, worst of all, bare foot of the other. Auntie Peggy, trying to get to sleep in the other bed, which she herself was sharing cheerfully with Auntie Bet, lost patience with us and snapped, 'Whisht now, you two. Settle down and bloody well go to sleep. Sure weren't we all plaited in the bed when we were youngsters, and it did us no harm.'

My dad's dad died of a rare cancer when he was just into his forties. In the final months of his illness, he was forgetful and irrational and took to sleeping with his bicycle chained to the

25

wrought-iron bedstead. In his altered state he viewed his sons and daughters as enemies within and he was convinced they were there to take all that was his. Great-granddad's beloved bike, bread and notes and coins all went to bed with him. It took several trips up and down the steep stairs with his treasured possessions before he was finally ready to blow out the candles and rest. His wife, my nan, decided to sleep on the stone-flagged floor downstairs when her husband started sleeping in his overcoat with his shotgun cradled in his arms.

Curls equalled loveliness in rural Ireland in the 1940s, and Mum said all the sisters tried everything to wake up with ringlets in their hair. Even potatoes. They once tested small round pota-toes of a similar size as makeshift hair rollers. The spuds were scrubbed, pinned and tied into place and covered with a hair-net overnight in a quest for bouncy curls at dawn. 'You'd suffer *anything* for a few curls,' Mum said when I asked her how she'd managed to sleep with a scalpful of raw spuds. The potatoes worked themselves loose as they slept and ended up down the bed, on the floor and even inside their clothes by morning. Every single one had to be hunted down and accounted for because their mother had them in her sights for the boiling pot over the fire. 'We had to find them and be sure they were in the pan the next day, and there was no codding her, Mammy had counted them before she went to bed!' And the girls' hair hadn't curled either.

My mum said that one of the greatest things about coming to London was the availability of soft, spongy hair rollers. She wrote a letter home enclosing one as proof because she didn't think her sisters would believe that such a divine item really existed. And every week after, she put two in an envelope and posted them home until the sisters remaining behind had enough for a fine head of curls and a good night's sleep apiece.

In my growing-up years, the staples on our kitchen table were a stainless-steel cruet, an orange Bakelite butter dish, an ashtray and a plastic plant pot piled high with sponge rollers frizzy with old hair and spiked with V pins. When the sisters convened around the table at our house, they would reflex-reach for those rollers and twist them into their hair for a curl boost, even if they were dropping by just for a cup of tea. No curling opportunities ever went unseized.

One thing they imported from Ireland to London was their love of dancing. 'When we weren't working or asleep we were danc-ing!' Auntie Peggy told me. Dancing was their second religion. My dad claimed he had danced with Mum several times in Ireland before they met in Woolworths on the Edgware Road in London, but she would squash his claim with the words, 'And I never noticed! You must have been an awful long way down the queue of fellas who were waiting to dance with me!' Dad also said he remembered seeing Mum get a ride home from a dance on the crossbar of another lad's bike and getting a 'fizzing' feeling in his chest. 'Fancy. And I never noticed ye at all,' she said with her nose in the air, but with a teasing half smile.

They always made time for dancing. My mum said she was step-dancing even when she was nine months pregnant with my brother, her eldest child. First stop in London was the dance hall, and fresh-faced and in some cases still swaying from the ferry crossing, Mum and Dad's brothers and sisters would blend for afternoon tea and evening dances. These were the highlights of their social scene. My dad loved the quickstep, the tango, the jive, but the waltz especially. For an unskilled, unsophisticated man, he was mercury in the ballroom. His brothers called him Paddy Astaire and he gobbled up the compliment.

Dad had only one real dance rival in the family: Sweet Feet Bill, as he was called, who made up his mind to marry contrary Clodagh, after just one dance in hold. It was more a musicality merger than a marriage. This pair danced to win and became 'champeens', and their home became known in the family as Trophy Town. After their first introduction my mum said Clodagh's confirmation name must surely have been Grandeur. My sister once visited with my dad. In sock feet and with clean hands, the prerequisites for entry, Julie said visiting that house was like stepping into a giant Battenburg cake. Every wall was painted pink or yellow and some both. First stop was the trophy room where their ballroom-dancing awards were displayed on purple velvet and lit from above in a bow-fronted, bespoke glass cabinet. According to Julie, all that was missing was a church kneeler for visitors to pay homage. Clodagh had a notepad, with which she used to take the potato order for dinner. 'How many do you want?' she would demand of her guests. 'I don't want to overpeel,' she'd say, making it sound like an illness she could catch and die from.

Newly married Mum and Dad's Bayswater bedsit was a hovel – and they were quite delighted with it. They had the thrill of electricity, an indoor toilet – shared with a dozen others – and one another. Most of their waking hours were spent at work; Dad was a porter in a grocery shop that did a roaring trade selling cigarettes singly at a premium to immigrants, and Mum was a cleaner in any number of private houses. She used to say that the women she worked for could never remember her name, even after she'd been on the staff for months, or years. Most of them just called her 'Irish'.

Precious time off was largely spent queuing in the post office sending things home. Andy and Annie had become Mrs Pick 'n' Mix but they both managed to get the sack from Woolworths just after their wedding for deliberately stopping the noisy, iron-framed service lift between the stock-room and shop-floor levels. Their manager suspected there was unholy slap and tickle taking place in the lift, but in fact the newly married couple were engaging in other deadly sins: gluttony and theft. They were busy between floors filling their faces with chocolate and their pockets with suitable goodies to post home to their siblings.

Posting things home was their solemn emigrant duty. English newspapers, especially the *News of the World*, plus Turkish Delight and Fry's Chocolate Cream topped with ten-bob notes were dispatched weekly to Ireland in brown envelopes of various shapes and sizes. On first receipt of the *News of the World*, my nan wrote by return post and complained about the stream of 'filth' it contained. Mum apologised in a letter back and promised she'd stop sending it. Quick to pen a reply, Nan told her not to do that, but instead to send two copies – one for herself and another for her friend and neighbour Mrs Flood.

My mum knew that her mother adored fresh tomatoes, a rare and expensive treat in rural Ireland at the time, so she chose two of the hardest greenest tomatoes she could find in the shops and posted them home. They were tomato purée memories by the time they crossed the Irish Sea, but her mum assured her thoughtful daughter that she had licked and sucked the envelope dry and got a good taste of them, and even kept the pips to try and grow on.

ME AND MINE

Milo the postman at home in Ireland had one of the best jobs in the county. He was the first to know any gossip from home or overseas, and there wasn't a woman in the village who didn't want to know everything he did. Milo would be offered tea and cake at every stop and pumped hard for rolling news – which he shared at a price. The contents of parcels were listed on the outside for customs purposes and my nan said he would often hand over a parcel reeling out what was inside it. He'd linger over the description of something he wanted to taste, like orange pekoe tea or shortbread biscuits. As more people went to America and England and posted more and more luxury foodstuffs home, Milo got fatter and fatter – even though he was cycling all day long.

When my mum was fifteen and still living at home in Ireland, her elder sister Theresa returned from London without warning. No explanation for her surprise visit was needed. The lump that sat high under her unbelted coat spoke for itself. Her baby had been conceived in an alleyway on a walk home from a dance in London. Her suitor pulled, Theresa pushed. And afterwards she cried for weeks. Her mother gave Theresa home-made chicken soup with a hug and then shooed her wet, pale-faced daughter upstairs where she waited with her five sisters and braced herself for news of her pregnancy to reach her father's ears.

My nan picked her time with great care. Her husband was replete after a sizeable hot dinner and halfway to a doze in his fireside chair when she spoke. 'There's a baby on the way ...' She cleared dishes noisily, bashing pans to try and lessen the impact of her words. Eyes half shut he replied evenly, 'Whose?', meaning which friend or neighbour was expecting. There were footsteps on the steep wooden stairs and then, 'Hello, Daddy ...'

My grandfather cussed his eldest daughter inside out, spraying spittle as he ranted. He keened about what Milo the postman, family, friends and neighbours would say and how he would be forced to hang his head in shame when he saw the parish priest, and all because his daughter was a shameful, good-for-nothing tart and a nobody. My mum, listening from the top of the stairs, said it was as if the normally mild-mannered man had been possessed by the devil. All the time he spoke Granddad was pointing, with an arm that was trembling so violently it drew circles in the air, at the low-set front door of the cottage.

'Alright now, Patrick. Calm yourself. What else can we do but take her in?'

'You shut your stupid mouth if you want that hair to stay on your head! I'll hear not another word. What I say is *law* in this house and it'd be wise for you to remember that!'

'Tay, Patrick? I'll make a cup of tay,' my nan said, trying to distract him.

'The little English girl whore and her bastard child need to be off this property in the next five minutes or I won't be responsible for my actions ... and feck you and feck your tay,' my grandfather declared, shivering with temper and disappointment.

Theresa, her face blanched, stood and wrung clammy hands in despair. With a wide stare she pleaded wordlessly with her father to show her some mercy. She wanted to tell him what she had earlier told her mother: 'But I *swear to God*, I didn't let him touch my belly button!' In a house that had welcomed thirteen babies, not one of the young women in it understood how a baby was made. When Theresa got her first period she thought it was something to do with the beetroot she'd eaten the day before. Their sex education had been compressed into one

31

sentence delivered by their mother when they each reached fourteen and were making plans to leave home to look for work in London: 'Be sure to keep your bottom drawer shut until there's a ring on your finger.'

My grandfather got two shocks that night. The first was learning that his unmarried daughter was heavily pregnant. The second came when his wife, expectant daughter and her five sisters all filed past him as he sat in his fireside chair, and disappeared, one after the other, through the front door. They were carrying clothes, bedding and crockery piled high in their outstretched arms. It was dusk and the seven women were dressed for outdoors. They didn't look at him or speak to him or bother to shut the door behind them.

In a slow procession, heads held high, they made their way up the lonely dirt road, on foot, towards the nearest town. My mother told me they had been walking in silent single file for almost an hour before they heard Granddad's bicycle bell trill some distance behind them. When he caught up with them he cycled ahead and then got off his bike, allowing it to fall sideways onto the road, wheels still spinning. His heavy breathing was all that broke the silence. My nan said it seemed the crickets fell quiet because they were as keen as she was to hear what my granddad had to say. Nothing. He said nothing. His wife and daughters had lined up to face him and fast-moving currents of hard stares and dark glances rushed between them, finally slowing and reducing in intensity until it was just Nan and Granddad's eyes that were doing the talking.

Daylight was fading fast and the two curt nods exchanged between husband and wife after the long silence – he nodded first – were barely visible to their daughters. 'Home it is so, girls,' declared my nan. She turned and led the way down the road back to their cottage through the mosaic dusk. Granddad picked up his bike, climbed on and carried on cycling away from his family in the opposite direction. He was heading into town for a pint.

On the walk home, my mother asked my nan where they had all been heading that night. 'For disaster, if he'd not come for us, Annie,' she'd said with a tight smile.

3

Buns Drawn

And they all did find work, plenty of it. They had two and three jobs apiece in shops, bars and restaurants, on the buses, on the trains, driving milk floats, digging roads, cleaning and labouring. They were a cheerful, tireless, unskilled workforce. Taxes and national insurance were paid, and Green Shield Stamps, which they collected with gusto, were their second currency. Green Shield Stamp books were as valuable as cash and they got stored under the mattress alongside any money that was being saved.

My sister and I still have some matching Chitty Chitty Bang Bang bedspreads and pillowcases that we got from the Green Shield shop in Chiswick High Road. This was paradise *circa* 1970. Through my innocent eyes, it was the place my mum and I went to on Saturday afternoons to get *free* stuff. Admittedly, I had to do a whole lot of licking to get at the goodies, and many a Friday night was spent spitting on the gum on the back of the stamps to secure them into the books. No spit? No shop.

My dad would have been a serious contender for the *Guinness Book of Records* in the category 'Irishman in London who had the Most Jobs'. There weren't many building sites he hadn't worked on, and on the occasions that we travelled through Central London by bus he would point to various buildings and airily claim, 'I built that!' As he told it, my dad was single-handedly responsible for the erection of the Hayward Gallery, the National Theatre, City Hall, London Bridge and even St Paul's Cathedral. On a primary school outing when my class travelled by coach to visit St Paul's Cathedral, I stood at the front and announced, using a microphone no less, that we were on our merry way to visit the place my dad had built. The nuns in charge of us that day snorted with unChristian laughter, but my classmates, like me, were too dumb to know any better. It was only when I studied history at secondary school and learnt about Sir Christopher Wren that I realised my dad had a well-developed gift – not for cathedral building, but for storytelling.

Dad may not have built St Paul's Cathedral but he did contribute a lot to the London economy. As well as being a builder's labourer, he was a bus conductor, a milkman, a baked-beans custodian at a Heinz factory, a park keeper, a petrol-forecourt attendant, a council gardener, a hospital porter, a handyman, a barman, a shop assistant in a car-accessories shop, a baker and an ice-cream maker.

Their weekly wages came in little brown envelopes. Pay day was always on a Thursday, and in our house I knew it as 'counting into piles' night. Small piles. Cash was divvied up to pay the rent, the milk and school-dinner bills and fares. And columns of coins were stacked to feed the gas and electricity meters – and the all-important one on the back of the TV. My dad, a sports fiend, never got over the disappointment of missing the end of the 1966 World Cup Final because the screen went dark. He used the last shilling piece in the slot on the back of the TV, but minutes later the electricity meter ran dry, and there were no coins left to feed it. My mum said it was the first time she'd seen him nearly cry.

Years before, the landlord of that first house in Cricklewood had purchased a television set for himself. The first my dad had ever seen, although he had heard them talked of. A TV was a rare luxury at the time and one that generated huge excitement amongst the lodgers, who were tantalised by the very sound of it every evening as they passed the landlord's ground-floor rooms on the way to their own. Lengthy listening-in sessions took place, the only clue they had been there the greasy Brylcreem patches at various heights on the hall side of the landlord's wooden door. Over a period of a few weeks the tenants were mesmerised and lured in ever closer. They progressed from listening to viewing through a small crack in the wood panelling of the door. This crack not only allowed them to watch the screen, but to note that after 9.30pm their landlord was always sound asleep and snoring in his armchair, TV blaring unseen.

This knowledge made the tenants very brave and twenty or so of them would sneak in nightly and stand in silence at the back of the room, watching whatever was on the screen. Those huge-shouldered, sweaty navvies all agreed on their favourite programme – *Come Dancing*. Sadly their viewing was prematurely curtailed. Not by their landlord waking up and discovering them in his room – but by the bracket giving way. An Englishman and a white-collar worker, the landlord would have been well advised to seek advice from one of the many tradesman sleeping under his roof before placing his precious

TV high in the corner of his sitting room on a cheap bracket that he had drilled, cack-handedly, into the wall. The tenants got away unnoticed by the landlord, but their hearts had dropped along with the TV set that had held them so happily in its thrall for weeks.

Wages night was the highlight of the week. Auntie Mary's husband Niall would bring his pay packet home, unopened, and rest it against the salt and pepper pot on the kitchen table as they ate tea together. Both would eat and watch the other across the table watching the packet of wages. When the meal was over, the teapot empty and the grease from Niall's mouth wiped away onto the back of his hand, it was finally time for him to reach over for the little brown packet and peel back its gummed-down flap. Niall would make a drama of turning his back to Mary and hunching over so she couldn't see the size of the bundle in the pay packet. Strumming his nicotine-stained fingers along the notes, he'd count out what he deemed to be the necessary amount for housekeeping each week. 'If ever I murder anyone it will be in my own kitchen on a Thursday teatime!' Mary once spat with fury to her sisters. 'Not a mention that my pay packet, with just ten pounds in it, was sat on the table too. My wages went unopened into his pocket and then taken for walkies to the pub. The auld bastard.'

I heard her cry tears of frustration at our table, and if she saw me looking at her anxiously she would put her hands on my shoulders and say, 'I'm only pretending, Anna May,' in an unconvincing voice. 'What's the point? What's allotted can't be blotted,' she'd add with a sigh that seemed to settle her. Perplexed as well as worried, I would nod in agreement and smile – without the first clue what she meant.

They only ever dealt in cash, even much later in life. I once suggested to my parents, when they were in their fifties, that they should get a debit card or a credit card to make life easier and they both reeled back as if they had been punched in the face. My mother was so appalled she blessed herself and said, 'Jesus, Mary and Joseph, the very idea! Sure isn't it only thieving!' My auntie Winifred acquired a credit card in the 1980s on the order of some bossy bank clerk. She whispered to me, 'I have something very, very dangerous in my knickers.' By this she meant that she had taken delivery of the card and then triple-wrapped it in a pair of her huge pantaloons, trussed it up further with her skin-coloured 80-denier stockings and slid it beneath the deadweight oak dressing table in her bedroom. Several strong men would have been needed to shift the furniture and get the credit card out from its hiding place. Satisfied she wouldn't be overtaken by the evil urge to impulse-buy, she was happy as long as it stayed right there. 'Temptation is a terrible thing,' she would declare and roll her eyes backwards in her head. Credit in any form was their anti-Christ.

They called the Irish good workers as well as immigrant scum. My dad worked seven days a week. At weekends he did numerous casual jobs in the local area. One job was for a Mr Brown, an Englishman who wanted footings dug cheap for an extension he was building. A Billy Bunter lookalike, Mr Young insisted that Dad call him by his first name. 'They do that, the feckers. Get friendly and then they rip you off,' my Dad prophesied when he got home that evening. The pair shook hands on a price and Dad worked so fast that he managed to finish the job almost a week early. Without any discussion, Mr Brown slashed Dad's pay in half. 'I should have known you'd be quick! The ability to dig fast is in an Irishman's genes. I believe it's to do with having to get the potatoes out of the ground fast before you starve or something, isn't it?' My dad was an even-tempered man but that rare day he actually considered taking his jacket off and scrapping for fair wages. When my dad didn't move or smile but kept his hand outstretched for the rest of his money, Mr Brown started to bluster about calling the police and accused Dad of pocketing winter bulbs, and claimed that Dad had looked at his wife's legs for too long when she'd brought him out a mug of tea. He then grabbed a rake and ran him off his property, but not before Dad got in his parting shot, 'I've seen donkeys with less hair on their legs than your missus!'

By the late 1950s, only Nan, Auntie Nellie and 'Auntie Bet' remained back home in Ireland. Three became two when Theresa sent Bet the passage money to join her in London. Bet wrote thanking her, still ignorant of the fact she was her real mother. My aunt Nellie called her home town 'Ballygobackwards'. The second youngest after Bet in Mum's family, she was easily the most beautiful of the girls. Soft-skinned and generously curved, Nellie 'pure crackled with life' according to my mum. She was a dynamo who stopped working, shopping, dancing and singing only for the few short hours she needed to sleep. Nellie bewitched men of all ages and types. Local boys wore a track outside the house cycling past in the hope of getting just a glimpse of Nellie.

It was the talk of the village when a gentleman with an English accent turned up in a car to take her for a drive. He called her 'Miss Nellie' and had brought her a dozen oranges and a huge bunch of sweet peas. My grandmother was sure to relieve him of his gifts before calling up the staircase to Nellie, 'Are we going for a drive today, Miss Nellie?'

'Tell the gentleman no thank you, Mammy,' she replied, and

her admirer waited outside in his car for two hours in case she might change her mind. My grandmother fetched him out a cup of tea. 'I know he's a Protestant but it's only manners.' Nellie and my nan then sat inside at the table watching the wavy-haired, pink-skinned man wait outside as they express-sucked four of the oranges dry and then ate them, pith and all. My elder relatives always ate the core of apples, too.

Sometimes two or three hopeful suitors would arrive at the same time and scuffle to be the first to knock on the cottage door to ask to take Nellie out. Her answer to every invitation – to dances or for walks – was always 'No thank you'. Nellie the beautiful was dreaming not of a man, but of a city. London.

Nellie wrote in letters to her sisters abroad that the stillness of the country air was choking her, and that she would suffocate and die if she didn't get a bit of life soon. 'She craiks a bit of action, that one,' my grandmother would tut. By life, Nellie meant London. Trinkets, stockings, magazines and sweet treats arrived in the post for her each week from England. They were intended to serve as consolation but only persecuted her further. Against her mother's wishes, and burning from inside out with shame that she was leaving her, Nellie booked a ticket to join her sisters and brothers in London.

The summer morning when she left home for the last time, Nellie got up before dawn, but her mother was ahead of her waiting at the foot of the stairs. The old woman got down on her knees and begged her daughter not to go. Nellie had no answer for her. She turned her back on her weeping mother and walked the long road to the train station alone. Her cardboard suitcase was packed to bursting with all she had – including her winter coat – and tied closed with string. She had no plans to come back any time soon. No goodbyes were spoken but there was a lot of silent pleading from both women. A note blotted and limp with tears, propped against the sugar bowl on the scrubbed kitchen table, lied that Nellie would come home for a visit very soon. She signed it, 'I do love ye so much, Mammy, but I can't breathe here. I want to be me. Your loving Nellie xxxxxxx'

Nellie went down a storm in London. Within days of arriving she had three jobs, in a shop, a pub and babysitting. A model scout approached her in Regent Street on her first Saturday in London and she agreed to an appointment with him at his offices – on the proviso that it would be held on a Sunday so all her brothers and sisters could come along with her for a bit of company. My mum and dad welcomed her into their flat in Bayswater where her bed was the sofa in the front room. It was their second London home, still a slum with shared kitchen and bathroom facilities, but bigger than their first and on the top floor of a grand porticoed house in Westbourne Terrace with Hyde Park as its back garden.

Nellie faithfully wrote home to her mother each week and always started with the same phrase – that actually she wasn't in London, she was in <u>Heaven</u>. On her ninth Sunday afternoon in London she went to Mass early and told my mum and dad that she had a date with a new boyfriend, a dentist. They planned to have lunch and afterwards take a walk together in Kensington Gardens. Nellie said to expect her for tea around 5pm. When the bell rang at 3.30pm my mum said she remembers thinking Nellie couldn't have liked the fella all that much as she had come home early. Rocking me in her arms, Mum opened the front door to find a policeman standing there on the doormat. She dropped me down onto her feet when she heard what he had come to tell her. Nellie had been killed when a motorcycle she was riding pillion had turned over on Park Lane and smashed into a concrete street light. As he was turning to leave, the policeman hesitated and told Mum that he had heard that Nellie had been a very beautiful girl and he was very sorry. His voice wobbled, she remembered.

There were no telephones to spread good or bad news at that time, so a telegram was sent to my grandmother to inform her that her youngest daughter, aged nineteen, was dead. My dad went in a police car to the hospital mortuary to identify the body. Afterwards he told the gathered, stooping sisters that Nellie had looked just like she was sleeping, and that her face was unmarked by the accident. No one believed him. Aunt Peggy tried to slap Dad for insisting time and again that Nellie's face was perfect and peaceful in death. She cussed him for the eternal torment of telling a lie and making her imagine the dreadful truth. But Dad was resolute. Only he had seen Nellie dead, and he insisted she was flawless. If he had seen anything different it was a secret he suffered alone for the rest of his life.

There was no money to send back to Ireland for a ticket to England for the funeral, so Nellie's burial took place in London whilst her mother knelt alone at home in Ireland, elbows resting on a kitchen chair as she rolled rosary beads between her trembling fingers. She crooned prayers for the repose of her daughter's soul. The farewell note from Nellie, written only weeks earlier, was folded and tucked deep into her mother's prayer book. After the funeral, whenever her dead daughter's name was mentioned, my nan blessed herself, looked heavenwards and said in heartfelt tones, 'Dear Lord, be good to Nellie, and I wish you had taken me instead.' It was the day of Nellie's funeral that the brothers and sisters started a fund in a cat-shaped teapot to fetch their mother over. They wrote to her with their joint intentions and she didn't say no, which meant her answer was yes – although she never said that, either.

After Nellie's death, my nan said she thought she'd gone deaf the house fell so quiet. She wore her hands out writing letters. Letters were everyone's lifeline. Short, misspelled pages that were peppered with the abbreviations TG and PG, for Thank God and Please God. My mum and dad had married in London and there had been no money to bring Nan over for the wedding. There is a precious letter, so old now it's like a piece of lace, that Nan wrote to my mum, sending her wedding blessings. It is loaded with a mother's love, and heavy with the pain of separation. Both widowed very young, Nan and Grandma spent long lonely days in Ireland watching their letterboxes for news from England of their vanished families. Nan was my mum's mum and Granny was my dad's mum.

Nan joined us, a life's belongings in a lone half-empty suitcase, to sleep in our front room. Mum said she watched her unpack and she had one of everything: underwear, cardigan, dress, coat and shoes. Her entire wardrobe was neatly arranged on the back of a hardback chair by her single bed, with her brown leather lace-up shoes and her patterned plaid pompom slippers stowed neatly beneath. A wire-thin wedding band, a plastic comb, a set of wooden rosary beads and a row of holy statues in painted chalk were all else that she owned. She had been a tenant in Ireland, and the shabby furniture in her cottage was sold as firewood when she left. On close examination I noticed that all the male saints in her statue collection were from the same plaster mould and just painted differently. I never told her that though, because she loved them. She carefully arranged Padre Pio, St Martin de Porres, St Joseph, St Anthony and

St Francis of Assisi, along with two others, the Child of Prague and the Virgin Mary, just as they had been on her mantelpiece in Ireland, so that the sacred woman and child were flanked by the holy men. There was quite a crowd on that fire mantel. Nan's collection jostled for space with Mum's framed pictures of JFK, the Sacred Heart of Jesus and St Vitus, the Patron Saint of all things Dance.

Our flat offered more room above our heads than on the floor because the ceilings were so tall. 'A stilt walker and his wife would be happy in this place, so they would,' was my nan's opinion of the property. Nan sat up to the table for her meals but when the chat and confidences began among her daughters around our kitchen table, she creaked over to her fireside chair just a few feet away. Pretending to doze, she made sure never to miss even the smallest whisper.

Nan was a tiny dynamo around our home. Always neat and busy-busy, she built the best and brightest open fires in the sitting-room grate. Dad used to say, 'That woman could get a fire going with just a glass of water,' and she loved to sit and stare into the blaze when all her work was done. She promised me that if I looked hard enough into the fire I'd find the face of my future husband there in the flames. For years I fretted I was destined to be an old maid because I searched and searched in the fire until my eyeballs were so hot I thought they would dry up and drop out, but still I couldn't see anyone. 'Did you see him yet?' Nan would ask. 'No, but I am trying,' I would answer. 'Maybe there's no one there for you and we're going to have a nun in the family!' she'd chortle. That made me scour the flames with a renewed determination. I didn't want to wear men's shoes when I grew up, or have a wart on my chin with a pubic hair growing out of it. I was sure of that.

Buns Drawn

Every morning Nan would line up a row of four teacups, one each for my brother, sister and me, and one for herself. A golfball-sized knob of butter went into each one, along with a shake of salt and pepper and two eggs apiece. She stood the cups in a pan of boiling water and stirred the golden eggy mixture until it collapsed into a scoopable goo. Sat up at the table, we'd hurry it to our mouths using the pile of hot buttered toast fingers she'd neatly stacked on a plate and covered with a white tea towel to keep warm. Whilst we gobbled, Nan would circle the table, using her fingers to eat her own egg from the cup, pausing between mouthfuls to tell us a mix of things that she said we were always to remember. I recall the slide of the buttery egg on my tongue and a few of the random pearls of wisdom that came with it. 'Always eat the fat off your chops – it'll grease your lungs.' And, flying in the face of the Catholic Church, 'There's no such place as Hell. God loves us all too much to send us there so ye can do what ye like and don't be afraid. But don't ever kill anyone.'

The only times my nan missed an opportunity to fatten us up and make us wise at the same time were when she was too busy because she'd invited herself along to my dad's driving lessons. As his self-appointed best friend, whether he liked it or not, she climbed into the back of the car when he set off with his instructor. Those driving lessons were a regular love-in. Dad was the instructor's favourite client as he had weekly lessons for over ten years, and his business alone paid the deposit on a three-bedroom semi in a leafy road in Kilburn. Before a lesson, Nan would roller her hair and polish her best shoes to 'Go for a little spin' as she called it. She liked to live dangerously and would overrule the instructor and urge Dad to drive fast, and then even faster. All the while she would be necking Milk of

Magnesia straight from the bottle because she claimed his driving gave her indigestion, especially when he changed gear. 'Is this a feckin' car or a rabbit?' she would yelp as Dad grappled with the gear lever.

It was around the same time my nan came over that my dad's mum was shipped over to England, too. Before they came to London neither of them had ever travelled more than a few miles outside the places where they lived – they had gone as far as they could on a bicycle and no further. They were both content to make the move to follow their families. 'The life went out of me when they were all gone,' said my grandma. My mum once asked her if she missed her little house in Ireland. 'I'd rather be anywhere than in those four empty walls,' she replied, tears daring to fill her fiercely independent eyes.

Grandma and Nan were two women with a lot in common: they shared a name, Elizabeth, had lived less than ten miles apart in Ireland, and had each borne the same number of children and been widowed young. But, inexplicably, they didn't like the scent of one another and kept a respectful, yet suspicious, distance. If they had been two dogs they would have fought viciously, but they were sweet grannies, so when they were in the same room they squeezed their eyes and raised the corners of their mouths in grim growl smiles instead. It was a case of buns drawn.

On the surface their exchanges were always cordial, but actually they were just swapping lies or insults. Their conversation followed a set silent-spat pattern. They began with one another's appearance. 'Your hair is looking grand, so it is, *mad* curly!' Or, 'Now there's a lovely cardigan on you and a grand fit, and there's a colour not everyone would be able to wear . . .' Translated that meant your hair is an almighty mess, and could you not have got a bigger size in that shite-coloured cardigan, you fattie?

Each of them believed they were outright winners in the 'Aren't Mine The Greatest Children' stakes. 'Is your Annie still enjoying the bingo on a Sunday?' This question, with its implied criticism of my mum's Catholic observance, would cause Nan's eyes to glitter with anger. Satisfied she had pissed her off, Grandma would pat her hair and smooth her skirt before taking fire again. 'And your Tony, is he still very fond of the pint? Does he manage to find time every night to have a sup, still?' And referring to the first ever union in the family between an Englishman and an Irish girl, she'd enquire, 'And how is Bet's *mixed* marriage? Getting on alright are they?'

The pair of them would keep going with arrow-tipped one-liners until it was time for both of them to have a restorative snooze. Then they would wake up and move onto spiritual matters. 'Are you still keeping up with the Angelus since you came over, like myself?' my nan would enquire.

'Oh and I am, of course. I never miss.' The clock struck six, Angelus hour, as they spoke, and the subject was swiftly changed.

'Shall I get one of the childer to fetch you over another gin?' my nan cooed.

Grandma's cheeks were raised to meet her eyes but it wasn't a smile. 'No, no, not at all, sure I'm only having just a sup of boiled water here for wind. I couldn't drink gin, no way. It would give me terrible gas altogether.'

'Isn't the water in London terrible altogether?' Nan enquired with one arched eyebrow. 'The fumes off of it.'

'Shocking,' agreed Grandma sniffing her gin and pulling a face.

As Nan listened to Grandma lying, she breathed down upon her Pioneer badge, the one pinned to her cardigan that read

'Total Abstinence', and gave it a flamboyant polish. Pity there wasn't a sash and crown to go with the badge. The taking of alcohol was like a conversational boil between them. Nan never drank and in her head that made her far superior to Grandma, who secretly did.

Daughters and grandchildren or the lack of them were fertile competition territory. 'I see your Mary likes the fashion for meanie skirts . . . I know what they all say but I don't think they are tarty at all . . .' would be countered with, 'Your Lizzine is a fine-looking mountain woman, so she is.'

'Poor Peggy – so no danger of a child now she's on the change?'

So it went on, and to any observer it looked like two silver-haired women who were getting on like a house on fire, when actually they were flaying one another with words.

Baking was another battleground. Nothing terrified the wider family more than an occasion where two of their cakes would be stood side by side on the same table. Flattering them equally whilst smiling and swallowing required a lot of concentration and tact. They both had recipes for cakes and breads that had been handed down over the years, which meant that preferring one scone to another was the equivalent of sticking two fingers up to your forebears. The two of them weren't beyond the employment of dirty tricks either. Grandma once baked a Victoria sponge that had a surprise third layer instead of the standard two and dwarfed Nan's effort. In revenge, Nan added grated laxative chocolate into Grandma's icing mix when no one was looking.

Granny was like a cardboard cut-out from a sepia photograph. She wore her white hair in a tidy bun low on the back of her head, and coin-sized round steel-rimmed spectacles fronted deepset eyes. For thirty years she wore widow's weeds, black from her throat to her heel, and she smoked a long clay pipe. I once innocently remarked to Granny that she reminded me a bit of Popeye, and got a slap on the back of the head from visiting Uncle Patrick who overheard my comment.

His blow knocked me forwards and resulted in me catching my protruding-teeth braces on the wool of Granny's cardigan. I was left there, hooked onto her in a kneeling position, for almost an hour until my mum got back and extricated me. Granny smelt of buttermilk and boiled bacon and didn't move or speak once during our lengthy attachment. She seemed unaware that I was even there and although I desperately wanted to prod her and ask her to set me free, I was worried that that might be disrespectful to my elder, and get me into more trouble than I was already in.

Uncle Patrick, ginger and swollen with self-righteousness, sat and read the *Longford Leader* for the entire time I was stapled to Granny. Every now and again he would mutter, 'Popeye, indeed!' Later he barefaced-lied to my mum and claimed he had no idea I was stuck and thought I had my forehead pressed to Granny's stomach because I was penitent.

As soon as my mum came back she rescued me with a pair of kitchen scissors. Instantly I was back on my feet, I snitched on my uncle about him hitting me and Mum puffed up with rage. Using the nearest thing to hand, a metal colander, she whacked him around the head with considerable force, nine times, to the tune of 'Don't-you-ever-lay-a-finger-on-her-again!' My odd teeth-to-belly embrace didn't stir Granny into wakefulness, nor did the noisy beating my mother gave my uncle. I made a mental note to myself that if I was ever playing statues with the cousins I surely wanted Granny on my team.

I loved that about my mum. You never had to fight a battle alone when she was around. Even now, aged fifty, I miss the certainty of that. And Granny did look like Popeye – but in a good way.

My dad and my nan were chums. They would watch the football, horse racing and *The Beverly Hillbillies* shoulder to shoulder on the settee – she would always save a space for him next to her. While their programme was on, at regular intervals she would press nut chocolate from her apron pocket into her son-in-law's waiting cupped hand. My mum would watch them with a face full of light.

Nan went to bed last and got up first every day she stayed with us. Bar one. On that one morning she wasn't first up, her nocturnal wee bucket was splashed with fresh blood. 'I've got my period, Annie,' I heard her call up the stairs to my mum in a weak, scared voice. Ovarian cancer shrunk her to the size of a baby bird in her bed within weeks and was the starting point for a conflict between her sons and daughters. Weakened by fear and despair, normally so united, they competed and squabbled to be the one who was most upset by Nan's sickness and imminent death. It was a kind of pre-mourning contest.

The sisters and brothers jostled for position around her hospital bed. The closer they were to their mother's ears and lips, the better they felt. Each came to visit bearing edible gifts trying to tempt her to eat and drink. They had tried all the standard fare and were branching out into the exotic: kiwi, a choc ice, a pineapple, pots of tangy yogurt. There was a vicious argument over an Israeli melon. Tony had bought one and my mum wouldn't allow him to give Nan any of it. She'd never seen one before and thought it might be poisonous. The pair of them had a heated disagreement about the properties of the melon until my nan raised her tissue-thin hand, cupped it against her ear and grimaced. Tony surrendered and put the melon on her bedside locker. It was bigger than Nan's head. Late one evening, close to the end of visiting time, persuaded by Theresa, Nan took a tiny bite out of a lime jelly sweet. Its green syrup burst over her lips. Nan seemed to like the taste and her stiff tongue journeyed out to try and lick it up. Aunt Peggy was so thrilled by this sliver of a sign of life that she fell to her knees, joined by Theresa, and they cried, 'Thank you, God! Thank you!'

The day my grandmother died they were all there around her bed, doing their best to try and talk and stroke her flat body back to life. Exhausted and strained, each of them severely aggravated the next. A going-nowhere chain-squabble started about ciga-rettes, money, children, dogs, husbands, wives, jobs. Everything and nothing. Amidst the cacophony of raised voices of her adult children and whilst their hips bumped for pole position at the top of the bed, my nan slipped into a deep and private sleep.

'It's disgusting! Who do they think they are? Look at them Irish, all over the street!' That's what I heard one passerby say to another on the afternoon of my nan's funeral. There were hordes of people, too many to fit in the house. Red-faced and dressed in black, they filled every space in the back garden and on the front pavement. Nan's bed was treated like any other sofa in the sitting room that day, and when I saw that I cried in my throat. There were empty glasses in among the holy statues on the fire mantel. A lot of the visitors wanted to press their palms to my ears, squeeze hard and lean in and kiss me. They all said the same thing with whisky breath, 'Haven't you got very big!'

There was a ring of people in the front room taking it in turns to sing. The songs were all maudlin and most of the men and women, hung with weathered flesh, had grimaces and half-closed eyes as they listened. I slid in as Uncle Tony finished the last verse of 'The Old Rugged Cross', which was always Nan's favourite. He had a full mug of brandy at his feet with a burning cigarette laid across it. It happened fast.

'Are you laughing at my mother's favourite song?' Theresa asked a second cousin, who was sat across from her in the crooning circle.

'Of course and I'm not. What in the name of God's the matter with you?' asked the velvet-jacketed relative who was only ever spotted at wedding and funeral buffets.

'Don't you speak to my wife like that, you bandy little quare ...'

This was rich coming from Con, who barely spoke to his wife Theresa himself other than to tell her to shut up. Some forward-thinkers slipped out of the room but the rest of us were a captive audience as hair and buttons and dentures flew. A window was broken in the rolling fray and so was Nan's statue of the Child of Prague. By the time the police arrived – a neighbour had made the call – the two worn-out warriors were in a slobby, split-skinned embrace, apologising and saying drunkenly each to the other, 'You're a gennelman, so you are.'

Auntie Katsie turned up at ours at the same time as the police. Mick, her husband who drove everywhere at eight miles per hour and was convinced he was the world's greatest driver, had managed to lose the funeral procession after it left the church. He had unwittingly joined another cortege, which took him twenty miles out of London to the graveside of a complete stranger. As usual, he refused to admit he was wrong and insisted on following the mourners in their cars from the graveside to the funeral buffet in a nearby pub because he wanted a free lunch. He ate several rounds of cheese and pickle and gammon with mustard sandwiches and downed two whiskies whilst Katsie sat outside in the passenger seat of the car praying for the repose of her mother's soul. He drove home at crawl speed again in a defensive rage, blaming the 'stupid fecker' who was responsible for the phasing of London traffic lights and Katsie for being too thick – which he pronounced 'tick' – to read an A–Z. Katsie was mortified that she'd missed her mother's burial. She sobbed big tears that she flicked from her eyes with long, perfectly manicured fingernails painted dark red for the occasion.

Dad's mum died soundlessly in her fireside chair some time after a weekday lunch, but the family didn't notice she was gone until they tried to rouse her at bedtime. They thought she had been quietly watching the fire and napping, as usual. Her body was taken back to Ireland to be buried in the same plot as her husband, escorted by five of her sons, including my dad. It was the first time any of them, including Granny herself, had been on an aeroplane.

The five brothers had been in Heathrow airport for less than thirty minutes when they were mugged. They had a neon naivety and may as well have worn shamrock-shaped badges that read 'Rob Me, Quick'. Their wallets, watches, cigarettes and even neckties were taken by three teenage boys. The brothers went to the airport help desk to report what had happened to them and the uniformed clerk sniggered, 'Oh yeah. And who am I? Inspector Clouseau?' Then he asked the brothers, 'Why are you lot all standing so close together?'

When they finally made it onto the plane, a gorgeous, high-shine air hostess in a full mask of make-up asked my dad if he would like a drink from her trolley. Virtually teetotal but overwhelmed by grief, fear of flying and the shame of having to tell my mum that he had been robbed at the airport, he decided that on this occasion he would take a drink. He asked politely for a pint of Guinness, saying both please and thank you as he wasn't used to being served anything, anywhere. He hoped the Guinness might steady his shredded nerves. The stewardess seemed surprised. Dad said at first he thought she was impressed by his good manners. Wrong. She answered his request with a withering look, leant in close to his big right ear so that none of the other passengers could hear and hissed, 'What do you think this is?' And before he could answer she continued, 'Let me tell you what it isn't. A pub, you Irish peasant!' My dad said he apologised to her for asking, and for having offended her, and told her he'd do without a drink, thank you. Satisfied that she had sufficiently terrorised him, the hostess then sashayed off down the aisle.

4

Six Weddings and a Funeral

Mum's sisters didn't choose their husbands as wisely as she had done. Perhaps being so far away from home and needing to belong steered them into the wrong arms. Or the terror of being left untaken, an old maid. 'There'll be white blackbirds before them ones find themselves a fella,' were the words my nan used to describe the unmarried women of the parish she counted in and out of Mass every Sunday. She could pity the spinsters of the parish from her lofty position as a woman with no daughters left on the shelf at home. 'All six of *my* girls are married,' she would say with a reflex triumphant chin-to-chest movement. Marriage, be it good or bad, was a permanent mark, and rotten husbands were better than no husbands. Divorce was a Tammy Wynette song, not a real-life option for them. Down the years, 'Stand By Your Man' became their sad anthem.

My dad was like the North Star of decency amongst them. The sisters, in ones, twos or threes, would turn up at our door at any hour of the day or night for tea and consolation. Our kitchen table was where my aunts' despair spilled over. Gathered around the teapot, they would tell all in low, flat voices.

The tea wasn't just for drinking; it was for reading, too. The meaning of life, the answers to problems and predictions about the future could be found at the bottom of a teacup, according to the women in my family.

The tea got swallowed at speed in preparation for what surely followed. 'I'll read your cup!' one sister would declare to another, reaching over to grab it. The cup would be placed rim-down on the saucer and turned twice in a clockwise direction. Only then would the reader study the pattern of the loose tea leaves left inside the cup and take a thrillingly long time to announce her revelations. Information about the present was in the leaves close to the rim of the cup and insights into the future were found down at the bottom. 'Do you see a baby for me?' was always Auntie Mary's first question, asked in a voice that trembled. 'I'll come back to that in a minute . . .' was the standard answer from whichever sister was doing the reading. 'Find a few bob in there for me,' was Theresa's request. 'What age will I be when I have a child?' was Peggy's charged-with-optimism baby enquiry. 'Is he doing a line with that fat barmaid?' Katsie wanted to know of her lusty husband. They asked questions but were afraid of the answers. Reading the leaves allowed the sisters to make comments and remarks about husbands and family that would have caused a riot in general conversation. 'But wasn't it the leaves that said it? Not me!' was their defence after a husband had been described as 'unfaithful' or a close first cousin as 'treacherous' or a beloved child as 'backward'.

Christine was a secondary-school friend of mine without any Irish connections – she was posh English and lived in Richmond. Christine's mother knotted her scarves at her neck and used a gold tiger-shaped clasp (according to Christine, one that had real rubies for eyes) to hold it in place. My mum made a triangle out of her scarf and wore it on her head, tied tight in a ball knot beneath her chin, sometimes with a rack of hair rollers on show.

One afternoon Christine came to my house after school and witnessed one of the sisters' sweet-tea-and-steadying sessions in full flow. Unnoticed by the huddle of aunts in their usual positions around our kitchen table, in crisis over something or other, I prepared orange squash and arranged biscuits on a plate for my chum and me. Their conversation continued in urgent, low voices whilst teacups were passed around the table for double-checking eyelash-meets-tea leaf scrutiny. Those women did nothing in moderation – their oohs and aaahs were good enough for a pantomime. I noticed Christine giving them anxious sideways glances and taking big nervous swallows as she waited for me to complete my hostess duties.

When we left the kitchen my friend was clearly 'afraidagog'. Afraidagog was a word we'd made up in school that very same day in RE to describe how the disciples might have felt after the resurrection of Jesus. 'Are they having a séance?' Christine asked me, her mind clearly flipping from terrorised to thrilled. She was rapt and didn't even notice the chocolate digestives I offered her. 'No, no, they're just reading their teacups,' I told her. 'Doesn't your mum do that?' Her bug-eyed silence answered my question. Christine, of course, sprinted home to her mother and reported what she had seen going on in my kitchen. And that was that. She was forbidden ever to cross the threshold again and the playground talk was that my mum and her sisters were witches.

★

Theresa, the eldest sister, blocky and green-eyed, was married to Con, a man-mountain builders' labourer. He was like a caramel-coloured version of the jolly green giant, only he wasn't jolly at all but the Patron Saint of Contrary. Nothing Theresa ever did was right. My mum said that Theresa's husband Con hadn't courted her, more like hunted her down. 'That bastard stood in her way and wouldn't let her pass.' I saw a photograph taken at Theresa's wedding. Regret was already large in the bride's eyes. Con was stuffed into a borrowed brown suit a couple of sizes too small and he'd had a haircut for the occasion. 'You can put a shine on shit but it don't last long,' sighed my auntie Peggy when she saw him spruced up and ready to wreck her sister's life.

Two sons arrived in two years, inexpicably called Tony One and Tony Two. Con regularly used their strawberry-coloured curls to lift them off the floor with one hand and then beat them hard with the other. 'I'm their father and I'll tan their arses if I want to!' he would bellow at anyone who dared to challenge him.

Theresa's big heart wobbled constantly like a jelly in her chest because she never knew what she was coming home to after work. Con grew bloated with booze – and the days, weeks and years of her family life were lived out according to how much he'd taken. Too much was awful, but quick, because after a drunken rage about slippers or sausages or anything at all of no importance he would snuff out at speed into a long sleep. Just right meant tug-of-war games with the boys in the garden whatever the weather, and fish and chip suppers. But worst by far was not enough booze. Then Con was sweating, shaking, vicious and watchful. It was on the not-enough nights that he tore up his sons' school exercise books bellowing, 'The buildings were good enough for me and they'll be good enough for ye two pair of scuts, too, by God!' Theresa baked her way sane through the early years of her marriage. A production line of apple pies, soda breads and buttermilk scones in the oven was her excuse never to sit with her husband in the evenings. She and her sons, a tight and terrified threesome, would occupy the steamed-up kitchen as Con and his foul mood filled the front sitting room. Theresa turned out the cakes, pies and biscuits as she watched her sons do their homework and whispered to them that it would be lovely to be an airline pilot or a shop owner, wouldn't it?

I hated visiting Theresa because Con always pursued me for a farewell kiss. 'Gimme a birdie!' he would demand, pushing his dry, pursed lips against mine. His breath was toxic – it reeked of a blend of fresh fart and stale smoke. And rubber bands. He insisted that Theresa wait up for him each night he went out to serve him a post-pub sandwich. 'With plenty of Daddies sauce!' he would holler to her from the sitting room where he was sat crooked in his chair. Arms folded, Theresa stood watching as, Adam's apple bobbing, Con struggled to swallow the bacon-and-rubber-bands sandwich she had made him. All liberally doused in Daddies sauce.'You enjoying that?' she would call in a loud cheery voice. 'You shite face you,' added under her breath. As usual Con ignored her.

Theresa was Amazonian in body and spirit. She wore men's shoes because there were no women's shoes to be had in size ten in those times. Her hands were like a pair of baseball gloves that puffed up bigger each week, cupped with spongy fingers. They were swollen because they reacted badly to the chemicals provided by British Rail for her job as a train station toilet cleaner. She didn't dare complain or suggest a change in case she got the sack. Her sons grew into giant balloon-faced young adults and once clubbed together a small portion of their dole money to buy her a secondhand fireside chair, which she placed by the washbasins in the toilets where she worked. Her boys loved her but had no idea how to show it, so said it with cake every Friday. Tony One or Tony Two would deliver a fresh cream sticky rum baba and Theresa sat in her chair and enjoyed it as people in the cubicles broke wind, flushed and did everything in between. Friday was also pay day – she got cash in a small gummed envelope – and it was the one day of the week her boys were sure to get out of bed in time to collect her after work. Linking an arm apiece, the two Tonies would walk her partway home, peeling off three-quarters of the way there to nip into the pub for a few Mum-funded pints.

Father and sons clashed constantly. 'It's often a man's mouth that breaks his nose,' Theresa would say. When Con turned on Theresa, that was the cue for Tony One or Tony Two to jump their father, who fought back like a lion. And on the rare occasions when Con was calm, Tony One and Tony Two would attack one another instead. 'Why didn't I have daughters?' Theresa would ask the moon as she stood in the garden smoking. Indoors her clench-fisted menfolk leapt and jelly-rolled around the house, wrecking it. Kitchen chairs, side tables, lamps, frying pans – anything at all that could be lifted was used either in attack or self-defence. Theresa was the never-never man's best customer because she ordered, reordered and paid off the same items of furniture into perpetuity.

It was whispered that after a bad night on the drink Theresa's boys would piss into their wardrobes, believing in their drunken stupor that they were in the toilet. Once Con took aim over Theresa's dressing table, soaking her powder compact and lace mats. His pee hit the mirror and ran down the back of the drawers, soaking a prayer book and wooden rosary bead set her mother had sent her as a gift on her wedding day.

Tony One left home at seventeen. He got a job as a deckchair attendant on a beach in Jersey. Theresa told friends and neighbours that her son was an international businessman because she'd heard someone described as that on the radio and thought it sounded marvellous. On his first triumphant visit home, Tony One startled his mother. Jersey sunshine had turned his skin from the colour of vanilla ice cream to the colour of milk chocolate. 'It was like all his baby freckles had joined up,' she said fondly. He was the bearer of gifts: four used deckchairs, one apiece for each member of the family, and hundreds of duty-free fags.

Theresa once appeared at our table after yet another fight. 'Leave the blaggard for once and for all,' my mum implored.

'But who'd look after him?' Theresa replied, without a trace of irony. She left our house that day with a handbag bulging with donations from the others: cosmetics, cash, cigarettes and rosary beads.

Tony Number Two never left home. He claimed he stayed to look after his mother. Quite how he did that from his bed – he was always in it – while she was at work cleaning the town's station toilets is difficult to say. He was a man of few words and worked out a finger-clicking system for his mother to respond to. One click meant fetch tea, two clicks meant fetch food and three clicks meant fetch fags. One day my mother was visiting when Tony two-clicked for Theresa, who was pegging out washing in the garden and temporarily out of earshot. Mum turned up at the side of his chair instead. She grabbed her nephew's nose in her fingers and twisted it full circle as she leant in close and whispered into his ear that she would pull that same

61

nose right off his face if he ever clicked his fingers at his mother again. 'Sorry, Auntie Annie. I won't do it no more.' Mum said she had to steady herself on the back of his chair when she heard that because she had fully expected him to respond to her warning by punching her lights out. 'Tea, Tony Two?' she asked him sweetly before dashing, mighty relieved, out of the room.

All the sisters and brothers had shared the spoils of Theresa's bake-ins. But they knew the pain that inspired the shortbread and sponge cakes and for that reason found them hard to swallow. 'She was a great baker but I couldn't enjoy any of it because of the lump in my throat,' my mum once said. To try and stop her baking her life away, they pretended to Theresa they didn't like her cakes because they weren't as good as their mammy's, which drove the puffs of flour from her mixing bowl even higher as she tried to improve.

After she'd had a cream sherry or a win at bingo that got her all excited and philosophical, my auntie Theresa would reach out with her huge hands for my tight mirror-shine ringlets. She would squeeze and pull my curls and bend down to me so that we were nose to nose and say in a voice cracking with emotion, 'Anna May, life is there for the grabbing. You go get it. You go get it.' I look back now and realise the words that went unspoken from her were, 'Do it for me because I'll never have a chance ...'

Theresa lost all interest in the baking as her boys grew up. She still hid in the kitchen but later she boiled, not baked. She was feeding hulks of men who were mostly so drunk they didn't even know if the meat they were swallowing was raw or cooked. She'd make my sister and me squeal as she dropped what we considered household pets into her pan. 'In this house if it's got eyes, it goes in the pot. What do they care?' she'd snarl of the men in her life. Looped in steam and stationed next to a giant boiling pot, she killed hours in the kitchen – wishing and stirring. Chicken, rabbits, mince, sheep heads and pig's trotters were all tossed in the pot and dished up with troughs of potatoes. 'Just look at them lovely spuds, laughing up at you they are,' Theresa would lie to her trio of drunkards, as they leant against each other and the wall, struggling to stay upright to eat, while she banged Smash or tinned potatoes onto their plates, claiming they were Ireland's best and prepared by her own fair hands.

She preferred to eat at my mum's table. Always with her eyes closed and in a state of bliss. At ours, macaroni cheese was Theresa's favourite meal, and when she tried that recipe at home for her boys, Con pitched the oven dish into next door's garden, shouting, 'Don't ye ever insult me like that again or it'll be you going over the fence! I earn enough for meat every night and I feckin' well want to see it hanging over the edges of the plate, so I do!' I often wonder, if it had been possible for her to keep Bet, her first-born baby girl, whether Theresa's home would have been a sweeter place.

The glamorous, high-shine Katsie was very figure-conscious, and even if she couldn't have tasted the tears in Theresa's cakes, she still would have eaten only a fingerful at a time for fear she might end up the same pillar shape as her hefty sister. She married Mick, a Belfast man she met at a bus stop in Waterloo. He had been transfixed by her 'God Almighty undulations', as her boss in the clock factory in Cricklewood had described them, with a dribble.

Katsie was like a rainbow on legs. At least that's what I saw when I was small enough to have to bend my head back to take her all in: the yellow hair, blue powdery eyelids, traffic-light-red lips, egg-white dentures and multicoloured finger- and toenails. This trapped peacock spent nine hours Monday to Friday and half-day Saturday perched on a high stool in a factory in Cricklewood, her Hollywood-long legs with apple knees plaited beneath her as she stuck the second hands onto clock faces. I asked her once if she liked her job. Katsie answered, 'I like the money,' and, after a pause, 'It's easy work,' and then, with a big smile because she'd remembered the best thing about it, 'And I spend all day thinking about what's in my make-up bag!'

Katsie treated my sister and me like her make-up apprentices. My mother used a wipe of lipstick and a dusting of face powder before facing the world and always plucked the hairs from her chin on Sundays whilst the potatoes were roasting. But although she was lovely, she wasn't even close to being glamorous. Katsie was *à la mode* for all things colourful and gloopy – and ever willing to share. Every item she bought on a market stall or in a department store was, according to her, even more fantastic than the last. If she saw a picture of something cosmetic she liked in a newspaper or in a magazine she would, in a near swoon, fan herself with her exfoliated and moisturised hands and declare, 'I'm having that, make no mistake!' or she would stab a glittery high-polish fingernail into the newsprint and say, 'Come to Mama, darling!' in a mock Russian accent that she believed she'd perfected but always sounded Scottish to me.

Once, she turned up midweek with a new acquisition. She used her perfectly manicured almond-shaped nails to prise the lid off a big plastic tub that she had plonked right in the middle of our kitchen table, already laid with cutlery and cups of milk ready for dinner. Like a magician she revealed it to us, very slowly and with a series of eyelash flutters and daffodil-coloured curl bounces. Breathless with excitement, Katsie generally carried on like she'd placed the Holy Grail there in among the ketchup and brown sauce bottles. My mum stood by the cooker boiling bacon and forking cabbage, watching from the side of her eye and pretending not to be interested.

The creamy blancmange product she finally unveiled was dismissed as 'goo' by my sniffy, low-maintenance mum but was 'pure gorgeous' according to Katsie. It was Colette hair conditioner. She explained its hair softening and shining principles to my mum, who at first thought it was a shampoo substitute. 'So it's washing your money down the plughole, ye are?' asked my puzzled mother when she realised the conditioner had to be rinsed out of the hair after use. 'And what's wrong with a wipe of Vitapointe that stays in?'

There were a lot of hair-washing rules and regulations in our house. Among them was that it could only ever happen on a Saturday night, in readiness for Mass on Sunday. And even a time of day was designated. Shampooing had to happen early because, according to my nan and mum, any girl who went to bed with damp hair would wake up with a permanent shake in her head, just like Bridget from Ballinasloe. 'Left like a turkey she was . . . never married,' my nan muttered darkly. And when my period started I was warned about the perils of washing my hair for however many days it lasted. 'Do you want all the milk in the house to turn sour?' was my mum's baffling reply if I pleaded for a hairwash at that time of the month.

The evening Auntie Katsie arrived with the Colette she managed to sweet-talk Mum into a partial swerve of the rules. My sister and I were allowed to apply the Colette conditioner onto our midweek hair, but to our dry heads only – and we had to leave it in because there was no way we could rinse it out with any precious, expensive hot water. We didn't care. We were proud to leave it in until the weekend came. Our hair was coated white and crackling stiff, but so what? We were sophisticated.

Mum's idea of a beauty routine was purging, scrubbing and the enthusiastic application of petroleum jelly. Every night before we went to bed, my mother would coat every female mucous membrane in the house with Vaseline. I never asked or even wondered why. It was just our routine greasy lullaby. And one particular night – when I was six years old and she was water-proofing my posterior as usual before sleep – she started to retch. Clearly panicked, she called my dad to come and look at my bottom. 'No,' he called back, 'that end of her is women's work.'

So my coat went on over my pyjamas, my bare feet into cold school shoes and I was hauled to Aunt Peggy's for an after-dark bum inspection. I had to bend over and touch my toes whilst a silent Peggy and Mum blew cigarette smoke all over my back-side and gawped. 'I've never seen anything like it!' was Peggy's summation. 'There's definitely something alive in there, isn't there, Peggy?' my mum asked in a stage whisper supposed not to worry me.

The doctor in casualty issued my snivelling mother with a tube of cream and a pair of white cotton gloves, which she started to pull on. 'They are for your daughter to wear,' the doctor said, tugging them off her hands, 'when she is asleep and may be unconsciously scratching. To get rid of the worms we need to break the cycle from anus to mouth. Like I explained before? Do you understand what I am telling you, Mrs Mangan?' She blew her nose and nodded and then shook her head. When we got home late that night, I heard my mum telling my dad I was being eaten by worms from the inside, and it was all to do with bicycles.

I am surprised Mum and Peggy went squeamish when they saw my worms. Mum, Dad and all my aunts and uncles liked nothing better than to terrorise me tight with tales of bugs, beetles and parasites that had lived on their skin *and* in their hair *and* in their beds *and* on their clothes during the growing-up years in rural Ireland. Like fishermen's stories, at every telling these cling-ons grew more enormous with ears, teeth, dangling genitalia, claws and wings. They claimed they were never afraid of any insect, and believed the bigger they were, the better to keep their scrawny, hungry bodies warm.

Every week at bath-time I voted with my feet for defying my mother and the Pope and staying stinky in Hell. I would run away and hide as soon as the tin bath appeared. This strategy worked for the amount of time it took for everyone else to get dipped. After that, my impatient mum would track me down and lift, lower or slide me from my hiding place. Using only her eyebrows and forefinger, she would scowl me into undressing and climbing into the by then grey and greasy water. Once I was in as deep as I could go, which was navel high, she would drop a bar of pink Lux soap in with me, which splashed the now freezing water upwards. It felt like flying needles on my scared skin.

Directly after the bath came senna pods. This was a herbal laxative to ensure we would be clean inside as well as out. The concoction smelt, to my junior nose, just like the poo it was guaranteed to induce. It was prepared by steeping the dry senna pod leaves in hot water and leaving them to stew until it was toxic to your bowels and cool enough to swallow.

Giving the entire household a potent laxative at the same

hour, when there was only one outside loo, was very poor strategic planning. Dad, Michael, Julie and I made a groaning queue in the back garden outside the toilet door, all with our foreheads pressed to our knees. It was the job of whoever was at the front to kick the wooden door in frustration and plead 'Huuuurrryyy uuuuuupppp!' through clenched teeth with an 'I am going to die this minute' intonation.

Mum was never in the toilet queue herself. She only dished out the senna, and never swallowed a dose of her own. If any of us were brave enough to ask why that was, she would go all haughty, flare her nostrils and reply, 'Do you ever hear *me* pass wind? So there you are.' Her restless guts were capable of performing the 1812 Overture when she was relaxed and asleep on the settee, so the answer to her question was, 'Hell yes, and often.' But no one dared tell her that in case they got a double senna serving for being cheeky.

Auntie Katsie had competition in the 'most brightly painted sister' stakes from Auntie Mary. 'Miss Westmeath' Mary would call herself in a giggly voice with an undercurrent of threat – daring anyone to challenge her claim to fame. She believed she deserved the title because she had once been declared runner-up in a London heat of the Rose of Tralee beauty pageant. Mary felt she was the dead-cert winner but claimed the judging was fixed because the youngest daughter of Ireland's richest pig farmers had taken the title. 'And her with a snout big enough so you'd know for sure whose daughter she was,' was Auntie Mary's oft-repeated bad-loser barb.

With her stacked bottle-blonde hair and penchant for sequins, Mary was Danny La Rue's doppelgänger. Although she lived in Ireland, she was still at our table often enough to have worn a groove in it with her elbows. Her style was always shout-it-out-loud! Mary and Katsie competed to have the longest, sparkliest nails and the biggest hair in the family. Once I caught them in the kitchen holding hand mirrors to check their make-up, and noticed that they both had them angled to watch what the other was doing. Mary was the clear winner when it came to outré nightwear. My mum, sister and I went to bed every night trailing yards of floral winceyette that concealed our toes and tickled our chins. Mary had baby-doll nighties that were made out of pink or red netting with matching frilly knickers and tottered into the bedroom, her Nivea-creamed feet clip-clopping in feathery, high-heeled mules.

Mary's husband Niall was toothless, bald and string-shaped. He proposed by asking Mary, 'How would ye like to be buried with my people?' As his family were dirt poor and buried mostly in paupers' graves, it wasn't much of an invitation. He was a butcher and would load her suitcase with Irish meat before she set sail. She'd arrive from the boat train with her brown leather suitcase dripping blood from the corners. Inside, wrapped in greaseproof paper, were steaks, sausages, black and white pudding and chops. These were real treats because all the sisters considered English meat to be 'dirt'.

My mother would roll her hair before bed at night and watch house guest Mary, corseted and frou-froued in neon colours, out of the side of her eye, and sigh loudly. She would tap herself on her temple with two fingers and raise her eyebrows – this was a secret message to me that Auntie Mary was 'touched in the head'. 'Don't mind her. She's waiting for God to send her a baby,' was my mother's whispered explanation for the bawdy bedwear, which was a bit of a waste considering her husband was sleeping on the other side of the Irish Sea.

Mary yearned for a baby. She had five stillborn babies before at last delivering a healthy son, Declan, whom she loved and feared in equal measure. Mental collapse had followed each stillbirth and ECT treatments were prescribed by doctors. In her wild and grieving state of mind, Mary believed she was being punished for being too weak to deliver a live child. ECT subdued her pain but not her determination to have a baby. When Declan arrived, all his food was lovingly mashed by his mother until he was eleven years old in case he choked. Four times a year, in the company of a trusted neighbour, the boy got shipped to England so that my mother could cut his toenails. His own mother was too scared to do the job in case she hurt him, and too petrified to travel on the boat with him in case he fell over the side. We had linoleum floor coverings all over our house and I can still hear the clip, clip, clip of a barefoot Declan walking around on it like Big Bird. His nails had grown out, over and under his toes.

To get at his toenails, my mum would have to lock all the external doors and then chase a terrified Declan right through the house. He ran through every room, over sofas and under beds, before she could catch him. When she did she would first press his feet into a basin of warm water to soak. Then she would set about sawing off the giant scoop of nail cupping the underside of each toe with something long and sharp she found in my dad's toolbox. 'Sing, Declan, sing!' my mother would grunt as she grappled with his fast-kicking feet.

Mary was an army wife and one afternoon at the shops she overheard the telling of a terrible tale by the wife of a soldier who had just returned from the Congo. Her man had been taking a pee in the jungle when a leech attached itself to the back of his thigh and, according to her, sucked him completely dry of blood whilst he was sleeping. 'He's never been the same,' she told her audience of rapt women outside the Bon Bon, a local café.

At that time the barracks where Mary lived had communal toilets which were reached by a short walk across stony scrubland. The accessory for that particular walk was a roll of loo paper on a loop of string that had to be worn either around the neck or sideways like a satchel. The worst-case scenario was to leave the loo roll behind for someone else to enjoy for free.

Mary was made weak by the prospect of her Declan's worshipped and adored blood being siphoned away by a parasite. Instantly she decided any risk had to be immediately eliminated and an indoor toilet installed by the end of the week – no matter the cost. This toilet – the first indoor domestic one in the entire town other than in the priest's house – was fitted. Smack square in the middle of Declan's bedroom. On a platform that was nine inches high to allow for all the necessary pipework and drainage beneath. Mary showed off Declan's toilet to all-comers, like it was a piece of antique Chippendale. 'Toilet tours!' her jealous neighbours would cackle.

When we stayed, every one of us would use that toilet, even if Declan was in his bed, awake or asleep. If he wasn't sleeping he would watch us and say proudly, 'That's my toilet,' and we would agree, flush and say thank you for letting us have a turn. His mother taught him to reply, 'You're very welcome. Do come again.'

Mary was Katsie's matron of honour at her wedding to Mick. They spent the day happily touching up one another's make-up in a brief confetti-inspired truce. My mother claimed that Katsie married Mick because she couldn't see what it was she was

71

taking on through the blonde curls that were always hanging over her face and the weight of the false eyelashes that were stuck to her eyes before breakfast every day. Mick himself was no looker. He was grimy and round, but he was the cleverest man in the universe. According to himself. A speed talker, he began every sentence with 'Ya Bollox!' and was self-proclaimed 'as good as any fecking professor, I can tell you'. Animal, vegetable or mineral, Mick was the last-word authority on it all. Sport was his speciality subject and no one knew anything about it better than him. Television sports commentators rendered Mick apoplectic. 'David Coleman's balls should be roasting over my feckin' fire – was there ever a man who spouted so much nonsense?' And it wasn't just sport – he loathed Reginald Bosanquet the newsreader, too. Mick described him as a 'shittin' know-nothing poncer'. The television, no matter what it was tuned to, made Mick so furious he would writhe in his chair as if his arse was on fire and hurl abuse at whoever appeared on screen.

They had one son who was treated like a little prince when he was a baby, but as soon as his legs would carry him, he was off. 'Head for the Hills' my mum used to call her nephew, who was always off somewhere in the middle distance. Katsie didn't care much. She believed it was his know-all father's penetrating voice that drove him away. 'I married it. He didn't,' she would say, with an envious note in her voice of her son's ability to roam free.

But the love of her life wasn't her husband or even her son. It was Sparkle, a Yorkshire terrier the same colour as a Caramac chocolate bar and as sweet. Her baby nose was chill with good health and high shine. Twice daily Sparkle's mini face was caressed clean with a ball of cotton wool soaked in Anne French cleansing milk. There was no struggle, her little dog leant into Katsie's touch.

On the night of the first moon landing in 1969, Mick went into a high rant. 'Fecking Yanks! Who do they think they're codding? Taking the lot of us for eejits, they are! Not me. Not this Mick Moran, and that's for sure, do you hear me??????'

Katsie lifted Sparkle from her lap and whispered into her glossy ear that she believed the astronauts were on the moon because President John F. Kennedy himself had pledged to make it happen years before. Then her evening upended. Mick lumbered and Sparkle scampered in the direction of the front door and the pair collided. Her husband kicked the dog high out of his way. Two of Sparkle's broken ribs punctured a lung and she died cradled in Katsie's arms an hour – or three pints – later.

Mick didn't notice his wife's little dog was missing for nearly a week, and tight-lipped and full of rising loathing for her husband, Katsie swore she would say nothing of the dog until he asked after it. 'Where's your little fleabag, Kay?' Mick finally wanted to know one morning as he tucked into a pyramid of fry-up breakfast. 'Sparkle? You kicked her and her ribs broke and she couldn't breathe and then she died. The night of the moon landing,' Katsie answered him as tonelessly as she could manage, with a longing eye on the bread knife that lay within arm's reach on the table. 'Bollox! There was no moon landing, haven't I told ye?' Mick yelled, slid his plate to the floor and set off on his well-worn path to the pub, even though he'd have to wait outside for it to open because of the early hour. He kicked over the hall table as he went.

One time, after yet another clash with Mick, Katsie slow-hiked the stairs to our first-floor maisonette. She had tried to stop him taking her housekeeping money to the pub. He told her the money was his and that she couldn't count because she was stupid. She was weeping that night, not because her husband had left a boot-shaped bruise on her hip, but because her black roots were now on full display to the world as she couldn't stand straight. The sisters bleached her hair and passed the hour before it was rinse-out time by swapping shoes with one another to make sure Katsie had the most comfortable pair, and playing card games for money. That evening Katsie cleaned up at cards, and the sisters complained so much about how much money they had lost that she was almost convinced they hadn't just conspired to let her win the housekeeping back. Mick died, growling, in his early forties and Katsie didn't even pretend to care. She spent so much time fixing her make-up the day of his funeral she was late to church.

They were all in a world of troubles of their own, and busy trying to laugh them off. Mary heard a saying on the wireless that struck a chord with her and she kept repeating it. 'The happiest people don't have the best of everything but they make the best of everything they have!' Her sisters often told her to 'Whisht' or 'Shut your gob!' after she'd interrupted a tale of woe with her signature quick cheer-up phrase.

Peggy, my favourite aunt, was always so warm and soft to sit with. When I was very young, she listened with her eyes as well as her ears to my tiny troubles. One winter evening she arrived in a taxi at our house and I heard the driver shouting, 'From the hospital to here it's £1! You understand English money? £1!' Then louder again, '£1! You should have hailed a horse and cart if you can't afford a fucking taxi, Paddywack. Fucking Irish! Beggars, the lot of you!'

Peggy called up the stairs in a muffled voice for my dad. He paid her fare for her and stood firm on the pavement, never taking his eyes off the cab until it was out of sight and around the corner. Then he carried her bag inside. I heard a noise. It was her dentures, broken into jigsaw pieces and wrapped in the floral-printed scarf she held in her hand, and clacking like castanets because she was shaking so violently.

'Bwuising's normal after bweauty surgewy!' she said as I stared at her split face. 'Three months' wages to get those bags sucked out, Anna May. Worth every penny! What's with that misery-gut face of yours?' Holding the tip of my little finger she let me trace the black nylon thread that had been dug into and dragged across her velveteen face with a doctor's needle to repair the work of her husband's knuckles.

Some time later Peggy confided that the bags from beneath her eyes had been posted back to her mother in Ireland with instructions that they should be fed to the chickens. I pretended I believed her to make her feel better. I was expert at reading my aunts' glances, and the way their eyes could argue with their smiles.

A year later, when I was in hospital after having my tonsils out, I acquired a serious infection that travelled all the way to my imagination. It was Peggy who volunteered to keep watch over me so Mum didn't miss work. She owned only one book. It was about St Thérèse of Lisieux and called *St Thérèse of the Roses* and she would read it to me, finish, and then start from page one all over again as I lay there semi-conscious. Peggy took root at my bedside, reading to me day and night. Thinking back, she was probably making up the story in her head because she couldn't read very well. After three days I finally opened my eyes and spoke. What I said to interrupt her long, lonely vigil was, 'Could you please be quiet? You are upsetting me.' She wasn't in the least offended. In fact, she laughed and then danced a jig next to my bed until the nurses intervened and strong-armed her to the front door of the hospital and slung her out with orders to go home and sleep. I got orange jelly to eat when she was gone. It was the first thing I'd eaten in a week. The sun shone in through the high ward windows down onto my jelly and made it glisten and soften. I thought it tasted like soft gold and I cried with the thrill of being back in the world as I ate it.

The sisters always turned to one another first for chat and consolation. Marrying into that cast-iron clique meant a challenge that most of their husbands couldn't, or weren't allowed, to rise to, and I understand how the husbands could have felt short-changed. Every marital secret was pooled, from the opening of the wage packet to what happened after the closing of the bedroom door.

My aunts believed there was no alternative to what they had, and maybe because they had one another to cling to they could endure being beaten or let down. Even when the emotional and marital climate was set fair, their men were still the 'outlaws'. Until the band played. Dancing was the one thing that brought them all together. Ceili music, a waltz or a jive had the power to close down any disagreements. 'The head's for thinking, the feet for dancing!' Auntie Peggy would say as she jumped up to dance with her husband, the Timer – a giant of a hurling player, given the nickname because he was always in the right place at the right time on the playing field. All arguments would be forgotten as the first bars of the ceili music reached her ears. On the dance floor the same pair of hands that had beat them would hold the sisters, throw them and sway them. And when they were dancing it was always as if it was for the first time and those men wooed their women all over again.

Sometimes the men's cruelty delivered a punch, but wasn't one. Aunt Peggy craved a baby. Month in, month out for almost twenty years she had to cope with the giddy disappointment that she wasn't pregnant. And when she was thirty-nine years old, Peggy missed her period, and then another one four weeks later. She confided her news first to the table and exclaimed that she felt like a big tree was growing up through her. The Timer was ecstatic when he heard. His face – the one that had been set in a constant snarl for decades – melted soft before her eyes. After asking how she liked it and how many sugars she wanted, her husband of twenty-odd years headed into the kitchen, virgin territory for him, and made her a cup of tea. The first ever. He stood over it and blew on the tea to cool it down before serving her the delicate pink and gold cup and saucer with his big doughy hands. The Timer even bought Peggy cherries and made a crimson mess trying to peel and stone them before sliding the mush into a china bowl and presenting it to her on a tray with a napkin and a fork. 'I heard my mother say cherries are good for your kidneys when you're having a child,' he said gruffly to the wall behind Peggy as he served them, his face as red as the contents of the bowl.

She stumbled to my mother's table to report to her sisters what the doctor had said. 'What baby? It's just the menopause you silly, silly woman!' she'd told them, large-eyed with unshed tears.

Later, speaking to the floor, she told her husband what the doctor had said. The Timer bent and took a step towards her with pursed lips. She thought he was bending in to kiss and console her. Instead he spat at her face and missed. Yellow phlegm shot past Peggy's ear, stuck first, rolled and finally slid down the picture of the Sacred Heart of Jesus that hung in a nook in their hall. 'Hahaha ! Sure I should have known. You couldn't have kittens, girl!'

The Timer disappeared into the toilet, slamming and locking the door behind him. Peggy waited in the hallway for half an hour but her husband didn't emerge.

At a loss, she walked back to our house and updated her sisters on what had just passed. The most shocking part, and she rocked back and forth on our hard kitchen chair as she told it, was that she had heard her husband crying in the lavvy. Crying. Hugged hard, kissed long and face wiped often by her sisters, Peggy walked, heavy-legged, back to her life.

Peggy was tall, graceful and didn't know how to be cross. She was my mum's echo in the bringing-up years because she never did have a child of her own. If wishing could make babies she'd have had a dozen. At times I felt like I had a two-headed mother. If I wanted to go anywhere or do anything I was required to ask permission of them both, and their opposite answers were entirely predictable. If it was safe and legal my mum would answer, 'Do it. You are only young once. Look after yourself,' and Peggy would chime in, 'Ohhhh noooooo, Annie! That sounds very dangerous. Can't she just stay at home and read a book?' Joining the school netball team and teaching catechism classes on a Sunday morning were the wildest of my requests at the time.

Aunt Peggy was devoted by nature and lived close by my first primary school. Even if she hadn't been only a short walk away, I think she would still have been stood on the other side of the playground railings keeping watch over me every morning and afternoon playtime. She would stand guard and chain-smoke and rattle the railings and shout, 'Eh! Oi oi! Mind out!' to anyone she judged was playing too rough with me. If I tried to approach to chat with her, she would shoo me away and hiss, 'Go away. I'm not here.' Her vigilance continued through secondary school, when she would often be waiting outside to meet me with an umbrella if it had rained unexpectedly during the day, or if she had been shopping and bought me a small but always perfect gift: a pencil case, a pen or a hairslide. Either that woman never got bored listening to me, or did a great job pretending she didn't.

Peggy had a unique culinary gift. She made the best hot apple sponge in the world and regularly walked the mile between her house and ours carrying it in a jumbo-size ovenproof dish. Her lilac mac coat had a permanent stewed apple stain under her left breast where the fruit seeped out as she walked. The sponge that hovered above the apples was so light I fretted that the breeze would have it away during the journey between her house and ours. It was paradise in Pyrex. 'What makes it taste so good, Auntie Peggy?' I asked her. 'Love,' she replied with a shy smile.

5

The Bacon and Cabbage Brothers

My nan was barely five feet tall yet she gave birth to thirteen babies. One simply slid out of her onto the stone-flagged floor she was scrubbing with a wire brush at the time. Shared thirteen ways, family traits got diluted: tall, thin, short, fat, smart, crazy, cross-eyed. All that was in them somewhere in different measures. Later in life their enthusiastic use of hair dye was another factor that made them look unrelated. From blonde to ginger to jet and every shade inbetween, each one claimed their current hair shade as genetic.

I don't remember, as a child, ever experiencing silence in the hours when I was awake because aunts and uncles in various numbers would always be gathered around our table talking, arguing or laughing. In three, four, five decades they never once ran dry of conversation. And it was face-to-face talking, no telephones for them. We were the second in the extended family to have a phone installed in the 1970s – Bet was always the first to have everything. My dad never touched it and kept our telephone number on a slip of paper at the bottom of his tobacco tin: 'In case I get hit by a bus.' Ours was a red telephone with a dial on the front and secured to the wall with a length of curly wire. The foot of the stairs was where we sat to use it, and how we coveted Auntie Bet's stylish dedicated telephone seat. This was a Formica-topped table with a connected stool that was upholstered in padded and buttoned burgundy PVC. Bet also had central heating, which meant she could lounge around chatting and smoking on her telephone seat in winter without seeing her own breath in the air or having to wear a hat, scarf, coat and gloves in the icy hallway like we did. A long hot radiator by her telephone table was the reason she always wanted to talk for longest. Our telephone was on a party line with a complete stranger, commonplace at the time. Shared line rentals were half price and meant we had to take turns making calls and could overhear all one another's conversations. The man who shared with us complained to British Telecom that he didn't want to share with Irish people because there were 'hundreds' of us and we'd always be on the phone blocking the line. He actually told this to my mum, too, when they both happened to coincide on a call. My mum answered him that she quite understood. 'I don't want that telephone jinxed with any arguments. It might start ringing with bad news,' was her excuse for not straightening out our line sharer in her usual forthright style.

Dad gave the phone a wide berth, almost like he was afraid of it. The closest he came to using that telephone was when I saw him call out 'Hello? Hello?' to it when it rang one evening – but he didn't pick up the receiver. Mum had a special English telephone answering voice. She spoke 'Hell' and 'Oooooo' into it like they were two separate words. When she heard the voice on the other end was family, she'd launch into a belly laugh and, 'Howaya?'

Face to face the family did argue – about who owed what to who, about horse and greyhound racing bets, card games, whose children were the loveliest, and which men were the most useless. Table banging, raised voices and flouncing out were quite routine, and then back they'd come later the same day or sometimes the next day, all smiles greeted by all smiles. Their allegiances were solid. The brothers and sisters in my mum's family loved one another all the same – except for Mum and Auntie Peggy, who had a special grip on each other's hearts and everyone understood that.

Bet, my aunt who was really a cousin but didn't know it (the secret of her birth had turned, over time, into truth), broke with tradition by marrying an Englishman. They met in a dance hall in London and she explained his immediate *zing!* attraction to her as hard evidence of the benefits of a good-fitting brassiere. Hers was the only white wedding of her generation, with a proper bridal dress and veil, a tiered cake and a row of scowling sister bridesmaids who all had lovely flowers and a severe attack of sibling envy.

The groom was Ken, a cheeky chappy Cockney cab driver. He was monied, by their standards, which probably meant he had a Post Office savings account. As the only child of two only children, the poor man was mystified by the hordes of people who were Bet's immediate family. When Ken's neat little mother was introduced to Bet and her sisters and their husbands and children, she paled and blurted out to her son, 'Are you sure you're sure about this?' My aunts and uncles had Irish accents so strong that for many years Ken didn't believe they were actually speaking English to one another or to him, which is why he never answered them when they spoke. But he smiled a lot.

Ken was the first car owner in the history of the entire extended family, and this car, a Humber, was revered by all the sisters and brothers, assorted husbands and wives and all of us children, who would very occasionally be allowed to sit and play in the vehicle. To be clear, playing in it meant washing our hands and faces, emptying our pockets, removing our shoes and sitting still with our arms folded tightly in front of us. Not moving a muscle had never been so much fun. My sister and brother and I would whisper *vroom vroom* softly through the sides of our mouths and pretend we were going places – usually to Mallory Towers or to rendezvous with the Famous Five for a super adventure that would end up with imaginary home-made lemonade and macaroons. To be consumed outside the car, of course. Only my grandmother was allowed to be a real, moving, proper passenger in that car. She would be driven to the shops or to Mass or to visit friends she wanted to piss off because they didn't have a daughter with a husband with a car. Her showing-off glee was contagious and would often manifest itself in celebratory slabs of nut chocolate or sherbet dips all round. If there was such a thing as a car-shaped crown, she would have worn one all her waking hours.

Imagine, then, the day Bet announced that she and Ken were the proud owners of a caravan. My mum said that caravan was bigger news than President Kennedy being assassinated. Theresa, jealous to the point of hospitalisation over the caravan, called Bet a 'proper little English girl' because she dared to own a car and a caravan, albeit only by marriage. She jibed that as Bet was still peeing in a bucket in the caravan, just as they had at home in Ireland, she hadn't gone that far up in the world after all, had she? Bet's response was to shout back at the top of her voice, 'The bucket's got a lid, with hinges! So what do you say to that, you big fat bitch?' All was forgiven when the sisters convened to a caravan park on the Isle of Sheppey for a bonding weekend. They sat sunbathing in dresses, scarves, cardigans and nylons, arranged in a fairy ring, backs to the sea, all facing the coveted caravan.

Bet was easily the most prosperous. She and Ken had their own house in Kilburn and visits there were without any doubt the highlight of my pre-teenage life. There was a constantly changing list of why Auntie Bet and Uncle Ken were a fave rave visit. Number one for a long time was their coffee table. A piece of highly polished driftwood with holes in it that were meant to be there, it was a coffee table extravaganza. Abstract and so deliciously 1960s. My sister and I played the game of trying to throw cocktail sausages, peanuts and crisps into one another's mouths, one of us positioned at each end of the table. We often missed and our nibbles would fall down the cracks in the wood. Our tongues weren't long enough to retrieve the lost treats, but, oh, how we revelled in trying. We would kneel down and press our faces against the highly polished wood, leaving sweaty imprints of our faces, cheeks and lips as calling cards. Auntie Bet would see what we were doing and laugh, saying gaily and loudly, within certain earshot of her sisters, 'The mess you two are making will surely keep my cleaner busy tomorrow!'

All her sisters heard was the word 'cleaner'. They all worked as cleaners but their sister actually had one of her own.

Auntie Bet had *two* toilets in her house, one upstairs and one downstairs. To get to the downstairs toilet you had to walk through an area that my mother thought was a Washing Wonderland. Bet had handwritten a sign, coloured it in with felt-tip pen and stuck it on the door so that there could be no mistake. To access the down-stairs toilet it was necessary to enter the door marked 'YOUTILITY ROOM'. In her 'Youtility' room there was a washer and a dryer – heaven on earth according to my mother, who at that time still washed sheets and towels in the tin bath. I witnessed her press her forehead to that washing machine and croon, low and needy. She scared me. And there was more – Bet had a steam press for ironing clothes. My mother couldn't resist flicking the 'on' switch to see how it worked and the powerful press hissed and shot steam straight into her left eye and made it bleed. She was conveyed to casualty, in Ken's car, with a monogrammed towel that read 'Ken and Bet' pressed to her oozing eye. 'Lucky thing!' said Theresa about my mother as she drove off to hospital in luxury.

Their pièce de résistance was made of red-cushioned PVC and chrome: the bar in the corner of Bet and Ken's sitting room. This was a much-photographed bar. Snaps of it were posted, or delivered in person, to relatives, friends and neigh-bours in our street, Ireland, America and even Australia. Uncle Ken would get common-or-garden plastic ice trays from the freezer and use his fingers to transfer the ice into a black and white ice bucket. Once he had used his hands to arrange the cubes in the bucket and his palm to press them down into place, thereafter the ice could only be handled using a pair of tongs. This was the Law. The smart and shiny tongs slotted into the bucket's pineapple-shaped knob. If guests refused ice in their drinks, Ken's disappointment was tangible. His shoulders and eyelids would droop. He so loved the forensic removal of a cube and its insertion into a glass so as to cause minimal splashing. He was King Ken of the Ice Bucket.

Bet and Ken's house was an Aladdin's cave of exotic furnish-ings and knick-knacks, but of all the shiny exciting things they owned, mine and my sister's favourites were the coloured glass balls in string cases that hung above the bar, apparently to give the area a Mediterranean feel. We begged them to take them down so we could hold and kiss these objects but the answer was always the same. 'No!' And the explanation? 'They're from Spain!' If we had asked to play with the Pope's testicles we could not have sparked more outrage. They were so tantalising, so green, so blue, so red, suspended in their string pouches . . . but they were forbidden fruit.

My little sister and I were as hypnotised by the glass balls as the adults were by the assorted drink bottles. Once, with great ceremony, Auntie Bet handed my sister and me a snowball to drink. A snowball is a blend of advocaat and lemonade mixed using a fork and topped off with a cherry flourish: a plastic-looking cherry speared on a cocktail stick. That snowball was gloopy and frothy and potent and elastic. It travelled up and down the back of my throat for days afterwards.

My mother's family exploded the myth that the Irish are all drinkers. Their husbands acted as 24-hour aversion therapy. The women chose tea every time. All bar Bet. She became an alcoholic in her late twenties, which was Ken's cue to leave her.

Bet brought up her two children alone and had a job she loved – sweeping up and washing hair in a hairdresser. No one ever left that salon without Bet exclaiming with a sunshine smile that they looked gorgeous. When her son and daughter left home she lived a low life, socially and financially, and her big treat twice a year was to shop in the local Marks and Spencer food hall. Tip money she'd saved up for months was excitedly exchanged for Viennese chocolate biscuits and jams with extra fruit and fudge, which she would eat with her eyes closed.

Once, for a college English A-level project, she agreed to let me interview her about a day in her life. It was an uneventful account that began with her cornflakes and took me through to *Coronation Street* – until the end when she pressed her hands, gnarled with arthritis, onto my knee. 'Be sure to put in that I'm not ordinary, Anna May. I had it all. Even a Teasmade. There's not many luckier than me.'

But her luck ran out. Bet had a shoulder replacement that went wrong and she kept telling the doctors that the pain was unbearable. 'I can't live with it,' she repeated. She meant it. On the fifth day after surgery she walked off the ward wearing pink floral-print pyjamas and took a bus ride. Her destination was Putney Bridge, where she got off and walked to its central point. She managed to lever herself up onto the bridge balustrade and roll over it into the River Thames below.

There were just two boys in amongst the thirteen on my mum's side who survived into adulthood, and they were so different that their own mother described them as 'bacon and cabbage'. Bren was the elder of the two and spent most of his life clearing the path ahead for his younger, champion-lazy brother, Tony.

For forty hours a week Bren was a bus driver and for another forty he was a part-time chauffeur to a big-cheese Irish businessman. Bren was a dashing driver, a smooth Terry Wogan-alike: clean shaven, sweet-smelling and impeccably dressed. That man made pyjamas look dapper.

Bren's second job brought him to Royal Ascot, Henley-on-Thames, Wimbledon and all the other playground locations of the very rich. Although not very talkative, he once told me proudly, 'Anna May, I've waited in my car outside all the best places, you know.' His sisters claimed that Bren's wife, Philomena, did so much talking it put him right off conversation. With one exception – he loved to chat to my mum, his sister Annie. He never missed a week without telephoning or visiting her and they had a gentle, undemanding relationship that endured without conflict of any kind all of their lives.

On the day my mother died I arrived at the hospice early in the morning to visit and found Bren already there. For her last few weeks he came faithfully every day, crossing London on public transport. He would loosen his silk tie and slip off his tasselled loafers, sliding them neatly out of sight beneath her bedside locker, and sit on a stool so he could get up close to her bed. Very quietly, and leaning in close to her left ear, he would read to her from the sports pages. The odds, the runners, the jockeys – he missed out nothing. He drew some betting slips from his jacket pocket and one of the stubby betting-shop pens that punters got for free and he asked her to do a bet with him. 'Go on, pick a few winners, Annie,' he urged, lifting her limp and yellowed hand and letting it drop gently onto the racing pages. 'Good choice!' he'd say to her as he wrote a horse's name down. A short, soft smile moved across her lips at his antics. The pair spent many of her last hours leant in together. They didn't touch or even look at one another. He brought no flowers or chocolates because there was no need. A light understanding hung between them. Bren spent five hours at my mum's bedside on that last day, and set off for home unaware he would never see her alive again.

She took us all by surprise. Due for discharge the next day, there was a sudden change in her condition and death crept up from behind. My sister arrived at the hospice that evening for her daily chit-chatty visit to find Mum semi-conscious and deteriorating fast. Julie was carrying a brand new, swanky chenille dressing gown from Marks and Spencer to replace the buttonless riot of cabbage roses that Mum had worn for over two decades. That robe started life in the 1980s as fleecy and was so boil-washed and worn out it had thinned into lace. Julie held up the new, smart dressing gown for Mum to inspect. There was just enough puff in her cancer-ravaged body for, 'I've got one. Go and get your money back.'

She died a few hours later and my brother, sister and I wept as much for her devoted brother as for ourselves. My brother made the dreaded telephone call to deliver the news to Bren. His face was twisted with pain as he spoke. Less than an hour later Bren's wife called us. 'It was the shock of Annie dying that did it,' she wailed. Bren was in an ambulance after suffering a massive stroke and was fighting for *his* life.

Bren survived the stroke, but as a miniature version of himself.

A bus driver for almost three decades, Bren made a serious mistake when he drove his double-decker bus beneath a low bridge and sliced the top clean off it. 'A miracle' is how he describes that all his passengers were seated downstairs that day and uninjured. But they all, including Bren himself, received a dangerously high dose of sudden shock. When my mum died, the top of Bren's life was lifted off and he was never the same again. As a brother, that quiet, steadfast man was beyond compare.

Tony was so different. A small-shouldered man with light brown hair that grew upwards in a wave formation. He would run his podgy hands, the colour and consistency of white pudding finished with yellow smoke-stained fingernails, upwards through it to make it tall and proud. He barely spoke other than to declare he wanted something.

His was the good hair, teeth and complexion of the always well rested. As the baby boy of the family, Tony got the cream of the milk and the top of the eggs and the fat from the bacon. A skilled darts player, he could light a match stuck into a darts board with the speeding point of a single throw. For this party trick he would collect not cash but liquid donations – Guinness, brandy, beer.

Another income stream came from scouring the streets early on Sunday morning for banknotes dropped by drunks on their way home on a Saturday night. His small, pale grey eyes would scan the pavement, lighting up whenever he found his free money. It was the only reason he ever left his bed early, and it also meant he could lie to his sisters that, yes, he had been to Mass. 'Where else would I be at that time on a Sunday morning?' he chided them if they enquired whether or not he had been to church.

Tony's moral compass was sent into a spin by the constant acts of kindness that rained down on him. His brother's and sisters' generosity didn't make him grateful, it made him greedy. All arms for taking, Tony was an unappreciative mute. On Sunday evenings, when Mum and Dad were at bingo, he was a regular visitor to our house. Alone or together, my sister and brother and I knew the drill. Whichever one of us was fortunate enough to be sitting in the prime position chair – the one with the best view of the TV and the greatest coverage from the gas fire – would leap out of it so that Tony could lower himself in. A sprint to the kitchen followed where the kettle would be taken off the gas just before it reached boiling point and the hot water poured into a mug containing two crumbled Oxo cubes. This stocky concoction had to be delivered to Tony's lap in double time, along with a freshly made Cheddar cheese (so mature it smelt eggy) and jumbo cooking onion sandwich.

Dessert was a teacup full of brandy. Uncle Tony would stare at us as he ate and drank then, rat-tat-tat, fart, burp onion breath across the room and leave suddenly without having uttered a single word. When he was gone my sister, brother and I would open the windows and flap them around to freshen the air before pummelling one another for the best chair. Whoever won would always turn the cushion before settling in.

Uncle Tony didn't need to speak – he always got what he wanted without words. As soon as his siblings were settled with work in London, they had clubbed together to buy him a suit and a sailing ticket so that he could cross the Irish Sea and come over and join them. He helped himself to a farewell present – the contents of his widowed mother's purse – before he left.

It was the pubs of London that twinkled for Tony when he arrived – not for him the harmless tea and twirling in dance halls that the others enjoyed. His brother and sisters were his adoring fan club: they supported him, dressed him, fed him and made heartfelt and convincing excuses for his bad behaviour. Writing letters home to their mother, they lied with love and made it sound like Tony was storming London. 'He's managing a pub already in Ladbroke Grove', 'He has a lovely girl, her name is Molly, she's a supervisor with Marks and Spencer', 'He never misses Mass, and always lights a candle for you ...'. The truth was that he was their best customer at that pub in Ladbroke Grove and not the manager. When he ran up bar bills and gambling debts so steep that even his devoted family couldn't afford to pay them off he was taken on as a pot man to work off his debts.

Tony had a spotless rent-free room in Peggy's house and would zig-zag his way back there some time or other after midnight, seven days a week, fifty-two weeks of the year. Peggy's husband, The Timer, the giant and always angry ex-hurling player, despised his freeloading brother-in-law with an unnatural force – even when he wasn't disturbing his sleep.

The last time Tony ever let himself into Peggy's house was in the early hours one Monday in December. En route to bed, he slipped and fell at the top of the steep flight of stairs that led to his room. Toppling backwards, Tony made a lot of noise as his skull strummed the stair posts before coming to a halt halfway down. The Timer, awoken by the racket, was crackling with fury that he had been disturbed and kicked the unconscious Tony down the remaining stairs and then dragged him into the centre of the front room before returning to bed.

A panicked Peggy was close behind her husband and when she saw the angle on Tony's neck, she tipped into hysteria. She wailed every time she remembered what she saw. 'It was like there was string beneath his skin, not bone.'

Barefoot she fled to the nearest telephone box to call an ambulance and then carried on running the mile to our house. I heard her calling for help in the distance as she approached; making a high-pitched yowling noise that woke all the neighbours, too. When I looked out of my bedroom window, Peggy was standing under a street light with her arms raised and outstretched in her floral nightdress. It was soaked and bunched on her body and legs. She was speed-pleading with God at the top of her voice. It had started to snow but she hadn't noticed.

Overnight my uncle Tony became a shouting head. Doctors delivered the news that he was permanently paralysed as a result of his fall. They left him no cause for hope. He would certainly never walk again and may have what they variously described as 'limited' or 'spastic' or 'spasmodic' use of his hands and arms.

As well as being clubbed around the head with that information, Uncle Tony was forced to dry out from alcohol during those first few weeks in hospital. His hospital bed became a wet cell, covered in sweat and blue plastic sheeting, the same blue as the livid veins that throbbed with fury on his neck. A pegged-out man, he was a windmill of tubes and wires and would stream sweat and contort his face trying his best to spit at staff and visitors.

Tony was transferred from hospital to a specialist NHS centre for the disabled – or 'Fucking Cripple City' as he called it. There was no ambiguity in its actual name: the Home for Incurables. All physiotherapy and rehabilitation offers were refused and jeered at by Tony, with profanities added for extra emphasis. 'No means no! Send me away if you want! Broadmoor'll do. Anywhere that Jimmy fucking Savile isn't is good enough for me!' Tony had developed an irrational hatred of Jimmy Savile, who at that time did a lot of voluntary work with spinal-injury sufferers.

He had made up his mind to sit out the rest of his life in a wheelchair and no one could change it. His was the soft and floppy grip of a baby and he had to wear a fireproof-style bib that staff tied around his neck so that he couldn't set himself alight struggling to smoke. He was powerless to rip it off but his livid chin did battle royal to try and repel it each morning as the nursing staff dressed him. When Peggy visited she could be seen flicking through a copy of *Ireland's Own* or *Titbits* with one hand and sliding a cigarette in and out of Tony's lips with the other so he could have a satisfying smoke.

Finally, with a spirit made gossamer by relentless rage after twenty-plus years in care, Tony killed himself by executing a carefully and long-thought-out plan. He painstakingly packed his upper body with newspapers that he had been saving up for days – with his powerless jerking arm it took him hours – and then dropped a lit cigarette from between his lips down onto them. The newspapers caught light and Tony used his bedcovers to cover the early smoke and smell of his body burning.

The suicide attempt did work, but not immediately. Fire alarms were triggered and staff discovered Tony alight, but in no pain. It was the one time his paralysis did him a good turn. The burns he suffered to his torso shrank his skin to purple floating islands above charred muscle and bone. It took almost a week for Tony to die from the infections that bloomed on his remaining wet-jelly skin patches. He was transferred to a room in a specialist burns unit that had mini sprinklers built into the ceiling to keep the air moist.

Those little jets extinguished what was left of the man's life spark as he lay there – paralysed, naked and seared. I recalled how the son of a patient Tony had once verbally abused years before had shouted at him in anger, 'I hope you burn in hell for what you said to my father!' Tony had cackled about how the man's father had looked like he was dancing when he was in the throes of a seizure. From what I saw, I believe Tony really did burn in a hell of his own making.

6
The O'Lottery

An uncomplicated woman, my mother loved and appreciated all she had and her wants were always for the things that money couldn't buy. 'Pray for health, *never* for money' was her mantra. Being and staying well was top of her prayer list, as she believed fervently that once you were fighting fit, you could make good fortune come your way.

Sunday wasn't Sunday unless you went to Mass, according to my mother. But, once you had been to church, then the world and all its vices were there to be enjoyed. Sights firmly set on some Sabbath bingo and roulette she would speed-roast a lunch – and it was always a roast on a Sunday, even if it was just potatoes and parsnips in the roasting tin. After the meal she would clear the table quickly and head for the front room sofa where she had a legs-akimbo restorative nap that lasted two and a half hours exactly. At 5pm on the dot and without any need to consult a clock, up she'd spring to do her pre-bingo ablutions. These never varied: a rinse of her dentures under the hot tap, an application of Rimmel lipstick (in the shade 'Talked About'), several hearty dabs of Coty face powder and a jumbo squirt of 4711 cologne. Finally, a quick change of cardigan and she was good to go.

Mum linked one arm into Dad's and on the other swung her giant Jackie O-style handbag. This two-handled slab of plastic, lined with red nylon, had a clasp that delivered a finger-snapping bite as it clipped shut. Then the two of them would go prospecting for cash at the local Essoldo Bingo every Sunday evening. Her cavernous bag would leave our house empty but for a rosary beads and a lipstick, and return home within hours spilling over with silver coins won on the roulette or fruit machines. Toddling down the road they took baby steps, carefully sharing the weight of the handbag between them. Dad, a hod carrier on a building site at that time, could easily have scooped it up and carried it solo without any effort. But Mum insisted that would be too 'poofy' (she pronounced it 'poo' pause 'fee') and to avoid this fate-worse-than-death they painstakingly fetched the money home in her handbag together, carrycot style.

My sister and I endeavour to keep their Sunday bingo custom alive. Once a month we head off to a building the size of an aircraft hangar in Cricklewood and spend three hours in there happily losing our money. The prize we come away with each time is for being Beacon Bingo's most consistent losers. Regular bingo players often display lucky charms on their tables. We have no plastic Buddha, wooden elephant (with spinning tusks) or a wind-up dancing leprechaun as our table centrepiece. Some players with strong spiritual leanings even construct a mini altar in their space with holy statues and votive lights burning. My parents' bingo superstitions never involved ornaments. Mum's was that stamping hard on your bingo books several times – think flamenco – made them certain winners.

Dad was convinced that good luck was transferable from one bingo player to another and he would always try and give the head of someone who had just won money a vigorous rubbing if he could get away with it. It's testimony to his good humour and charm that more often than not he was granted his wish to rub the head of a complete stranger in a bingo hall. The fact that the lucky donor had just won a ton of money and was therefore in a very jolly place probably encouraged them to agree to Dad's head-rubbing request. The only time Dad got a thump on the nose for his lucky laying-on-of-hands was the evening he rubbed first, asked second, and ended up with the hairpiece of a man who had just won £250 threaded through his fingers.

Gambling doesn't pay isn't a warning I can't take too seriously, because in my childhood it did, and nearly all the time. It paid for plenty: my school dinners, school uniforms, school trips, fish and chip suppers and new shoes – sometimes even a couple of pairs at a time.

One event that is still lit golden in my memory that was paid for from bingo spoils was a taxi ride both ways, and tickets to see the newly released *Sound of Music* film in Tottenham Court Road. For one night only I was a Very Important Black Cab Riding Princess.

Nan had been selected by Mum, who had to go to work, as my chaperone for the night. Normally a stay-at-home sort of gal, Nan ventured out and accompanied me more out of duty than desire. Made miniature by the plush West End cinema seat, she chomped her way through a family-sized bar of nut chocolate and a pound of mint imperials before the film had even started. Too breathless with excitement to chew or swallow, I ate and drank nothing. Before she settled down, her dentures were pressed into my hand. 'Hang onto these, Anna May, in case I swallow them.'

The Von Trapp children hadn't even dressed up in their curtain clothes before Nan was snoring. Her thin, short legs were crossed at her gobstopper ankles and didn't reach anywhere near the deep-pile carpet beneath her seat. She was wearing a bottle-green plaid pompom slipper on one foot and one of her best brown leather lace-ups on the other. A giant, flaky, custard-coloured corn on one of her little toes was hobbling her and she couldn't wear a proper shoe on that side because it rubbed too much. I remember offering up a short prayer from the back of the taxi that no one in the cinema would notice her feet and laugh. On the way home she asked about the film she'd slept through, and was especially keen to know what had happened to the pretty young postulant Maria. I was in a sulk with her because she had gone to sleep and also about the slipper she'd worn on my big night out. So, in petty revenge, I told her that Maria had murdered her Mother Superior and ended up in prison serving a life sentence. 'Would you credit it?' was her shocked response before lapsing into deep thought as she stared out the taxi window. A few miles down the road she spoke again, breaking the long silence. 'Fancy Mary Poppins carrying on like that!'

We had nights out galore at the White City greyhound track. 'Shall we get a bit of fresh air?' was my mum's way of saying we were all going gambling. Greyhound racing is a fast-moving evening. The races are timed close together, the dogs race, the trackside bookies shout the odds out and tic-tac at speed. The evening would flash by in bright trackside lights and splashes of colour. The only way to tell if Mum and Dad had won big, or lost the housekeeping money, was how we got home. Dad hailing a taxi was the best of news, which always included a meter-still-running stop at the fish and chip shop for a hot supper to take home. We crushed onto the bus if we broke even, and walked the five miles home if all had been lost.

One summer evening my brother and sister and I, all aged under eleven, were sat on a row of suitcases in the hallway of our flat. We were rigid with excitement. Dad was on his way home with his holiday pay and as soon as he arrived we were setting off on a week's holiday to stay in a chalet by the seaside. I can still remember the address of where we were going – Sunbeam Avenue, Clacton-on-Sea, Essex. I'd never been before but I just knew it was going to be a tropical paradise.

My mum was kneeling on her case and looking out of the window, hoping to catch first sight of Dad turning the corner and approaching the house. The price label was still on the sole of her new, cork-soled cream-coloured sandals, and her toenails were painted bright red. She'd waggled her feet for us to see the shiny varnish and trilled, 'So I'll look pretty on the beach!' As she watched out for Dad, I was flooded with joy at the promise of the days ahead – our first ever proper family holiday.

We each had sweets in our coloured plastic sand buckets; Mum had put them there. My sister and I were saving ours for the coach journey. My brother's bucket contained only empty wrappers and he was keeping a close watch on ours.

But as the daylight faded along with our smiles and the

electric lights had to be switched on in the hall – the silent wait stretched and stretched from something fun into something frightening. I wouldn't speak or budge from my case, refusing to believe what the expression on my mum's face was telling me – that Dad wasn't coming home and our holiday wouldn't happen. I believed my willpower could make everything alright. I fell asleep sitting on my case in that dark hallway well after midnight and Mum had to carry me to bed. My brother and sister had accepted defeat hours earlier and unpacked their pyjamas and toothbrushes, climbed into bed and cried themselves to sleep.

What happened? My dad, in a moment of gambling gung-ho, had bet *all* of his holiday pay on a horse – called 'Sunshine Sands', which I admit is nearly funny – and lost it. When the horse let him down and he realised what he had done, he was too scared to come home and instead he went to hide out with his sister and her family on the other side of London in Clapham. He just couldn't face us. Three days later Dad finally walked through the front door and my mum welcomed him back by breaking every piece of china in the house. She threw it, single item by single item, against the kitchen wall as we three children sat at the table in front of a cheese salad dinner and watched. We had to pick shards of china off our plates and out of our hair. She broke every piece of crockery we had and it was paper plates at every meal time for months afterwards. Hot food would make a hole in the paper plate it was served on unless we were very quick. Eating stew from a fast-dissolving paper plate was a big challenge. Pacing was all. We got our ears twisted if we gobbled our dinner and our legs smacked if we made a mess on the table. No table manner concessions were available during those paper-plate months.

He knew better than to ever blow the holiday cash again and in later years we managed a few family seaside holidays. They always lasted three days. Never a week. I thought that the word 'holiday' meant three days away until girls at my school reported they had been away for one or two full weeks. I thought they must surely be millionaires.

Our seaside destinations would vary – Canvey Island, Clacton, St Osyth, the Isle of Sheppey – but the drill once we got there was always the same. Mum would pressgang my dad, brother, sister and me into a row of deckchairs that she had lined up to face the sun. She would supervise the rolling up or rolling down of any clothing that covered our mushroom-coloured skin: sleeves, skirts, trousers and socks. Then came the order, 'Lift your faces up to the sun and get a bit of colour!' To help bring along our 'bit of colour' she would coat us with a face flannel pre-loaded with vegetable oil that she stowed in her handbag. To this day the sound of anything sizzling in a pan brings back the memory of our faces frying in the midday sun. The reward for severe burns for us children was candy floss from the pier, which we would sick up later when we were freezing and overcome with sunstroke shakes.

My mum and dad had no interest whatsoever in travelling anywhere, but took great pride in the fact that their children did. My dad would boast to his family about my sister, 'She's been all over the world, that one!' His evidence for this claim was that whilst she was at university Julie had spent two weeks in Portugal and a long weekend in the Lake District.

Most of my uncles and aunts did their travelling after they died when their bodies were returned to Ireland for burial. 'All the Yanks want a plot where I'm going – but it's all full up. I have my space ready. And I'll be arriving there on an aeroplane!'

crowed my aunt Katsie, a woman too terrified to fly when she was alive but happy to brag that she'd be doing it when she was dead.

There is a picture in our family album of Mum, Dad and my little brother all dressed in short-sleeved holiday clothes looking like they were about to board a plane. They were posing in the aircraft doorway on top of a flight of airline steps, smiling and waving for all they were worth. Dad was carrying a BOAC holdall. Fascinated by this photo, I wanted to know where they had been without me. 'Shepherd's Bush. To the picture studio,' my mum replied. 'They borrowed us the clothes and the bag. Doesn't it look real?' she asked, delighted with herself.

My dad had a mini holiday all to himself every Derby Day – the highlight of his racing year. For three decades he threw an annual sickie and headed to Epsom. Dad was rubbish at subterfuge. He would get up as normal, dress as if he was going to work and set off for the bus stop with his usual two rounds of sandwiches and a thermos flask of tea. He would give himself away over his cornflakes by repeating, 'Another day, another dollar!' over and again. Or sighing, 'Same auld same auld . . .' These weary workaday expressions were only ever heard on Derby Day and were intended to convince us that yes, as usual, he was heading to work. The pair of binoculars he had found on a bus some years earlier only ever emerged from the bottom drawer on Derby Day. Dad would hang them around his neck and button his jacket tightly over them, believing that way they were somehow invisible to all of us. My mother knew everything Dad was going to do before he ever did it, so she was well aware of the charade that was being played out in front of her beady eyes. Dad would return from his daring day out with the racing programme and his train ticket sticking out of his sports jacket pockets and his sun-baked bald head glowing red.

But all the gambling highs and lows that went before were the equivalent of rolling pennies compared with the year that my dad drew a horse in the Irish Sweepstakes. The Irish Sweepstakes was the O'Lottery of its day and drawing a horse was the everyirishman fantasy. From all of the hundreds of thousands of people who bought a ticket, only a supremely fortunate twenty or so (according to how many horses were running in the race) would draw a named horse that would run on their behalf. If that horse was placed in the final four, it would earn the lucky ticket-holder a *massive* cash price.

The first notification that Dad had drawn a horse came in a telegram. In our house the delivery of a telegram always meant someone was dead. Dad spread the flimsy piece of paper on the kitchen table and placed the salt and pepper pot at either end to stop it rolling up. I half watched him from the other end of the table, lifting my Enid Blyton book to my face in preparation, using it as a shield to block the bad news that I was sure was imminent. Dad bent over the telegram, trying to read it and prodding the printed words with his big sausage-shaped finger. Struggling, he beckoned my mum over to help. She stared at the telegram for a long time and then snatched it from the table and whirled it around above her head. Transformed, she was dancing and high-kicking with joy around the room, vegetable peeler still in her hand. 'You've drawn a horse! You've done it! We're innnn the moooonnnnneeeeyyyy! We're innnn the moooonnnnneeeeey!' she sang. Dad leapt up, understanding now, seized her by the waist and the pair of them quickstepped around the kitchen, clacking as they went on the lino floor. Nan appeared in the doorway, one side of her face still snooze-pink. 'What's the racket about?' she wanted to know, and I did, too. 'We're in the money!' Dad cried, his eyes wild and wide. 'We're going to be *rich*! BIG MONEY is on its way! I've only drawn a feckin' horse on the sweeps!'

My mum suddenly went all floppy and backed into a kitchen chair. She started to weep and laugh at the same time and pledged in a fast, yet solemn, voice that we could all have duvets with bright covers and she even promised a round white sputnik colour TV on a stand for the front room. I remember feeling dizzy at the prospect and asking if I could have a Tressy doll and a hamster if we were going to be rich.

The horse that was running for our family, and our future wealth and happiness, was called Desperate Dee. Within hours of getting the sweepstakes news our tiny terraced house was crammed with friends and relatives smoking, drinking tea and speculating about how Desperate Dee might perform in the race to be held four days later, on a Saturday afternoon.

If the horse won the race, Dad would pocket £25,000. To put that into perspective – at the time it would have bought him an island in the Caribbean. It was life-transforming money.

The ticket had cost £10 to buy, which was almost a week's wages from one of the three jobs apiece they had at the time, so Dad and Auntie Peggy had agreed to share the purchase price, or 'initial investment' as my dad had preferred to call it. Dad and Peggy were therefore, formally and legally, partners in excitement and fear.

And then the two of them were presented with a tough gambling conundrum, one that was put to them by the two representatives sent from the bookmakers to persuade Dad and Peggy to sell them a stake in their potentially winning ticket before the outcome of the race was known. The wide-shouldered men filled our front doorway. They had patent hair and shoes and wore matching pinstripe suits. £7,000 was the amount they offered for a half-share in the ticket. The eternal silence after my dad suggested they bid a bit more cash was how they explained – using no words – that there would be *no* negotiation on that amount.

Dad and Peggy told the bookmakers that they needed time to think. Hands, legs and chins wobbling, the two of them headed out into the yard for a conflab and left me alone in the company of the no-chuckle brothers. I was nine years old and sat doing my homework under the bookmakers' disinterested gazes.

They sat stock still, observing all the excitement and consultation that was going on only feet away. The sash window of the back room that looked out onto the yard was thrown up as far as it could go and the thirty or so relatives and friends who were jammed into that little room jostled to take turns offering their opinions. These were delivered via the open window. It was the most thrilling dilemma, especially for a room full of skint, diehard gamblers – to sell or not to sell?

The buy-in amount the bookmakers had offered Dad and Peggy was enough for a sizeable deposit on a house and a new car apiece, and it was assured, even if Desperate Dee hobbled in stone last on three legs. But if the horse ran the race of his life and was placed in the top four and scooped a massive prize, half their joy money would have to go straight into the bookmaker's account. Should they put their dreams up for sale?

A car was a big want for my dad. He yearned to be a driver. He had a pair of leather driving gloves hidden at the bottom of his underwear drawer that had been there for eight years in wait for the big day when he finally passed his test. They were easily the most expensive thing he had ever owned. Earlier in the same week that he drew a horse in the sweepstake he had failed his driving test for the thirteenth time. The consensus amongst the extended family was he should stop trying to pass his driving test. Only his elder sister Kathleen – who herself failed twenty-seven times – urged him to keep on going. Kathleen would insist to anyone who would listen that she simply had to pass her test because, 'My husband only has the one lung.'

Dad was working in Selfridges when he drew the horse on the Irish Sweepstakes. And if he and Peggy stood strong and didn't accept the offer, he could have bought almost everything in the store. It was the enormity of the prospect of that kind of cash that made the 'to sell or not to sell' decision painfully slow in coming. Pot after pot of tea was made and paired with round upon round of tomato sandwiches or soda bread with straw-berry jam and disappeared into the crowd of aunts and uncles and neighbours who congregated in and around the house. The smoke intensity increased. This was a sure indicator of the seri-ous nature of the discussions. Still the bookmakers played statues in the kitchen where I sat. They declined food and drink with a single simultaneous shake of their heads, and fixed their steady gazes into the middle distance.

Aunt Peggy cried a lot during the proceedings and kept saying by way of explanation, 'I'm on the change.'

Finally they reached a decision. The pair came into the kitchen and sat down at the table. One of the men raised a single eyebrow in their direction, which was the question asked. Dad answered, 'Yes,' Peggy said, 'Please,' Dad said, 'We'll' and Peggy finished off in a rush, 'take it, £7,000.'

The word gobsmacked was created for what happened next. The taller of the two men stood, smoothed his suit trousers and slid his attaché case onto the kitchen table. It opened with an authoritative click. The case sighed quiet air into the room as it slid open. I noticed it had the same sort of gold satin lining as my dancing ballerina jewellery box upstairs. *And the cash was already in there.*

Auntie Peggy's knees started to bounce up and down, her shoes making a tapping sound on the lino floor. £7,000 was more money than they had ever seen in their lives and it didn't seem to make them happy ... just very, very nervous. Dad grabbed the knitted cosy from the teapot on the centre of the Formica-topped table – it was a woolly Cheshire cat wearing a tartan waistcoat – and he used it to wipe his forehead, which was bubbling with sweat. Peggy snatched the tea cosy from him and jammed it first into the left of her cardigan, beneath her arm, and then moved it to the right. She groaned like she was in physical pain. 'Me oxters ... they're soaked,' she cried as the men continued to count out the cash into tall piles.

When race day dawned the front door was left ajar from 7am for family to let themselves in and get into position to watch the race on TV in our front room. There was an early morning fag- and cornflake-fuelled summit when it was decided that my nan was too old, and entirely of the wrong disposition, to watch the race. It was decreed that all the excitement might just finish her off. So, directly before the 'Off', she was ambushed from behind, frogmarched into the back yard and locked out of the house by three of her loving daughters.

'It's for your own good!' my mother shouted at her through the keyhole.

'You mare! May God forgive you!' my nan called back, but I think she was relieved because too quickly she stopped complaining, settled onto the back doorstep and stuck her fingers in her ears as she hummed 'Star of the Sea' over and over again. She said later she'd chosen that particular hymn because it rhymed with Desperate Dee, the horse's name.

That afternoon was a stringent test of cardiac function for my family because Desperate Dee was a bit of a joker. He hung back, came up on the inside, led the field, stumbled, recovered and finally put on a speed spurt that brought him home in fourth place. They had won. Not huge money after all, but big money, nonetheless. They roared, they groaned, they gripped and stamped and cheered. One neighbour accidentally yanked the front-room curtains down in a moment of passion; another set fire to a sofa cushion with a cigarette in all the excitement, and the glass lightshade got smashed and smashed again by several pairs of waving arms during the race. When it was all over the front room looked like the Hells Angels had stayed over. But no one cared; they laughed heartily and jigged around outside in the street.

They were told via another telegram that their portion of the winnings, twelve and a half thousand pounds, would be delivered on the Wednesday of the following week by special post. My dad and Auntie Peggy were both waiting on hard-backed chairs by the open front door for its arrival. They expected a parcel containing banknotes, and were puzzled by the thin, medium-sized brown envelope that turned up. Dad slid a banker's draft from the envelope and they both stared at it in dismay, their mouths making the same 'O' shape.

'Do we tear it in half?' asked a bewildered Peggy. 'Will the shops accept that?'

Dad had nothing to offer her in the way of sage advice. He had never in his life been in a bank and was confounded by the meaning of this 'banker's draft'. It was finally agreed that when Peggy went to work that afternoon she would ask the advice of her boss or his wife, who both worked in an office.

The news from the white-collar worker wasn't good. He explained that turning the draft into hard cash would require a visit in person, or in their case in persons, to the bank. When the extended family heard about the necessary visit to the bank, they all swung into action to help with the preparations. Not one of them had ever visited a bank, and they had various notions about what might be required. My dad would definitely have to wear a suit, it was universally agreed, but a buttonhole was ruled out as overkill.

Dad's younger brother Patrick lent him the necessary suit, because his was newest and only a size and a half too small. 'Hmmmn, Teddy-boyish, if you close one eye and squint with the other,' observed my mum when she saw Dad clamped into the shiny jacket and trousers. His shirt collar was starched and pressed and his shoes shined into submission so they looked smart in spite of their age. Another brother, Joseph, trimmed Dad's hair and dutifully wet-shaved him on the morning. 'You'll be as good as anyone else in that bank,' Joseph declared somewhat doubtfully as he studied his handiwork. Dad's chin was a patchwork of newspaper pieces secured to his face with blots of blood. Joseph had enjoyed a fierce dancing and drinking session the night before and his hands had wobbled as he wet-shaved. A criss-cross of nicks covered Dad's neck, chin and upper lip and his sideburns differed so drastically in length and thickness that, side on, he looked like two different people.

Whilst Dad was being groomed in the kitchen, Peggy was having her make-up done in the front room. A hat that one of her sisters had 'borrowed' from a woman she cleaned for was secured to her head at a jaunty angle. It was a black velvet hat with netting and crystal droplets, a perfect choice for a royal funeral maybe, but several sizes too big and a complete mismatch for Peggy's lightweight beige suit.

Dad carried an empty suitcase with him and Auntie Peggy toted a hat box because the sisters agreed it would be a suitably chic container for hard cash. They were worried about whether the money would be issued in coins or notes and whether they would have enough room in their bag choices to get it all home. One of the brothers suggested they bring a wheelbarrow into the bank, and after a long, deep think this suggestion was voted out because it would be unwieldy on the bus home.

The bank was situated in the Strand and it was a vast, wide and high building with walls of glinting glass. Peggy described it to us later as like 'a train station, but for only money'. Clinging to one another Hansel and Gretel style, the intimidated pair went three times around the revolving door before getting inside. They made their way across the vast tiled floor of the banking hall and joined a queue behind regular clients who were bearing cheque books and paying-in forms – sure signs that they had been here before and knew what to do.

When it was their turn, Dad and Auntie Peggy got closer than strictly necessary to the grille that separated them from the male bank clerk and simultaneously tried to explain why they were there. 'Do either of you speak English?' he interrupted in a loud, slow voice. The bank teller had also lifted his right hand to shoulder height and was showing them his palm to silence them.

When my dad saw the teller's upturned palm, he jumped to the very wrong conclusion that he was being asked to take an oath, like he had seen people do on television programmes when they were in a court of law. This is why he raised his right palm back to the bank clerk. A very flummoxed Auntie Peggy saw the two of them with their palms exposed and she quickly followed suit. For a few moments the three of them, separated by a metal grille, stood there Big Chief/Hiawatha style.

The bemused bank clerk broke the confused silence. 'How. Can. I. Help. You?' He spoke slowly and one decibel short of a shout. He lowered his hand. Dad mirrored the move and dropped his hand, too. He bent down to reach into his sock and withdrew the rolled-up banker's draft.

It was passed over to the clerk who stamped, signed and countersigned the piece of paper in duplicate before filing it away in a mahogany velvet-lined drawer. Formalities complete, the crunch question came from behind the counter.

'How would you like the money?'

Dad had no answer in his head except 'Right NOW!' but he knew that was wrong. Peggy was perplexed but thinking hard she finally said, 'Oh yes! I understand what you're saying! We want it half for him and half for me!' Dad nodded at speed in agreement and one suitcase and one hat box slammed simultaneously onto the counter.

Dad's first purchase with his winnings was a pack of large brown envelopes. We set up a production line at the kitchen table that began with Mum and Dad behind a stack of banknotes. My brother did the counting and folding and made a list of how much went into each envelope. I addressed the envelopes as directed and passed them along to my sister at the end of the line. She licked stamps and stuck them on with giant concentration. The envelopes were addressed to each of Mum and Dad's brothers, sisters and first cousins, and there were over twenty of them. Cash in varying amounts, determined by how many children were in the household, was stuffed into each one and on the top banknote, using a green bingo marker pen, Dad wrote, 'from Andy, Annie and Desperate Dee'.

Gambling in all its forms was their only vice – if you don't count smoking forty a day, and in those days nobody did count smoking as a vice. Both my parents smoked constantly at home. It's so hard to believe now, but the three of us children were brought up wreathed in smoke. When the aunts and uncles were visiting, they all lit up, too. We could barely see the television or one another for the thick nicotine fog that permanently hung in our small sitting room. My mum offered me a huge long fag when I was just thirteen and urged, 'Gooooo on, try one. They're lovely.'

My brother, my sister and I have never touched a cigarette. In my teens I swapped contraband fags for sweets behind the bike shed at school when all my friends were living dangerously and lighting up. I knew I didn't ever want to smoke. My revulsion for cigarettes probably began when I was in nappies.

Cock crow in our house was replaced by cough crow. Mum and Dad's first fag of the day would be smoked horizontally, in bed with closed eyes, and it was followed by an expulsion of high-glaze emerald-green phlegm that would travel at speed across the room if it wasn't swiftly captured in a hankie. 'Bogey lacrosse' my sister and I would call it, woken from our sleep by

Mum and Dad's lungs shouting for mercy. I once heard Mum and Dad murmur agreement, between coughs, that it was a good job they smoked as it helped them to clear their chests first thing in the morning.

7

The Sea of Dennis

'He's a lovely man!' were the words I heard used time and again
to describe my dad. It was a compliment addressed to him and
a backhanded way of saying 'she's a right bitch' about my mum
by her sisters in-law. In any family gathering, she would do the
straight talking and he would do the smiling. Wading in was her
trademark. That and saying it like it was. 'Do you like this dress
on me, Annie?' asked my dad's sister Margaret, twirling in
peach-coloured crimplene. 'You're the full of it!' came Mum's
answer. 'Lend me a fiver, Annie?' pleaded her brother Tony.
'And why would I give a lazy article like you my hard-earned
money?' She once kicked a work colleague of Dad's in the shin,
an Englishman, because he dared to describe her husband as
'barely the right side of simple'. The expression 'least said soon-
est mended' was anathema to my mum. If she thought it, she
had to say it. Her own family loved and understood her, but in
Dad's family, especially among her sisters-in-law, she inspired
many a crooked smile.

My dad's sisters and brothers had kind hearts, but ones that carried plenty of troubles, too. On my mum's side it was cancer that ripped through their contentment, but on my dad's side, for some, their family curse came in different shapes and sizes – in a whole lot of spirit bottles.

My mum, a rabid gambler and in no position to judge when vices were out on display, would always arch an eyebrow when she saw a sister-in-law with a tumbler of gin at her feet or another lashing more of the Christmas brandy in her mouth than into the cake mix. She was Mrs Right and in her opinion gambling had a whole lot more charm than boozing.

Alcohol was a choice in our household. Mum was teetotal and Dad hit the hard stuff once a year. He had nine brothers and sisters who survived into adulthood and they convened in numbers at his brother's pub in Blackfriars every Christmas morning to drink to the season. A toast was always made to the three absentees across the waters in Australia, America and Ireland.

Having a publican in the family was second best to having a priest in amongst them, and it made them all so proud. Uncle Jim was a good publican. And he stayed that way because his family were charged full price for drinks just like everyone else. 'He's still got his first communion money, that one,' my aunt Delia would grumble as she emptied her purse out on the bar, making her brother wait as she counted out coppers for her glass of brandy and Babycham mixed. A true lightweight, Dad would be poured into a cab before midday and arrive home boss-eyed after just three drinks. Mum always chose to stay home on Christmas morning and babysit the turkey.

Every year, two roast potatoes and a sprout into his Christmas lunch, Dad would end up face down in his plate, fast asleep. We all did a valiant job ignoring him, chattering, pulling crackers and arranging his paper hat on the back of his head instead of on top. After the Christmas pudding and custard had been cleared, Dad would wake up with a start and look over at Mum in her cracker hat with a seasonal sparkle in his eye. 'Shall we go and have a lie-down?' he wanted to know. 'No. We have to watch the Queen's speech. We live in England, don't ya know?' Mum would then marshal us all into the sitting room and into position for her majesty's address. It was as though the room filled with sleeping gas as soon as the Queen's face appeared on the screen. Speech unseen, a couple of hours later we would all wake up refreshed in plenty of time for *Coronation Street* and a good film.

I think my sister, brother and I got our physical bulk from Dad's side of the family. The men and women, bar one, had the same tall, broad-shouldered silhouette. The Mangans were built for work and depending on.

As they processed over to London, because of sheer weight of numbers it became difficult for either Mum or Dad's family to assemble under one bedsit roof. Their landlords at the time papered the walls of their lodging houses with lists and these all began with the words '<u>Do not</u> . . .'. My relatives couldn't read what was on the lists but were smart enough to guess that bringing home nearly twenty visitors, even if they were brothers and sisters and their partners, would be forbidden.

Their preferred meeting places were quickly established. The La Bamba and the Galtymore in Cricklewood and the Blarney Club in Tottenham Court Road. 'It cost two shillings and sixpence to get into a dance, and if I had to choose between the gas and the electricity meter and dancing, off I'd go. Even if it meant getting ready in the dark!' my dad's sister Auntie Rose told me. She mystified me by telling me that she used to keep her beauty spot for dancing in her make-up bag. Answering the question in my eyes, Rose showed me how she had applied the sharp tip of an eyebrow pencil to her face, in the space between her upper lip and cheek, twirled it three times and got the perfect face decoration. 'Eat yer heart out, Marilyn,' she'd say as she admired her beauty spot in the mirror before dashing off to a dance.

They went dancing several nights a week and twice on a Sunday when there were afternoon sessions, too. A little snack bar did a roaring trade in orange squash and biscuits, with scones and jam on offer at weekends. Men wore their Sunday best to the dances and my dad claimed that in place of Brylcreem he would nip into the gents and slick his hair back with a palm wipe of urine to stay looking dapper. He was envious of the lads who substituted butter for Brylcreem because he couldn't afford either. But the pee got good results. 'The girls always passed remarks on my lovely shiny hair,' he told me, laughing into my gurning face.

It all sounded so innocent, but ceili dancing was actually a form of frantic foreplay. There should have been a dance called Shake Those Childbearing Hips or the Husband Hop, because that was what the dances were all about. Boy Meets Girl.

The best-known dance of the night was the Siege of Ennis, which for years I mistakenly called the Sea of Dennis, and a few of my cousins thought was named the Seed of Venice. Dancing it wasn't a whole lot easier than getting its name right. This set piece for hordes of people arranged in pairs started with some mannerly to-ing and fro-ing, hand holding and body weaving.

It moved up a gear to some medium-paced side-to-side skipping and then came the moment of truth – the *spin*. 'You wanted a fella who could get yer heels up near yer shoulder blades as he span you round with a good auld grip on yer waist!' my aunt Rose explained. 'Hands like shovels were a great sign of big spin ahead . . .' I did the Siege of Ennis often in my youth, and it is one big dipper of a dance. Once I dared to turn down an invitation to dance it with a man who looked like a billy goat. I had broken the rule. He looked at me with disgust 'No? No? So why didn't ye bring yer feckin' knittin then if you're not here to dance!'

There were strict Rules of the Dance Hall. The first was that when a male asked a female to dance, she couldn't say no. If she refused, the spurned man could report her to the Master of Ceremonies. All important, the MC stood up on stage and called the dancing into a microphone, strutting and marching around as he did so. The MC was not a man to be disobeyed. Close to a girl's ear and microphone covered he would issue a warning, 'Dance or feck off home for yerself!'

Second was that a pair had to dance together for three dances. This was known as a set. My mum believed a set was something to do with religion, the Father, Son and Holy Ghost, but it was more likely a way of giving the live musicians a short breather after every third dance. Three dances was like winning the jackpot if the man who wanted to step out with them looked 'like oh good God, that Robert Mitchum', as my mum used to say. But not so good if he looked, as many of them did, in Aunt Theresa's words 'like a horse's arse'. They dreaded the oldies. There was nothing worse, they claimed, than being coupled for a whole set to a clicky-hipped, hairy-eared hoofer. A young and free Katsie had always been happy to dance and even occasionally date older men. 'There's more juice in a ripe raspberry,' she would say, arching both her heavily pencilled eyebrows.

So dance the lovely young women did, with whoever asked. Even if they had to cling onto a man who danced like a wild horse as he jumped and kicked around the dance hall for three long tunes, they did their dance-hall duty.

My mum and aunts would sit around the table reminiscing about their dance-hall days and nights and screech with laughter about the men who in their words 'queued up' to dance with them. 'Howaya, and can ya milk a cow?' and 'Me mammy would love to meet you, so she would' and 'How's about a bit of jiggy jig, me and you, down the alley afterwards?' were some of the conversational overtures the sisters received from men on the dance floor. 'Do you fancy coming out for a slide?' was the question the men asked, and 'Yes please' with a sigh or a smile depending on who was asking was the obligatory women's answer. Going for a bit of a slide was no exaggeration. Soap flakes were sprinkled on the dance floor at regular intervals to make the dancers go faster. 'You couldn't beat a bit of a skid,' sighed my aunt Peggy with her eyes half closed and a half-smoked cigarette hanging from the corner of her smiling mouth. She would be twirling around the Galtymore in her memory and loving it all over again.

My dad's brother Bill, the family's champion ballroom dancer, was teasingly described by his loving brothers and sisters as being the meanest man alive. If he opened a pack of twenty cigarettes he would take one out for himself and never offer them around. 'Aaah, give us a fag,' one or other of his siblings would beg. 'I only have nineteen left,' was how Bill refused them.

119

Bill's wife Clodagh had lacquered hair as tough as a crash helmet and a cat's-bum mouth lipsticked in fuchsia. She thought that every one of her brothers- and sisters-in-law was simply too vulgar for words, which was why she rarely spoke to them. In the dance halls, the Master of Ceremonies would often issue spot prizes to the couple he thought danced the best, the fastest, the cutest. When they were competing, Bill and Clodagh would dance like they had been plugged in and they were certain there was no one to equal them. If the couple didn't bag a spot prize, Clodagh could be seen, bent forward with her hands on her hips, berating the MC at regular intervals for the remainder of the evening. She and her husband were dance maniacs and on the rare occasions they joined family celebrations down the years they would make a grand entrance, hands joined and held aloft, and then immediately start rolling back any rugs so that they could give a rictus-grinned dancing display.

Even though Clodagh was a smooth mover, she had a bumpy figure, and when she entered herself time and again into small beauty pageants that were organised in pubs and clubs but never once made the final, she sought out my dad's sisters for solace. 'What's the matter with them bleedy judges?' she asked, scowling. 'What is it I have to do to get them to notice me?'

'I know!' said my aunt Rose brightly. 'You could change your name from Miss Riordan . . .'

'To what?' Clodagh demanded.

'Miss Tayto?' Taytos were a new but already well-known brand of Irish crisps.

'Or maybe Miss Kimberley?' joined in Aunt Delia, referring to the famous biscuits.

Clodagh didn't speak to her sisters-in-law again for three decades, and they didn't miss her either.

'A punch-up was the icing on the cake after a grand night out,' claimed my uncle Patrick. I asked him what the dance-hall fights were about. 'Nothing at all,' he answered cheerfully. It was enough for one man to say to another, 'And what do you think you're feckin' looking at?' Aunt Rose said fights sparked because the men were grumpy – they hadn't had enough to drink. Sometimes it was more than a skirmish over a look or a good-looking girl. Vicious county wars could break out after some dances and gangs would assemble waving hurling sticks as weapons. 'I saw a few of them set-tos from a distance, alright,' said my dad. From a distance, because he would be heading off in the opposite direction. 'The best way to win a fight is to run away from it,' he would always tell his son. 'It's better to be a coward for a minute than dead for the rest of your life.'

The dances were mainly for loving, though, not fighting. One hopeful suitor once asked my mum did she fancy a bit of 'rooting' after a waltz. She said she didn't even know what he meant and assumed he was talking about gardening.

At the end of every dance night came the Irish national anthem. Everyone present stood straight and silent for this, even the few fellas who had popped out to the pub in the interval and had a Guinness lean on them.

One summer night my uncle Joe walked the considerable distance home from the Blarney Club in Tottenham Court Road to his lodgings in Cricklewood after a dance. Halfway there another chap fell into step with him, a Londoner of about the same age. They chatted about dance halls and jobs until his companion suddenly changed the subject. He said, 'You look nice tonight ...' and Joe realised the man was after more than just small talk. Shaken to the core, he told his brothers afterwards, 'If I'd had a *five*-pound note and I'd dropped it that night, let me tell you I would have kicked it all the way home!'

'And what in the name of Jaysus is that?' screeched Aunt Rose when she saw a man with his fly unzipped and his manhood on full display. She was on the top deck of a bus on the way home from a dance. The exposed man was muttering about God and being Spanish and he stood and thrust his hips closer to Rose's eyeline. The woman Rose cleaned for had given her a stale and almost empty bottle of Youth Dew perfume as a gift and Rose removed it from her handbag and sprayed the 'Spanish sausage' with it. 'Beeeeech!' the man shouted before running down the stairs to the lower deck and jumping off the moving bus. She agonised all week about whether or not to tell the priest what she had done at her weekly confession. Truthful by nature, she did. The priest coughed and spluttered in response to Rose's telling of her sin before asking her to repeat it while he considered her penance. Her penance was to pray a decade of the rosary for all Spanish men that they might become more God-fearing.

All my dad's sisters met their husbands in London dance halls. Their haul was mixed. Rose met her husband, an Englishman, in the Hibernian in Fulham. Fred was there delivering beer and as soon as she looked down at him – he was almost a foot shorter than her – it was a done deal. She said her heart did a jelly roll. He was a part-time drayman and, in keeping with his height, a small-time gangster too.

Calamity struck when four children into their marriage Fred ended up serving a long prison sentence in Wormwood Scrubs.

Collectively the aunts and uncles told us children fantastical lies as to Fred's whereabouts. According to the grown-ups he was simultaneously on a cruise, training to be an astronaut and working as a missionary in Africa. Even his own son answered the question, asked by a nun at primary school, 'Who is omnipresent?' with, 'My dad.' 'The Lord our God is the correct answer,' she reprimanded him, with a rap of a ruler across the knuckles.

They all clubbed together to give Rose housekeeping money whilst her husband was in prison. I think some of them felt it was good value for money because they were spared listening to Fred crooning 'Gimmee the Moonlight' by Frankie Vaughan at family gatherings and interrupting their standard fare, 'A Nation Once Again' and other assorted rebel songs.

I don't think Auntie Delia's husband John was ever young, not even as a baby. His belly was his personal table and he balanced his huge dinners on its highest point. Uncle John's glasses frequently slid down his nose and landed in his food, which is why the lenses were always greasy. 'I noticed him because he was a couple of dances behind everyone else on the dance floor,' Delia told us. 'He was a bit different.' Uncle John managed always to live life at a pace a few days behind everyone else. Delia was devoted to him but very soon bored senseless, too.

She was drowning in dull even before the last of her four babies was out of nappies. The gin bottle provided her entertainment. 'Unhappy ever after,' my mum used to say about the family.

Auntie Marg ran away with an American serviceman called Randy she found in a London dance hall. She was the tiniest of all dad's family and her 'Yank' dubbed her his 'Irish pocket doll'. Her brothers and sisters never used Randy's name; he was for ever, after that first introduction, the 'Yank'.

They met and married fast. At their wedding my uncle John toasted the couple with tea and said, 'A man isn't complete until he's married. And after that he's finished.' Within five weeks they were the other side of the horizon in the United States. The young couple continued to live like they had to beat the clock. Five children arrived in five years and after that her Yank speed-walked out of his family's life. Marg boxed her way through life, working more hours than she ever slept and remarried when her children hit their teenage years. Her second husband died young and left her financially comfortable just as her own health was failing and she spent her last years in a big puffy armchair ordering from the TV home shopping channel. 'I don't even open the boxes when they arrive. I want none of it,' she would happily confess. 'The pleasure I get is just being able to order the stuff up, after having nothin' when I was a little girl . . .' Auntie Marg would pay astronomical postage charges to mail bulky imitation Tiffany Lights and chalk figurines of British Fusiliers over to London to her brothers and sisters as gifts. My mum, who hated knick-knacks with a passion, unless they were holy, shooed her presents from the States from the box to the shelf to the bin within weeks.

Dad's family were suspicious of Mum. Her crimes were that she didn't drink, and as the years passed she grew grittier and more determined for her children. They took this as an indirect criticism of their lifestyle and offspring and started to view her as the enemy within.

It didn't help that whenever they played cards – which was whenever they all got together, and carried on from dusk to dawn – Mum cleaned up. Twenty Fives was their game and I think Mum and Dad often won at cards because they were the only ones around the table not seeing double with drink by the end of the night. Rent, clothes, shoes and even a car were staked. My mum once left a card game folded into a navy cashmere-mix coat she had won from my aunt Rose. It was pure luxury and had become Rose's pride and joy after being left unclaimed in the cloakroom of the restaurant where she worked. Her manager held a raffle amongst the female staff for the coat and Rose was ecstatic when she won it. Mum abandoned her tatty caramel-coloured C&A mackintosh on the back of Rose's settee without a backward glance.

No pity was shown or expected. If you bet it and lost then you paid up in full. There was No Mercy for lightweight gamblers. It crossed my mind that in those smoke-filled front rooms in the early hours, with a scratchy Val Doonican LP playing low on repeat in the background, that one night Mum and Dad might actually consider staking me or my brother or sister.

Uncle John always sat the card games out. He was too slow for them and dedicated his evenings to reciting monotonous riddles that only he thought were hugely entertaining. 'A duck before two ducks and a duck behind two ducks and a duck in the middle between two ducks. So how many ducks were in it?'

'Who gives a fuck about the duck,' cackled Auntie Delia over from the table. Not her. She had deliberately sworn out loud in the vain hope she might temporarily distract the other card players and improve her chances of winning. She failed. There was a deadly silence. Their concentration was unbroken. My cousins and I dozed on, draped and disinterested all over the settee and floor, waiting for the interminable card games to end. John in a sulky voice announced to the couldn't-care-less room, 'Three ducks. The answer is three.'

8

May Queen Mayhem

I went to a Catholic primary school and the first thing I realised was that I wasn't there to learn how to read fluently, write clearly or add up. I was there first and foremost to compete to be the May Queen. That was the Holy Grail for every immigrant Irish mother with a daughter. We were subliminally instructed to forget any nonsense about education – just be sure to get crowned the *May Queen*. For the uninitiated, it's a beauty pageant with prayers.

The May Queen's job, eight years in the hoping and planning stage for their mothers, took just forty-five minutes to execute. Resplendent in a floor-length blue dress and new white shoes paid for by the good people of the parish, her mini holy majesty would lead a procession of parishioners, climb a stepladder decked with spring flowers and place a plastic crown on the head of a statue of the Virgin Mary. Hymn singing, having bouncy fresh rollered hair and looking not-at-all triumphant even though she certainly was were her other solemn May Queen duties. The May Queen mother's job was to wear something in a sickly pastel shade and occupy the front row of the church, strobing with pride and false modesty in equal parts.

'Whose daddy has a car?' came the loaded question from one nun or another stood in front of my class of forty eager children. Most of us would put our hands up even though our daddies didn't really have cars, just to try and please the all-powerful sisters. Hand stretched high in the air, I would pray under my breath that I wouldn't get picked and exposed as a liar. Whoever was chosen was given a very important message to pass to their daddy – he was to get a great privilege, and should be at the convent gates at 5.30am to transport one of the sisters to Euston Station for her to catch the boat train to Holyhead. If a daddy was very lucky, his child would put his or her hand up in answer to the question, 'Whose daddy has a car and comes from Mayo?' This was to obtain free return transportation of a nun and her luggage to Ireland for the summer holidays, and back. If this or any other favour could be granted, it was done with a smile. It was a great way to earn May Queen points.

Having a daughter chosen to be the May Queen was a beast of a brag opportunity. To put this annual event into modern-day parlance, combine the national significance of *The X Factor* and the World Cup Final when England is in it and multiply to the power of a thousand. Being the May Queen's mother was the highly potent stuff of hopes and dreams and guaranteed an infinite number of photographs to send home to Ireland, including, for sure, plenty posed with the parish priest. It would guarantee you a photograph in the local papers in London, and the so closely read county papers in Ireland, too.

By rights, a liveried footman and eleven pipers piping should have been involved in the weekly delivery of the local county paper from Ireland. It was an eagerly awaited dollop of home, stuffed solid with births, deaths, marriages, crime, and boom and bust stories. I should know, as I was regularly called on to read long, dull sections aloud. Bad news stories were received by my mum, dad and nan with a lot more enjoyment than the good news ones. Tales of violence, fraud, theft and sexual misconduct had the power to keep them talking all week. My help wasn't required with the photographs. These were black and white and on every page and all looked like they'd been taken in a snowstorm. Every inch of them was pored over and the commentary went, 'Jesus, Mary and Joseph, she's the full of that coat!' and 'Who stole his hair? He used to have a grand head of curls, so he did!' No story was too small for inclusion. Mrs Ryan had bought new plastic laundry pegs and much preferred them to wooden ones, Mr Butler's sow had seven piglets, and a new tractor, only a month old, and belonging to Farmer O'Shea, had sprung an oil leak. At the back of the paper was a section dedicated to news from overseas – a photo montage of baptisms, weddings, first holy communions, May Queens, confirmations and graduations. The expressions of the adults in these photos were always the same: 'Take A Good Look At Us! How Prosperous We Are!' Sometimes a May Queen got an entire half-page photograph in the county newspaper. Being Our Lady's attendant was big beans on both sides of the Irish Sea.

A powerful panel of selectors decided which girl was to be declared May Queen: the parish priest, a gaggle of fat, flat-chested nuns with glossy black moustaches and the ever contrary school headmaster.

An annual summit meeting was held behind closed doors in the presbytery. Rumour had it that the panel, even the sisters, were sustained throughout by Gordon's gin and Woodbine cigarettes. On this sacred occasion, smoke escaping from the windows and doors did not mean a decision had been reached, it just meant the panel were going heavy on the fags.

The experts would be scrupulously fair and apply the numerous selection criteria to decide who should be May Queen. These criteria included ... who knew? Not the CIA, nor Interpol, and not a single soul in Vatican City had any notion of what those self-selected selectors were looking for in a May Queen. This perpetual and vexing mystery sent the mothers of the parish rabid – each of them convinced that their daughter should be the chosen one.

My mother openly scorned all the other desperate, fawning women of the parish who were bribing the priest and baking for him. Some were apparently even trying to flirt to win.

When the name of the May Queen was finally announced, from the pulpit at 8am Mass on the prescribed Sunday in April, there was the usual annual uproar. Prayer books got slammed shut in disgust and hymns went unsung in protest. The girl chosen was called Mary. How fitting.

On May Queen Sunday, Mary was attended to by a sulky straggle of leftovers, called handmaidens, all with royally pissed-off mothers. Their daughters' hair hadn't been judged shiny enough, eyes not bright enough, complexions not clear enough to be the actual May Queen. Their girls were the papal equivalent of the ugly sisters.

My own sister was chosen to be a handmaiden. Her task was to walk ahead of the May Queen carrying a basket of rose petals. The petals needed to be first kissed and then tossed on the aisle floor of the church to create a fragrant carpet for the May Queen to walk over en route to the crowning ceremony.

Sister Joseph, the May Queen coordinator, was perpetually delighted. The first time I ever saw her without a smile was when my little sister underperformed as a handmaiden. Vaseline, and my mother's fixation with it, were the culprits. When the big day dawned, Julie had a cold, and my mother had smeared Vaseline around Julie's red raw chapped nose and mouth, convinced it was a cure-all for every animal, vegetable and mineral complaint.

Standing at the back of the church, waiting for the organ to start playing 'Ave Maria' and for the procession to begin, Julie got her wild arm-waving cue from Sister Joseph, who carried on like she was bowling overhead at a cricket match when all she needed to communicate was the word 'Go'.

Concentrating hard on what she had been told, the step/kiss/toss routine began. But poor Julie only got as far as the step and kiss part of her handmaiden duties. Tossing was made impossible because the rose petals stuck to the Vaseline my mother had loaded onto her face. By the time she had reached the altar she had a thick beard made of rose petals. It looked a bit like she had tried to eat them by cramming them all into her mouth at once. And finally, realising it was all going horribly wrong, her flowery face crumpled as she stood small and alone with her back to the altar. She started to cry.

Sister Joseph had no Plan B, but my mother did. She leapt out of her pew near the back of the church and outpaced the May Queen up the aisle to rescue her bewildered, weeping and petal-faced daughter. Unfortunately this meant my mum and sister then had to make their way back down the aisle as the

May Queen was still wobbling her way up it, trailed by twelve slow-marching handmaidens. They were so well drilled by Sister Joseph that they were like automaton soldiers and were not going to make way for anybody until their job was done.

The May Queen's mother called for the entire event to be restarted. The congregation, who had never enjoyed the May Queen celebrations as much as this, were by now gawping, gossiping or guffawing.

Father Donal remained silent. His response was meditative. Joining his hands, he bent his head and closed his eyes in prayer, or despair. He was leading the way in turn-the-other-cheek-style spiritual contemplation. Reluctantly, and very slowly, the packed church followed his lead into silent 'prayer' and, finally, order was restored.

Next, it was my turn to mortify my mother. I had a bidding prayer to read during the service. Sister Joseph was to give the signal for me to leave my pew, walk reverently to the altar, genuflect and climb into the pulpit, where the microphone was waiting for me. There was a surprise on the floor of the pulpit in the form of a hard-backed chair. I was nine years old, a May Queen cast-off, and the eyes of the entire congregation were drilling into me, so I made a split-second choice *not* to move the chair out of the way. Instead my common sense failed me and I decided to stand on it. This gave the front few rows of the church an eyeful of my yellow daisy-print knickers. The pulpit microphone was pointing at my ankles.

I read my prayer, but only the lip-readers in the congregation could have understood me because the microphone was too far away to pick up my words. When I climbed down from the chair, descended the pulpit steps, negotiated my way off the altar and rejoined my mother, she immediately put one arm around my shoulder. Her other was pulling my sister to her, and she hugged us both very tight and said, in a deliberately loud voice that travelled around the church and didn't need a microphone, 'You were both brilliant!' But I noticed her zigzag smile that hinted she wasn't convinced.

Decades later, when my own children were at primary school, we got a letter about the month of May celebrations. I have to confess that my first thoughts were that one of my three gorgeous girls would surely be a shoo-in for the position of May Queen. I remember congratulating myself on being sufficiently evolved to at least feel a note of sympathy for all the other mothers. The ones with less beautiful children.

It struck me that, even today, if I was to visit my mum's grave and whisper the words, 'May Queen', her hand would shoot up through the earth Carrie-style holding a hairbrush and a face flannel for me to use to get her granddaughters competition-ready.

If there had been such a thing as a May King then according to the adults in my family my brother would have been a dead cert for the role. Michael was always – in my mum's, dad's, nan's and Aunt Peggy's adoring eyes – a little Prince, a King in waiting. If they could have afforded a sedan chair the four of them would certainly have carried Michael into adulthood in it.

Once a week a Mr O'Reilly, purple-faced from whiskey and yellow-fingered from fags, came along to our flat to give Michael his private accordion lesson. A lesson that lasted an hour and a half and for its duration everyone else in the flat had to sit out in the communal hallway for fear we would interrupt the mini maestro's concentration or creativity. My tone-deaf mum was convinced her only son was musically gifted, but Michael assaulted that accordion so severely it was he who disturbed us;

my reading, my sister's colouring and nan's darning. Tunes like 'Baa Baa Black Sheep' and 'Wild Rover' were smashed beneath Michael's fingers as my Mum stood taut, nodding her head to the mostly unrecognisable music. Mr O'Reilly never said Michael was good, or bad. With one wise eye on his wages he would merely say 'Sure the little fella's a natural!' Mum persevered with these music lessons until a neighbour told her that Mr O'Reilly was actually a bin man and not a music teacher at all. She only revealed this to me years later and begged me *never* to tell my brother. 'Michael might have been a great musician if I'd only got him a proper teacher when he was starting out.'

Aunt Peggy would say to my mum, 'Annie, we'll book a *box* at the Royal Albert Hall when Michael gets famous and is on the stage there!' She spent a lot of time daydreaming about what she could wear and what she might drink when her turn finally came to sit in a private box. Bet was disbelieving about the whole thing. 'Catch yerself on, would ya? How would you even see anything out of a box? A box has four sides you stupid mare.'

Michael was a busy boy. As well as private music lessons he had Irish dancing lessons twice a week in the back room of a pub given by *The* Mrs Ursula Purcell (the italics were her own). She smoked two fags at a time as she taught. One hung from the side of her mouth and the other was alight in her hand. A third was tucked behind her ear, a nicotine hairslide for her shock of dyed black hair. Piano accompaniment was provided by Mrs Embly, an octogenarian with breasts so large and pendulous that she had to position her stool a couple of feet away from the keys in order to reach forward and thump out the tunes. Her grey hair was like steel thread fashioned into candy-floss. Hard of hearing Mrs Embly played continually, never hearing *The* Mrs Purcell's calls for her to pause or start a tune from the top. Work–worn and weary, the mothers sat in a ring in one corner of the room and smoked. Somehow they found the energy for a weekly brag competition about whose children were the most marvellous. My mum declared herself the clear winner every week without fail. She never said the words, it was her victorious smirk that announced the result.

But poor Michael always appeared to be in a different time zone to the rest of the dancers. He was facing front when they faced back, skipping when they were still and jumping up long after they had come down. *The* Mrs Purcell finally lost patience. 'Yer lad is built for hurling not dancing' she ruled. Mum marched out of the class with her head held high and hauling my ecstatic-to-be-retired brother behind her.

9

The Best-Dressed Couple in A & E

Once a year, on the middle Sunday in August, a coach would leave from outside our church after early Mass and take the parishioners on a day trip to the seaside. Everyone on the bus looked like they were going to a wedding in new clothes, with suits and ties for the men and dresses and jackets or cardigans for the women. Even my vest, knickers and socks were new on the occasions we went for a day out. 'In case we have an accident and they have to be cut off ye in the hospital,' was my mum's rationale for the pristine outward-bound underclothes.

Our family only went on the parish day trip once. Partly because it was too expensive for all five of us, and it was the law that we had to go everywhere together on a Sunday. 'Yeese are like Brown's cows,' my nan used to say about us. But mostly because my mum decided that the company was much too common.

My brother Michael has always been a quiet boy. He speaks only when it is essential, even now. But he was as obedient as he was silent. Allocated a seat at the back of the bus with a family from our primary school, Mum warned him, 'Don't sit there and say nothing, they'll think you're a halfwit.' From our seats in the middle of the bus, my sister and I listened in amazement to our brother wear his voice out doing as he had been told. Telly, comics, dinners, dogs, football and friends . . . the family in the seats around him heard every thought he'd ever had since conception. Halfway to Margate, he was returned by his ear to my mum's aisle seat. 'He's a halfwit!' exclaimed the father of the family he'd been sat with. 'Won't stop talking. We'll swap him for her, she looks quiet.' He pointed at Julie. So Julie shifted and, genetically designed to be travel sick, spent the remainder of the journey throwing up into a plastic bag as quietly as she could.

First on the list of seaside things-to-do was secure a severe sunburn, followed by a swim for the brave, candy-floss, prize bingo and pumping pennies into the slot machines in the arcade. Only my brother went for a swim in the sea at Margate that day, wearing a pair of knitted swimming trunks that weighed more than he did when they were fully loaded with seawater. My sister and I waited impatiently on the beach, hopping waves barefoot, until Michael turned blue enough to want to come out. Once he was dried off, we clamped ourselves onto the penny machines in the nearest arcade. Mum didn't mind us playing on the machines – how could she, as she was so enthusiastic about them herself – but she insisted we used the ones nearest the arcade front door. That way, she said, we would all get plenty of sea air as we gambled the day away.

Included in the price of our parish-day-out ticket was a something-and-chips supper, served with tea and white bread and butter in a café on the seafront. I chose mushroom omelette as my something. I was nine and it was the first time I'd tasted mush-rooms and the first time I'd experienced a rubbery oil-loaded omelette. An hour later – another first. A projectile vomit.

My dad once took my sister and me, both aged under ten, to see England versus Ireland at football. It was a big game played in Wembley stadium and full to capacity. I remember the foot-high, green, white and gold felt hats he bought for us to wear, and how it took the three of us to raise the huge tricolour banner he'd fetched from home high enough for the wind to flap it fast over our heads. Dad went berserk when Ireland scored, celebrating with arms outstretched and both feet off the floor. We joined in. Our fun was shared by fifty thousand other people and made us feel giddy. And then later, when England scored, we felt disappointed and expected him to be, too. Instead, Dad clapped politely and made us do the same. 'It's only manners,' he said solemnly. After the match outside the sta-dium, half a dozen drunken lads wearing England shirts snatched our souvenir hats from our heads as they ran past. They dashed ahead of us with them, but stayed in sight. One took out a lighter and set fire to my hat and then used mine to light up Julie's before throwing them both down on the pavement. All of them joined in to stamp them to ashes. They were jeering and chanting, 'Paddywack, don't come back!'

My dad's face was twisted tight in annoyance. He couldn't take the six of them on in front of his young daughters, so seizing one of our hands in each of his, he straightened his shaking shoulders and, head held high, walked past the youths. 'We're just visitors in this country. Remember that,' he told Julie and me.

The biggest night out my mum and dad never had was when they were booked to eat at the restaurant in London's Post

Office Tower. Dad's sister was on a trip from America and this was her big idea. My mum had bought a new dress for the occasion, a peachy chiffon number, from C&A. It had several layers. 'Great value for money,' was how she described her fabric-rich party frock.

My dad was beside himself with excitement, getting ready for his gala night. Perspiring and breathing heavily, he could hardly do up the buttons on his new shirt because his hands were trembling so much. He kept counting the notes in his wallet and asking Mum if she was sure they would have enough money to pay their portion of the bill. He knotted and unknotted his tie several times and fiddled with a pair of cufflinks he had borrowed from someone at work.

'Calm down, would you, Andy. It's only a bit of dinner,' she chided him, and then, unable to keep her cool, she squealed, 'Right up in the sky over London! Oh Jesus, Mary and Joseph, did you ever? We're going to the Post Office Tower to a resteer-ant!' He half smiled and took his wallet out again and started to count. 'Andy. Stop it! You'll give yourself a heart attack, the way you're carrying on.'

Her words were a prophecy. Minutes later he clutched his chest and fell forward, face down onto their bed.

They were the best-dressed couple in accident and emergency that night. Dad had suffered a heart attack and his new shirt was left buttonless after it was torn open by the doctors who saved his life. The next day his brothers and sisters came to visit him in hospital and brought the menu from the Post Office Tower so he could see just what he'd missed. The talk was all of the view and the lights of London and the weighty cutlery and gleaming glassware. Dad's cardiac arrest was dull in comparison and barely got a mention.

Mum and Dad got me to read the menu aloud to them very slowly. After a lot of deliberation, they decided they would have had the prawn cocktail for starters, steak for mains and Black Forest gateau for sweet. In bed that night – I was sleeping with Mum to keep her company whilst Dad was in hospital – she whispered, 'Anna May, are you awake?' I thought she might want to confide how worried she was about Dad. Instead she said, 'I think I got it wrong. I would have had the lemon meringue pie you know, not the Black Forest gateau ...'

The Saint Patrick's Day Parade in London, the greatest day out of the year for London Irish, was off our social calendar permanently after the trauma of the year when we went along with Aunt Peggy. She was walking ahead in the crowds, dragging my brother by the hand. I was being carried through the singing, clapping, dancing crowds by my dad. The adults decided to hop on a bus to get ahead of the crowd to a better viewing point. At Hyde Park Corner, Aunt Peggy lifted my little brother onto the platform of a Number 73 bus and raised her foot ready to step on and join him. But the bus pulled off before she, or any of us in the queue behind, could get on. My mum and dad said the look on Peggy's face was pure panic, and she shrieked in horror as her four-year-old nephew started to move away from her at speed. Heroically, she gave chase and flung herself after the moving bus. Sheer determination helped Peggy to grab hold of the bus pole. Her grip slid from the middle to the base and, half on half off the bus, she was dragged a hundred feet long the road.

My brother, a solitary little figure in a belted mac, short socks and sandals, was squirting tears of abandonment on the bus platform; his auntie travelling below his ankle level was hanging on for her life. Mum and Dad scampered after the bus. When it stopped at the first traffic lights they were able to snatch back my brother. Peggy, seeing he was safe, rolled over into the gutter and lay there groaning. The tarmac road had acted like a cheese grater and left her feet a size smaller, skinned, bleeding and spiked with grit. We never saw one float or heard any music that day, and from then on my mum associated the St Patrick's celebrations event with the worst of luck. '*Don't* mention that bloody parade to me,' she would scream at anyone suggesting a visit. 'It nearly killed the lot of us, so it did!'

Another major event was my First Communion party, which meant receiving the body and blood of Christ and a lot of lovely money. We girls, aged six years old, were dressed as miniature brides in white dresses and veils but my white socks were tinged with red because my heels were shedding skin and bleeding. White patent shoes bought cheap in the sales – two sizes too small – were the aggressor. The boys in my class wore short trousers, shirts and a tie on a piece of elastic. I remember being dazzled by the row of shiny white knees on show. I knew the boys had knees, of course, I had just never seen them so sparkling clean before.

I was prepared in religion lessons to receive the communion host, and not to ask any difficult questions about exactly how God could fit into a wafer of bread the size of half a crown. 'Faith, Anna May!' was the answer to every query I had. The host tasted like half a flying saucer sweet but without the sugar or sherbet filling. 'I must not chew, I must not suck, I must receive the divine host with my eyes shut!' was what the nuns in school made us repeat time and again. And that the unjoining of our prayer-poised hands was disallowed for the entire duration of the church service.

After the church service we communicants retired to the

school hall. Our parents smoked and watched through the windows as the nuns served us Tizer in paper cups with straws, flabby jelly in corrugated card cases and fairy cakes iced with the symbol of a crucifix. Those same hands that poked, prodded, slapped and pushed us around the classroom every other day fluttered around us in hospitality on that single Sunday.

Some of my aunts and uncles drank so much at my Communion party that they forgot they had already given me a card with *paper* money inside and pressed on me another half a crown as they side-stepped home. I got several pound notes and even a gasp-worthy *five* pounds from Aunty Bet. When my Mum later heard of the five pound gift she warned, 'You'd better have said no often enough and not made a show of me.'

The high excitement of a Communion party was replicated on Christmas night, or if the parish priest was coming to visit. On the rare occasions the Lord's representative on earth dropped in, my mother turned into Hitler in a pinny. She was convinced the purpose of his visit was to inspect the cleanliness of her skirting boards and picture rails. These had to be bleached, scrubbed and rinsed in boiling water before his arrival. The front doorstep, every bit of the stairs and each hanging light in the house had to be sparkling, too. Plus, we all had to wee in a bucket in the garden in the hours before he turned up because Mum had personally cleaned the toilet and sink and wouldn't trust any of us with her pristine porcelain until after Father had 'blessed' it with his holy water. 'I'm not giving him anything to talk about!' was the driving force behind her micro-clean.

The best chair in the house was plumped for his already well-padded posterior and assorted relatives would gather around him once he was comfortably in position. 'That man eats like a savage!' my mother would tut tut, well out of his earshot. In my youth a tin of pink salmon was the ultimate luxury. Maybe once or twice a year we would get to taste its contents, and only ever on a Sunday afternoon. Shared out in a salad or a sandwich amongst all of us and any visitors – sometimes as much as fifteen ways – the pink salmon was bulked out with plenty of lettuce, cucumber and salad cream.

When the priest came, an entire tin of salmon would be bruised across one slice of thick bread and topped with another, both thickly buttered. The salmon sandwich was presented to Father on a tea plate fancy-trimmed with cucumber and tomato and resting on a lace doily on top of a tray. Eating our own salad-only sandwiches, we would all watch the fishy filling overhang the side of his bread and try to think holy, not resentful, thoughts. 'Are you all enjoying yer salmon sandwiches?' my mum would ask the room, pretending we were affluent enough for salmon all round.

With the salmon, my mum served the priest coffee. The first time she did this he looked puzzled and requested tea instead. 'Oh, Father, I am so sorry, but we do only drink coffee in this house,' she answered with a lying smirk on her face. One of the girls at work had told Mum that coffee was what all the fancy Yanks drank, and she should 'get with it' and do the same. Only the poor and unsophisticated drank tea. Thereafter any special vistors were offered coffee only, and we drank tea when they were gone home. Finding a coffee pot to impress was a problem. Mum once got Dad to glue the spout of a broken teapot onto our good teapot to give it the look of a coffee pot, but that didn't work as the hot liquid softened the glue and the spout went down into the cup along with the coffee.

Mum dispatched Dad to buy the coffee, expecting him to return with beans. It was a good job he didn't because she wouldn't have had the first clue what to do with them. He fetched home a bottle of Camp coffee – a chicory and coffee blend that was dirt cheap. 'Just add boiling water to make you and your family refined' is what it should have said on the label. But it was rejected instantly because on the front of the bottle was a picture of an Indian man in a turban. 'Proper coffee, I want,' my mum hissed at my dad, who on the power of her stare went scuttling back to the shops.

The priest would lead assembled friends and family in saying the rosary. This lengthy prayer required everyone to get into position, kneeling facing the fire mantel. There in our direct line of vision were the essentials for every London Irish Family at the time: a scroll of the Sacred Heart of Jesus hung in front of a lit votive light, a plaster statue of the Virgin Mary and a framed photograph of John F. Kennedy. These were accessorised by a stack of invitations to Benefit Dances. Younger family members would help aunts, uncles and neighbours, age-stiff and with knees that went off like firecrackers as they went down onto the flowery nylon carpet, into position. The Timer would kneel at the back for these rosaries. If ever I dared glance around he was always picking his nose with one hand and wielding a slipper to smack any miscreant children on the back of the head with the other. The salmon-sandwiches part of the priest's visit slid by in moments, but the mumbling, fumbling rosary took so long that the elders found it harder to get back on their feet than they had to get on their knees.

The fact that our priest had the most desirable car in heaven and on earth at the time, a white convertible with a soft black top, parked outside the door, didn't stop him enjoying an Irish measure of whisky to wash down his salmon sandwich and coffee. He would accept the tumbler-sized glass and say, 'A drop of this is grand for my digestion, so it is,' and talk about his family back in Ireland, his parents, his wants, his needs, and never seemed to show any interest in anything to do with us, other than what was coming next for him in a glass or on a plate. After the salmon sandwich always came a weighty slab of apple pie, buoyed up by oodles of homemade custard and more whisky. My brother, sister and I would be coming to quiet blows over who got to lick out the custard saucepan in the kitchen as the priest tucked in in the room next door.

My mum wasn't daft enough to think the priest cared a jot about any of us, but she wasn't dumb enough to cross him either. And she would tell us by way of an apology, after he had left, that his visit brought out the worst in her because it reminded her of the time their house at home in Ireland had been selected for the 'Stations'. This was when one house in the village was instructed to host a Mass for all, a local honour higher than any other. 'The time we got the Stations, my father started by whitewashing the whole of the outside of the house,' Mum recalled. 'And my mother sewed new curtains and table-cloths and we worked until our fingers bled to make every corner spotless.' In those days anyone who attended the Mass would also get breakfast, served after the priest had eaten his, and there were bread and boiled eggs all round. 'It was a grand thing, a great honour having the Stations,' my mum would say loudly in earshot of my dad, whose family never had the Stations.

'And that auld get ate six or seven tins of my salmon!' wailed my mother of our parish priest when it was announced he had done a midnight bunk from the presbytery taking the nun who was headmistress of a local primary school with him.

Every year we spent six weeks in Ireland at Auntie Mary's house. This was such a home from home it actually didn't count as a holiday, although it was certainly the farthest we ever travelled. On the same day that school broke up for the summer, we would take an overnight train and ferry journey that took sixteen hours door to door. Hauling cases and bags heavier than ourselves up the ramp onto the boat that sailed from Holyhead in North Wales to Dun Laoghaire on the east coast of Ireland, we were jet-sprayed with insecticide. This was a precautionary anti-foot-and-mouth-disease measure, but my dad used to say with glee on the outward journey, 'They're washing the smell of England off us!' He was miserable and had nothing jolly to say when we were coming inward.

Those ferries seemed to have no stabilisers and bobbed and swayed around in the water, triggering sea-sickness in the majority of passengers before they had even set sail. Maybe it was the sheer weight of passengers that made the ferry wobble. There wasn't an inch of free floor space inside. Your suitcase was your seat. A delicate traveller, on one crossing I was on deck clinging to the handrail of the swaying boat and gulping mouthfuls of freezing sea air, trying to quell my constant nausea. Two nuns stood about six feet away from me, their black veils flapping in the vicious wind whipping around the deck. One of them was wailing, 'I'm going to die, Sister Aloysius! God help me!' She spilled the contents of her stomach down over the rail and a gust lifted it and sploshed it onto my face and neck. Gagging with revulsion I ran to where my family were sat on the floor in a corner below deck, picking my way through the crowds and the meshwork of outstretched legs to report my catastrophe. My mum leapt up when she first saw me but relaxed back immediately I told her that it had been a nun who vomited on me. 'That's a blessing for sure!' she said happily as I went alone, crying, to wash my pebbledashed face.

The ferries served drink all day and all night and that put travellers either in the best or worst of moods. There were so many fist fights on some crossings it was like being in a floating boxing ring. One year we travelled with Auntie Peggy and the Timer. She dozed most of the way, too seasick to eat or drink, and she used her new camel coat as a makeshift pillow against the humming walls of the boat. A fresh-faced couple and their new baby sat near by, tinkering with a wind-up record player they were bringing home. They had just one record with them and played it over and again. 'You're Such a Good-looking Woman' by Joe Dolan crooned from the horn-shaped speaker. After several pints of Guinness at the bar, the Timer was replete and ready to spend a few dead hours sleeping it off. 'Turn it off,' he instructed. The young man frowned and turned sharply to look at the Timer, whose red eyes were like slits in his face and whose torso swayed in a manner that was nothing to do with the boat. Even featured and even tempered, the man chose to ignore the instruction, rightly judging it as booze talking.

'Turn –' a pause – 'it –' another longer pause – 'off, I feckin' just told ye and won't say it again.' It was characteristic of the Timer's foul temper to snap, but it was always a shock. Rising like a threat from his seat, he snatched the record player from the lap of the young woman and barged through the saloon doors out onto the deck holding the record player aloft. Once at the boat rail he hurled it as far out as he could into the swollen sea.

The white-fringed waves reached up for it and it was gone in an instant.

With a running jump, the young man leapt onto the Timer's back and floored him, crunching his nose against the slimy wooden deck. The fact that the Timer was stocious drunk was the only thing that stopped that young husband joining his record player in the waves that night. The Timer crawled back to where Peggy was sitting. She had one consoling arm around the young man's wife and in the curve of Peggy's other arm lay the young couple's sleeping baby son. Golden and warm, wrapped in a crochet blanket, he was making prayer-like shapes with his miniature hands. As the Timer slumped on the floor next to her, Peggy covered the baby's ears with her long slender fingers and said, 'You filthy, rotten, lousy pig!' to his by then already unconscious body.

When we arrived in Ireland, within hours of the travel sickness subsiding we were in the grip of more suffering. With hives. Some the size of grapes. The milk, the water, the air were all blamed for the lumps that rose up in crop rows over our face and bodies. They made us look like mutants, but worse than that they screamed out day and night, interrupting every thought, deed and sleep to be scratched. These torturous swellings usually went down just in time for the journey home. I once caught my little sister with a knife trying to slice one of hers off.

We didn't dare complain of any ailments within earshot of Auntie Mary, who had inherited from Nan a saying for the ailing: 'Get down on your knees and be thankful you are on your feet!'

It was Auntie Mary who introduced my sister and me to the delights of Pongo, a number game that was played in her local church hall for prizes on wooden boards. The markers were caps from mineral (fizzy drinks) bottles. Our favourite mineral, which we thought so exotic, was red lemonade. This left a bright and long-lasting red ring around our mouths after just a couple of gulps. 'You look like a clown!' I would crow at my sister's stained face. 'No I don't – you do!' she would tell me back, and we would trade insults until we reached a plait-pulling crescendo when any nearby adult would intervene to separate us.

Dad would join us for two weeks of the six-week visit, either at the beginning or the end, because he couldn't afford to take any more time off work. The weeks he wasn't there, a brown envelope from England would arrive every Saturday morning for my mum with his week's wages inside, which took us just a couple of days to spend. After the initial excitement of being away from home had passed, I would sit on the third step of Auntie Mary's wooden stairs sucking my thumb whilst rubbing my nose with the edge of a blanket from my doll's pram and firing big ploppy tears. 'I want my daddy!' was my refrain, which everyone ignored.

One year, halfway through our summer stay of six weeks, we all took a train ride to visit a first cousin of Dad's who lived in a farm deep in the Irish countryside. This excursion was billed as a treat. The sound that welcomed us to the farmyard was squealing. Loud and panicked. Following the din, we children trudged behind Mum and Dad into a vast shed with a pitched corrugated roof. A city child, I was sure I'd stepped into Hades. Two men in there, overalls dotted with blood spray, held a live piglet apiece, belly up in the spit-roasting position. A third man was using what looked like an ice-cream scoop to castrate the animals in a single swipe. Piglet testicles, fresh cut, were dropped into a steel pail full of white disinfectant and the scoop got a cursory pink shake. The floor of the barn was a bubble of piglet backs as the panicked creatures bumped and shuffled and snuffled.

The drama was intensified when a wild-haired woman came running into the barn shouting, 'Ye bastards! Max Factor that is!' and snatched a lipstick in a gold case from the farm-hand, who was using it to put geranium-coloured crosses on the backs of the piglets who had been 'seen to'. It was a crooked column of colour, thick with grit and pig hair. She cuffed the lipstick abuser around the head before rushing back outside, muttering about being late for the bingo. The big-bellied farm dog was busy on bucket watch, snout bobbing into the bucket as he lapped up the fresh lychee-sized testicles seconds after they hit the disinfectant. For lunch that day we got a tin plate apiece weighted with a slab of buttered soda bread, a hard-boiled egg and a mug of milk, still blood-warm from the cow. The farm dog got mine because the sound of screaming piglets had killed my appetite stone dead.

Don't underestimate how sticky cow dung is. That would be my advice for any townie heading off to the country for an overnight stay. On my uncle's farm I was playing hide and seek with my cousins and had to run away quickly and find some-where to hide. I had a choice of going over or around the pile of 'earth' that was directly in front of me. In white leather san-dals and ankle socks and wearing a yellow floral-print cotton dress with a matching ribbon in my hair, I decided to scamper over the heap. There was a cracking sound and I sank down in manure to navel height. The hard brown surface was just a sun glaze. What was beneath was the colour and texture of dark toffee and its stench was enough to make my eyes spin in their sockets.

A cold hosing down and a bar of carbolic soap removed the solid matter, but it didn't remove the staining or the residues in my navel, fingernails and toenails. Or the smell. Sometimes when I sweat even now as an adult I think I can still get those vegetable and methane notes from that day on the farm when I was eight years old. 'It's Anna-Maynure,' my uncle Joe liked to say, over and again, whenever he saw me afterwards.

Back in town Auntie Mary was well known in her home town for refusing to pay the full price for anything. Carrying a deep wicker basket like a shield, combat-ready she would set out for her daily messages with me in reluctant tow. In the grocer's she would ask the portly Mr Butler to weigh out her sugar, tea and flour, and wait with menace whilst he packaged her parcels in a double layer. After all that personal attention, he would tot up in his head and announce the price. 'Goway owa dat!' Auntie Mary would say with half a laugh in her voice. Mary would reach into her basket and fish out a huge sparkly purse and count out what she thought the shopping was worth. This amount was hopped onto the counter and she would stalk off, with me scampering behind her, looking over my shoulder and apologising with my eyes to Mr Butler.

Mary's husband Niall was a butcher, but he was without a tooth in his head to chew meat. His dinner was always something soft, bruised in buttered mashed potato. His favourite meal was a poached egg and creamed potato. When we stayed, our plates would be stacked with bloody towers of lamb and steak and beef. Niall sucked as we all chomped. When in my early teens I decided that I couldn't in all conscience eat animals any more, I became a vegetarian. My mother was perplexed and unsure about what my conscience had to do with my dinner. Auntie Mary wept when she heard and predicted, 'Ye'll end up bandy!' The first year we visited when I was a new vegetarian, Auntie Mary did her best to yield to my principles and presented me with a special welcome dinner. On my plate there was mashed potato, boiled potato, chips and a scotch egg, all floating in beef gravy. For six fraught weeks she did her very best to rise to the challenge of feeding a veggie, and almost got it right the evening she served me a cheese and tomato pizza. Trouble was, she'd cooked it topping-side-down on the oven tray. 'Don't ye like your pisser?' she asked as I tried to chisel pieces off it with my knife and fork.

We spent almost every school holiday in Ireland, bar Christmas. But Auntie Mary was convinced that we wouldn't survive the festive season in London if she didn't truss up an Irish turkey in string and brown paper and post it over to us. One year it was livid with maggots by the time it arrived. Another time, my mother didn't even remove the brown paper from the turkey. There was no need. The fact that the bird stank of fish on the day it was delivered confirmed it was rank. And it was my job, every year, to compose the thank-you letter for the festering birds. Mum would dictate all kind of turkey compliments – juicy, buttery, melt-in-the-mouth, tasty – and so fast I could hardly keep up. I asked why she didn't just tell her sister the truth – that her turkey didn't travel well – so she could save her time and money. 'Whisht. It's nice to be nice, Anna May,' was her answer.

Christmas was a festival of food and my mother knocked herself out stuffing, peeling, soaking and setting. One year Dad arrived home with a turkey the size of a Labrador the full of his arms. A man in a van had bartered it for free petrol at Selfridges where he was working at the time. It was, he had claimed, the little brother of the self-same turkey that the royal family would be eating that year. Our kitchen table bowed when Dad banged it down. Mum looked at it, and then over at her small oven, and asked. 'And what do you want me to do with that?'

Together they lined the bottom of the oven with layers of tin-foil and tried to slide the turkey in but it was too high-backed to fit in. So they heaved it onto the kitchen table and stood on kitchen chairs to push down hard from above to flatten it some. This worked. Again they tried to get the bird into the oven. But although they had made it shorter, they had also made the turkey wider. Mum was determined not to waste the giant turkey gift so she ordered Dad to take his trousers off. 'Have you lost your senses?' he cried. 'Think of the childer – they're only down the hall.'

She curled her lip in disgust. 'Dirty auld man. For hygiene. Take them off.' She made him lie on the kitchen floor and clamp the turkey between his legs, squeezing as tight as he could, and at the same time she straddled him, pressing down on the bird with all her might. He squeezed, she pressed. Grunting with exertion, they leant on the oven door to lock the bird in. It took twenty-seven hours to cook.

10

Lucky Dip Dinners

Perks of the jobs that my parents did were few and far between. The last time my brother, sister and I were all naked together was in a vast house near Hampstead Heath, a full hour's bus ride away from our home. Our mum cleaned there three times a week. And as she worked, we bathed in one of its four luxury bathrooms. She considered dipping us whilst she worked a small benefit of the job, and it met with no resistance from the three of us. Sitting neck deep in scented water, in a house as warm as an oven set to high, was bliss – whoever the company.

The three of us, all primary-school age, were steeping in the vast bath, chins immersed in rainbow foam and wearing bright bubbly smiles. Resplendent at the centre of the bath – how posh was that! – rose the gold-plated tap in the shape of a fish. It gushed non-stop hot water from its open mouth. Through the glorious steam I could see my mum in the distance on the other side of the bathroom, a space so big it had its own echo. 'The Black Velvet Band' was the song she slaughtered as she scrubbed away at the floor and wall tiles. A steel bucket hung over her arm like a handbag.

Our communal bath was cut short when Mum's boss, a GP, returned unexpectedly from work. We heard his key in the front door and Mum reacted like she'd been shot. Using hysterical sign language she indicated we were to get out of the bath and get dressed – immediately – stabby-pointing to behind the bath-room door. She couldn't have been thinking straight because the bathroom had shuttered, half-length saloon doors. Mum looked like she was going to cry and was the only one making a noise as she pleaded with us over and over again to 'Sssssssh! Sssssssh!' Pointing to the pile of fluffy white towels she shook her head violently, miming the word *no!* One by one we slithered out of the bath, each three times our usual size with bubbles, and started to pull our clothes onto our wet skin.

The doctor was grumpy because he had forgotten his wallet and had to come back for it. It felt like a fortnight before we heard his footsteps on the stairs, this time heading down the stairs. Mum burst back into the bathroom almost drunk with relief and laughed and kissed us all. We jumped for joy in the puddle of bath water and fright-wee we'd made, and laughed right back at her.

Then, 'Back in!' she instructed, and we began the gargantuan struggle to get out of our wet clothes and dive back into the foamy water.

When I was at primary school, I wanted with all my heart to be a cleaner when I grew up. I went to work with my mum and aunts on the school holidays, and it felt like going to paradise in rubber gloves. The vast houses they cleaned had fridges the size of wardrobes bulging with food, shelves of books to read and lawns that were long, flat and neat – perfect for rolling around on. It was like having a park all to myself. Some of the gardens had swings and climbing frames and ponds with frogs on lily pads, as if the pages of a book had come to life. The rules were that we had to be ready to hide ourselves away quickly at all times – because of course we weren't meant to be there – be completely silent, and *never* touch anything in case we broke it. I prayed that one day I might be a cleaner in a big house, too, and then I could touch things.

My mum once took my then seven-year-old brother to her cleaning job at a solicitor's Victorian villa in Notting Hill. She had no choice but to bring him because he was off school sick. 'The size of a football field' was how Michael described the leather inlaid desk where he had been parked for the morning with a colouring book and some pencils. Mum went about her chores, repeating, 'Don't touch anything,' and he claimed she said it so much the phrase started to sound like 'touch anything don't' and 'anything don't touch'.

Later that day in casualty, Michael wailed that he had done what he was told and hadn't actually touched anything. He had merely waved his finger across the powerful industrial electric stapler that was on the corner of the huge desk and plugged in beneath. The stapler shot a three-quarter-inch staple through his fingernail and there was an instant geyser of blood. Mum, wild with annoyance, knotted his finger in a tea towel and made him hold it, still dripping, over her open handbag whilst she finished cleaning, before taking him on the bus to hospital to be stitched up.

My dad got a job at the Heinz factory in West London when I had just started secondary school. Workers there were given the chance once a week to buy damaged tins, all unlabelled, for a fraction of their normal shop price. Dad would struggle home on the bus carrying his bodyweight in mystery tin cans of all shapes and sizes. My mother, who considered wasting food to be on a par with infanticide, introduced a house rule that if a mystery tin was selected and opened, whatever was in it had to be consumed there and then in case it went off. Thank the Lord that Heinz didn't make dog food.

During the Heinz era, we lived on a culinary precipice. There were occasionally some nice surprises – treacle pudding for breakfast, tinned peaches for lunch and a lot of rice pudding with everything. After eating weekday dinners, my brother, sister and I would plead for the opening of a mystery tin for dessert. Pre-Heinz a sweet was only ever served on a Sunday. If my mother's mood was good and she was pro-tin, one would be selected and placed in front of my dad for opening. The first piercing could offer a clue. Clear juice meant fruit, custard and rice were cause for immediate celebration, and tomato sauce was universally bad because it meant beans, ravioli or soup. We would groan inwardly and kick one another under the table in frustration if our mystery dessert turned out to be beans and mini sausages, macaroni cheese or, worst of all, mulligatawny soup.

Once, a friend from down the street happened by at dinner time just after we'd played Russian roulette with an unlabelled tin, and lost. She joined us at the table after we'd pleaded for dessert, got it and wished we hadn't. In our house if you arrived during a meal you got a plateful of it, whether you wanted it or not. And an especially large portion if you said you didn't want any. 'Have some pudding!' my mum ordered, dishing out tinned spaghetti.

Nan was the only person in the house exempt from my

mum's many and various rulings concerning food, money and
absolutely everything else in the universe. She would construct
a double-decker fresh peach, salad cream and sugar sandwich for
herself, her favourite summer dinner. My friend looked at our
pastel-pink-stained mouths and my nan's sweet and savoury
bread tower and blurted out without thinking, 'Weird. My
mum said you Irish only eat potatoes and cabbage.'

'You can tell your mother that at least we don't eat jelly
heels!' retorted my mum.

The letdown of the decade from the discounted-tins lucky-
dip carrier bag was vegetable salad. A handful of diced mixed
vegetable: potato, carrot and peas all stuck deep into a ball of
solid mayonnaise. It looked like someone else had already
digested it.

The biggest dinner-table treat of all was leftovers. Not our
own, but whatever my mum and aunts had managed to clear
from the tables of some of London's poshest hotels, where they
worked as casual waitresses. And not just any old leftovers.
Celebrity ones. I once enjoyed a crème caramel that Henry
Cooper had left behind, and my sister tucked into melon and
ham – complete with a glacé cherry – that Cliff Richard had
toyed with but not eaten. A glacé cherry was the seal of sophis-
tication for any dish.

'This is international cuisine,' my mother would announce
proudly as she unveiled what was compressed onto the plates
she'd ferried home. Exotic delicacies such as eggs in curried
mayonnaise, prawn cocktail and lemon meringue pie were
squashed together onto one dish for ease of transportation. We
licked the plates they came home on clean, and over the years
acquired a good collection of fine china and monogrammed
cutlery from our takeaways.

We sent out food, too. If my dad had to work on a Sunday, Mum proved her love and devotion to him (and her determination to get to evening bingo on time) by dishing him up a full roast meal to go: meat, potatoes, swede, parsnips and cabbage, all submerged in boiling gravy. This dish was prepped for travel by the addition of a second dinner plate, which acted as a lid, and two tea towels which were a flimsy wrapping. The dinner was placed into mine or my sister's safekeeping for delivery to the garage where Dad worked. It was a thirty-minute bus ride away. Considerable skills were needed, especially when the bus took corners, to keep the hot gravy out of your lap.

Our reward for delivering dinner was to sit on a big stool in the garage and work the till as Dad ate. The till had giant buttons and a spring-loaded drawer that opened with a ping when you cranked the side handle hard and fast enough. Before I left to get the bus home with his dinner plate that was scraped clean, Dad would slam open the till and take a handful of notes and coins saying, 'Take these home to your mammy.' I once asked if he was allowed to take money from the cash register, and he smiled and said, 'Sure they're called tips, Anna May. Amn't I entitled?'

My dad was generous to a fault, and regularly redistributed his employer's cash and stock. When he worked in Selfridges garage he would encourage all family members who had a car, any old jalopy would do, to come and park it on the forecourt and he would shoo them off shopping for a while. By the time they returned, Dad would have filled their tank with petrol, their engine with oil and their car interior with goodies from the garage shop. Driving gloves, chamois leathers, car-seat covers, car mats, spark plugs, windscreen wipers and Feu d'Orange car fresheners. Feu d'Orange was the fragrance of my youth. Those little strips, compliments of Selfridges, hung in every space in our house: rooms, cupboards, wardrobes, even our dog had a fresh one hung around his neck weekly. No matter what Dad brought home from work, or gave away to family, he never looked on it as stealing. According to him it was sharing.

Whilst he worked in Selfridges, he did a lot of free shopping. He was of the jolly opinion that as a forecourt attendant in their garage he had full rights to help himself to whatever he fancied from all five floors of the shop. His only limitation was that any spoils had to be able to fit onto the Number-Six bus for transportation home. One December evening he helped himself to a cardboard box from the store room that had a picture of a beautiful luxury Christmas tree taped to its side. A new tree was exactly what we needed. Our old faithful, made of pink tinsel, was fifteen years old, floppy and suffering from an advanced case of mange. He pulled, pushed, rocked and rolled the box on and off the bus and along the pavement home, and with all of us behind him managed to shoulder it up the stairs. 'This is going to be one fine fecker of a Christmas tree!' Dad said as he ripped the box open. In there was a fine Christmas tree. Along with twenty-three others. Two dozen trees in total. Which explains why every relative we had in London had an identical luxury Selfridges Christmas tree that year, and for many afterwards.

For my wedding day, Dad did a deal with the men's tailoring manager in Selfridges in return for a bespoke suit. For a down payment of a few squeegees, spark plugs and some windscreen wash, he ordered a beautiful navy striped suit in a cashmere-mix cloth. 'Sean Connery admired that cloth this very week,' is what the man murmured in appreciation of Dad's good taste. After that Dad would take money from the till in the garage shop where he worked to make weekly payments to the men's tailoring cash register. He looked sensational in the hand-sewn suit, although the jacket pockets did bulge a little on the day because of all the betting slips he had in there.

'What is that?' my mother screeched.

'Ssssh, Annie, you'll frighten the poor dog!'

'That's not a dog, it's a cart horse.'

So went the conversation the evening my dad returned from his job as a park-keeper with a St Bernard called Dinky on a lead. His owner was going into hospital the following morning and couldn't find anyone willing to take care of his dog whilst he was indisposed – until he came across my sucker of a dad locking up the park at dusk.

Dinky was not only tall, waist high to an adult, but wide enough to fill up our council flat. He blocked the stairwell and doorways and, more stubborn than any of us, we always ended up climbing over him. That dog had a head the size and weight of a concrete block, which meant when he rested it on your lap you were pinioned to the seat until he released you. A four-legged slobber fountain, he left seeping wet patches all over the carpet and sofas. He had an appetite to match his size; he once ate our Sunday dinner roast chicken in one swallow. Mum pretended to complain about Dinky, but she had a special way of getting him to sleep by using her finger to make circles on the soft skin where his front leg joined his body, and she saved her best smiles for him, too.

News of Dad's willingness to board pets for free reached all four corners of the park and we ran an unofficial dogs' home for a year or two. Sometimes more than one dog would stay and they would take a four-legged-style shine to one another. Any copulation attempt was guaranteed to bring my mum to her feet. She'd cry, 'Don't look, girls, and bless yourselves!' and then, blushing at speed, 'People never do that of course!' We missed the dogs when Dad left the park-keeping job. Although I have lots of non-canine reminders in my garden of his time with the royal parks: plants, benches, signs and paving. Everything he helped himself to came home on a wheelbarrow in the dead of night.

Dad had the fastest turnover of jobs when I was at secondary school, maybe starting the week as a window cleaner and ending it as a porter in a hospital. He blagged his way into some jobs claiming he was skilled, and lasted as long as it took for his employer to find out he wasn't. But he always had the buildings to fall back on. 'Ah, it's a grand job digging holes,' he would say. 'The only one where I can start at the top!'

11

Bucketgate

It took a week's pay for my parents to kit my brother out in grammar school uniform. He was the first in our family to take the eleven-plus, and no one even knew what that meant at the time. When a letter later arrived saying he had won a place at the best boys' grammar school in London, my mum grumbled that it was a long way from home and thought he must have come bottom of the class to get allocated a school so far away. He set off to school on his first day looking like Just William's twin. He was carrying an empty cardboard plastic-coated brief-case that was a Green Shield Stamps purchase and dragging a PE kit holdall that was bigger than a body bag.

Once he started big school, my brother disappeared under an avalanche of paper. The school philosophy was to break the boys with homework and Michael was in his room studying almost all of the time. Whenever he brought home some recordings of Shakespeare plays as study aids, my mother would march her visiting sisters and brothers up the stairs to listen to a bit of *Macbeth* or *The Tempest* through his bedroom door. 'What do you think of that!' she would say proudly. 'What is it?' Peggy asked. 'How would I know?' my mum answered.

His school reports damned him, even though his chin rarely left the desk. He couldn't have been all that clever in those days because my brother would open his school report at the end of each term and read it aloud to my mum without any editing. I once heard him say, 'Michael is a very mediocre boy' and 'Michael is destined for a lifetime of unskilled labour'.

My mum kept right on smiling.

'Royal blue skull cap with gold hanging tassel, woollen beret, navy blue belted mac, navy blue crombie coat, kilt, cotton shirt (3), PE shirts (2), PE knickers, outdoor PE knickers . . . were the first of forty-seven items on my new school uniform list. I ran out of breath reading it to Auntie Peggy. 'Are ye joining the army or what?' she wanted to know. 'That school only takes the cream of the cream!' my mum crowed to Peggy for the fourth time in an hour.

She'd changed her tune. When I passed my eleven-plus and was offered a place at a convent grammar school, my mum wrote a note to my primary class teacher that read, 'No thank you to gramer scool for Anna May', followed by her line-of-loops-that-leant-sharply-to-the-right signature. She had no particular objection to selective schooling. I don't think she even knew what it was until we were in the thick of it. What put her off the idea of grammar school was maybe the danger of an unaccompanied daily tube and bus journey for me. My formidable, purple-faced and perpetually furious teacher didn't take the trouble to respond in writing to her note. Instead, at home time on the day he received it, he pulled me from the classroom by my plaits and half walked, half ran me to the school gate where my mum was waiting. He collared her and leant in so close the cigarette she was smoking dropped from her mouth to the ground. '*You* are an ignorant woman and this opportunity means your daughter doesn't have to be, so bloody well take it and don't deny her chance to get on in life!' And then he tore up her 'no thank you to grammar school' note in front of her shocked eyes. My mum said in later years that she wasn't angry with him. She was grateful he'd thought enough of me to put her straight.

That teacher was wrong about one thing, though. Mum was in no way stupid, and neither was my dad. They were without education but shot-through smart. As children they walked five miles each way to their respective village schools, barefoot or booted, depending on who fitted the few pairs of boots in the household that were shared between them all. They both said they were always early for school in the summer months when the tarmac roads were red hot and hurt the soles of their feet if they didn't pick them up and run to get on the cool wooden floors of the schoolroom. My mum told me she was the child picked to be her teacher's teeth monitor. Mrs Cready, fat, fretful and forty, daily left her dentures in a cup on the classroom windowsill. She told my mother to keep constant watch out through the window for a car approaching down the country road. Only the priest or the school inspector had a car and for a visit from either of those the school mistress would jam her dentures in just in time to greet them. Once when Mum was concentrating hard on her sums, she missed first sight of the car and the priest caught the teacher by surprise without her teeth in. After Father had left the classroom, the teacher's fake smile fell from her face and she lifted my mum off her feet by her hair and spanked her hard. 'There's a mess of curls on yer head and very little else in it!' was what she shouted.

In winter schoolmasters ordered their pupils to bring a briquette of turf apiece daily to burn on the classroom fire. The children who brought the most turf got to sit closest to the burner – and the master himself would spend the day sat *on* it. 'I hope he got piles the size of tomatoes!' my mum said in later years. My parents were so impoverished they could rarely bring any turf because there was none, or none to spare, at home. They would sit shivering with cold out of sight and earshot of their teachers. Any pupils who couldn't correctly answer the questions the teacher shot out at random like gunfire into the classroom were viciously beaten around the head and shoulders. In Mum's school, the master used a wide leather strap to scar the children; in Dad's, a piece of boxwood was used. And that's how the desire to learn was frozen and bludgeoned out of my mum and dad. They said they danced for joy when they left school at thirteen.

It was other mothers' reactions to all three of us getting into grammar school that alerted mine to the fact that she and her children were onto something good, and had something the others wanted but couldn't have. And she loved that. Some of our English neighbours told my mum that we had taken school places that their children should, by rights, have had. This didn't make my mum feel ashamed, she was simply delighted to have confirmed what she had always known anyway – that her children were special.

Miss Thomas, our downstairs neighbour, repeated to my mum what her nephew had told her, that the pass mark on the exam was set lower for the children of the Irish and the Polish because otherwise the eleven-plus would have been too difficult to pass for 'illiterates like you'. Having three out of three children officially declared as 'clever' gave my mum's status in the family and wider community a fillip that she thoroughly enjoyed. One of my dad's sisters, who was raging that her children were all trudging daily to the secondary modern whilst we were safe in grammar school, accused my mum of becoming an 'auld schnob' because she had put a few books on display in the front room. 'You're just showing off. You couldn't read any one of them!' she said accusingly to my mum who replied, 'No, but those orange ones are a good match with the wallpaper, aren't they?' Her sister-in-law snorted in disgust and my mum said brightly, 'Isn't it better after all to have your nose in the air than in the gutter!' She was rising fast to her new-found position as mother superior.

She developed a new confidence to fight our corners. Like the time my brother and all his friends applied for temporary Christmas work sorting and delivering at the Post Office. All six of Michael's friends were offered jobs and Michael alone was rejected. Mum was white-faced with fury when she heard about this.

'Can you explain to me why exactly my son is not considered good enough to deliver the Christmas mail? At *grammar* school he is a vice prefect, and on the waiting list for the choir and—' She was standing in front of the desk of the Post Office big chief, whose deep, well-spoken voice had interrupted her. 'Do you and your son talk often?'

'Of course we do. Isn't he my son? Why wouldn't we be talking?'

'So you would then, of course, know that your son is known to the police for being drunk and disorderly. And here at the

Post Office we do not consider juvenile delinquents as suitable candidates for employment. Permanent or temporary.'

After that shaming encounter, Mum gathered my brother, sister and me together on the sofa and demanded that when we had troubles we were to bring them home, no matter what they were. 'That includes babies!' she said, wagging her finger at my sister and me.

Providing my fancy grammar school uniform swallowed a week's wages for my parents. Did I appreciate it? Not a bit. Dressed in 100 per cent best quality wool I applied myself, not to learning, but to pointless rebellion and complaint. In truth, I had absolutely nothing to complain about. My life was wonderful because my amicable, hardworking parents worked several jobs apiece to make sure I had everything I wanted. I was disruptive in the extreme. 'Don't go breaking your shin on a stool that's not in your way,' my mum would implore.

I made my teachers' lives a misery and deserved any punishments I got. One thousand lines of 'I must improve my manners' was cramp-inducing and memorable. But there was one occasion when I got in trouble and was completely blameless.

My best friend at school was Fenella. She was even bolshier than me, and I was her biggest fan. We were inseparable for two years until Fenella had an operation to pin back her teaplate-sized ears. She came around from her anaesthetic convinced she was now a beauty queen and jettisoned me as her best friend. For a few cringe-making months I loyally straggled around in her wake, just in case she changed her mind.

My dad was working as a bus conductor at the time and had booked my sister and me hot, hot, hot tickets for the annual bus garage workers' Children's Christmas Outing to see *Snow White and the Seven Dwarves on Ice* at Wembley Arena. This was the biggest thing that had ever happened in our lives. The pair of us were sleepless with excitement at the prospect of this ultra glamorous trip. We whispered together about what it might be like day and night for months beforehand. What we would wear, eat, see and hear on the big day were discussed on a loop, and each conversation about our upcoming gala outing was even more thrilling than the last.

'She has very weak hair, this one,' my mother would lament of my sister as she set about flattening it with a comb and a wet flannel. It had a will-o'-the-wisp attitude and daily refused to stay close to Julie's scalp or settle in nicely behind her ears. She always took longer than anyone else to get ready to go out because her hair headed in so many different directions. Mum planned ahead and decided she would bunch and plait Julie's hair for the big day out.

As children, my sister and I had a brilliant free game that kept us quiet, not just for a few hours, but for years. My mother would give us an out-of-date mail-order catalogue. It came from a neighbour who was getting rid of it because her new one had arrived, and we used it to play 'I Like This and I Like That'. Thicker than a telephone directory, this catalogue was a source of endless joy for us. The made-up game was to be the fastest to point at the item we wanted in the catalogue in the full knowledge we wouldn't ever have it. It was window shopping but without the window and without the shopping.

Our shared bedroom, where we played this game sat in bed together, was like a holy shrine. A two-foot-tall fluorescent yellow, plastic statue of the Virgin Mary was the centrepiece on our dressing table. She glowed in the dark and one night we accidentally threw a petticoat over her as we tore our clothes off in the freezing cold and got our bums slapped the following morning. 'Our Precious Lady looks after you day *and* night. Don't you two dare to be so ungrateful and cover her up!' A china ornament in the shape of a book was painted with the words of a prayer we had to recite aloud to our mum every night. 'Now I Lay Me Down To Sleep, I Pray The Lord My Soul To Keep, Thy Angel Guard Us Through The Night And Wake Us With The Morning Light.' Julie could sometimes be heard repeating this prayer over and again from beneath her bed covers. Mostly after I swore to her that I had seen the eyes in a painting of the Sacred Heart of Jesus, which hung in pride of place above the fireplace in our room, come to life and swivel around to stare at her whilst she was sleeping.

We were homey girls – an outing for us was a rare and thrilling treat. Which is why it was so cataclysmic when tonsillitis cruelly felled Julie the day before our trip to the ice show in Wembley Arena. She was declared too sick to go by the visiting doctor, and that's how my by then part-time friend Fenella got a last-minute invite. I was wearing a half-velvet, half-glittery-satin (overlaid with beaded net) dress, which had buttons and bows and a sewn-in feathery boa. Maura, my mum's first cousin, had made one for me and an identical one for my little sister. They had been posted over from Ireland. The nursing staff in the mental hospital where Maura was a long-stay patient had helped her sew on the many and varied trimmings. Inside the package was a holy picture card of Jesus nailed to the Cross. My aunt had carefully added glitter to the crucifix part only, and it was signed on the back by her and all the hospital staff. They wished us both a lovely time and God's special blessings on our special day out.

On the day of the trip, Julie's new dress was hanging and pulsing neon colours on the outside of the wardrobe door. But instead of her finery, she was wearing teddy-bear-print pyjamas, accessorised by a thick woollen scarf to keep her tonsils warm. This scarf was tied tight in a double knot around her neck by my mum. From the expression on her face that scarf might as well have been a noose.

Fenella dressed down in slacks, sweater and a nylon anorak. This was a blow to me, and took away most of the fun factor in my new dress. But she was eager to see the ice show and had obviously calculated that it would be worth putting up with me for a few hours for the free ticket. She barely spoke and spent a lot of time checking her hair in a small compact mirror and making herself bleed by twisting the gold sleepers in her newly pierced flat-to-her-head ears. I was determined not to notice that she was playing cool.

The garage had arranged a special bus to transport all the children. It was a Routemaster in disguise. There were inflatable snowmen and reindeer on the roof and inside was a riot of tinsel, paper chains and balloons. Sticky sweets and lollipops were piled high on every seat and a magician called Mr Magico walked around, even as the bus was moving, and did brilliant card tricks and games for us. Mr Magico's assistant was a white rabbit called Mr Snowy. He was a poorly rabbit that day and Mr Magico let me cradle him, soft and weighty with heat and trust.

Heavenly – the only description for the ice show with its singing and skating and fireworks and sliding scenery. It took me out of my world and into another dimension of pleasure. A beyond perfect day. I was just thirteen but came home convinced there would never, in my entire life, be a better one.

When I got home I found my sister propped up in bed with

eyes like poached plums from crying. I jettisoned all my ecstasies and told her a dollop of lies. It had all been rubbish, the seven dwarves kept falling over and Snow White was old – at least thirty – and a wobbly skater and the bus ride had been freezing and boring and made me feel sick. She wanted to be convinced, so she was. The hardest thing was keeping Mr Snowy a secret from her because we always told each other everything, but I knew a magic rabbit – one that didn't wriggle and wanted to snuggle up – would have taken her to tonsillitis tipping point.

Back at school, I was still buzzing with post-ice-show excitement. First lesson was in the biology lab. I was working behind Fenella O'Leary and overheard her telling a group of classmates about our day out. 'She lives in a proper slum, and thought it was all amazing, silly cow. She's so easily pleased, and you should have seen the state of her dress, her loony relative made it . . .'

I turned to stone. I stood there trying hard to make what she said mean something else. I thought of my dad paying in instalments for ten months for the tickets and the return ride on the tinsel bus that was so thrilling. She had eaten Marks and Spencer steak pie and hand-cut chips and an individual strawberry mousse for dinner at my house before we went, and we hardly ever had that combination of special treats. My little sister was sick and diabolically disappointed. And all Fenella could say about the day was that I lived in a slum?

In those days on every school laboratory wall there were two hooks, one for a bucket of water and another for a bucket of sand. They were there in case of emergency, and this definitely ranked as one of those. I don't remember deciding to do it, but I do recall Fenella's face after I had. The bucket was very heavy and the water came out of it fast down onto her head. 'Don't you *ever* call my house a slum!'

171

Two hours later my mother and I were both standing in the headmistress's office. Sister Bunbury was a wimple-wearing despot. I was in my usual position on the rug in front of her desk and my mother was positioned to my right. The standard routine was that the headmistress would berate me and when I opened my mouth to reply she would seethe, 'Don't you daaaaaaaare speak!' This time was different. Sister Bunbury wanted to hear what I had to say. They both did. Four eyes drilled into me. They were waiting for an explanation, but didn't get one.

How could I repeat what Fenella had said about my house being a slum in front of my mum? She was always cleaning and polishing and generally cherishing the 'slum' and I was scared about how upset she would be and, worst of all, how hard she would try not to show it. I kept my silence, even though my headmistress and my mum, who were usually adversaries about my misbehaviour, were for once united in fury with me.

Sister Bunbury concluded the meeting by saying that this time I had gone too far and she had no choice but to expel me. A letter would be sent home to that effect. Shock replaced my mum's anger. Wet-cheeked, she clamped me to her outside the school office and whispered in my ear, 'It'll be alright, don't be worrying about anything,' when she clearly didn't think it was alright and was herself worrying about everything. I was in agony for upsetting her.

Later that day, which I spent in exile in the school library, the headmistress called me back to her office. It was just the two of us this time, and she asked again for an account of the events. She gave me a particular look that made me certain she could actually see inside me, through my bones and right out the other side. By then I was good and ready to crack, and she knew it. A cascade of tears crashed from my eyes. I ended up hot-snottering all Sister Bunbury's grey-serge-clad squidgy balloon bosoms. I told her everything about *Snow White on Ice*, the choc ices, my sister's tonsillitis and Mr Snowy.

That flinty but fair old nun did send a letter home to my parents. In it she said that on reflection she was going to give me a *final* final chance. Fenella was put on cloakroom-cleaning duties for six months. And Bucketgate was the last time I was knowingly naughty.

When my brother qualified as a teacher and became the first ever graduate in both Mum and Dad's family, it was a monumental day. Mum was inside out with joy. Dad was happy because everyone else was, but then he always was happy anyway. Dressed like we were going to a society wedding, we all headed up north by coach to my brother's university campus for his convocation ceremony. There were eighty-two people on that bus and by the time we pulled up at Leeds bus station, every one of them knew that my brother was a graduate and going to be a teacher. Mum stood at the coach door in the bus station and shook all of their hands as they disembarked, accepting their thanks and best wishes without a trace of modesty or shame.

Marbled with pride, both my parents studied the scroll that declared their son was a Bachelor of Science with genuine wonder. That piece of paper went to a specialist shop to be mounted in an ornate, expensive frame. A frame that my dad complained when he tried to hang it on the wall 'weighs more than a sack of spuds!' When Auntie Peggy heard of Michael's Bachelor of Science title, she asked in a worried voice, 'Does that mean he's too clever to get married now?'

With the Wimpy restaurant where we'd had our celebratory

meal as the backdrop, we all posed for a special set of com-memorative photographs. After they were developed, my mum carefully selected the best two and sent one to her and Dad's county newspaper in Ireland, who printed it, and the other to the *London Evening News*, who ignored it. I saw the letter she wrote by hand that went in the post with each photo. It said, '*My* son is a grajut and a scool mastar and here is snaps. Thanking you.' Her signature, a delicate row of dreamy slant-ing loops, read, Annie Veronica Mangan (Mrs).

Mum and Dad spawned three 'grajuts'. Whilst this was very brag-worthy, it had attached worries, too. Mum's big fear was that any high-faluting jobs might take us a long way from home. Occasionally she would lose patience with all the studying we had to do. She once urged me to pack in all the 'reading and writing' and get a job near home so I could come and see her at lunchtimes. She got application forms from Woolworths and Bata the shoe shop, both on our local high street, for me to fill out and submit.

A careers interview questionnaire at school had started with the question, 'And what does your father do?' In fact, most job and university interviews did in those days. I would reply in a puzzled voice, 'Oh, he has a job, thank you. This one is for me.' My adviser, a woman the full of a dogstooth-check skirt suit who had overdosed on coral lipstick, told me I was pretty, which meant at least I wouldn't be working for very long before I could get married. She put forward her suggestion like she'd pulled a rabbit from a top hat. An air-hostess for Aer Lingus. 'But only if you stay trim and don't get any taller,' she warned. Mum rubbished the air-hostess idea instantly she heard it. She claimed my lovely face would swell up from flying, never mind that I might die in a plane crash, and anyway dishing up dinners was what she did for a job – only not in the sky – and surely they could find me something a bit better than that after all the education I'd had?

I had a seasonal job as a Post Office worker over my Christmas holidays, and one of the kindly permanent posties would drop me off at home each lunchtime with my bulging postal sack and deliver me back to my 'walk' afterwards. This favour brought paradise to my mum's kitchen. Not me. My postal sack.

She would bounce-serve up my lunch and fast turn her attention to my sack. Letters got steamed open, read and carefully returned to their envelopes so the recipient couldn't tell they had been tampered with. But they were always very boring: water bills and train timetables. Parcels were her favourite. These were opened up, commented on and resealed. There was one that silenced her. It contained a PVC basque, eye mask and a cat o'nine tails. 'Protestant!' was all she said about that one. 'You shouldn't do that,' I would say to her. 'I'm only looking. Where's the harm in that?' was her reply.

Some fellow students at university experienced crushing pressure from their parents to study and get top marks, and they could scarcely believe that mine didn't even know what subject I was taking. My sister did a law degree and took Law Society exams, which meant being walled in by high stacks of dusty texts for months. Mum wasn't best pleased about that, and one afternoon she snapped and took the offending books and hid them in our garden shed. Her justification was, 'That one will ruin her eyes with all the studying and never get a man.' No pressure? Or smart reverse psychology on her part? I still couldn't say for sure. And although my mother was very proud of our eventual achievements, she always managed to keep us in place with a line about her friend from her home town. 'Molly Murray's daughter is a doctor.' I think if one of us had won Wimbledon or become Prime Minister, she would have been proud, but she would still have trotted out the line, 'Molly Murray's daughter is a doctor.'

12

Clock Soup

My sister never did make it to a splendiferous bus-garage
Christmas outing because Dad got fired from the bus conductor job and access to those golden tickets. Getting the sack was
commonplace for my dad. The announcement didn't even
merit a 'Not again!' from my mother. Unskilled jobs were easy
come easy go, and he always charmed his way into another job,
sometimes even two, before the week was out.

London Transport had good reasons for sacking him. The
first was because of the incident when a passenger tumbled
unnoticed from the platform of Dad's Routemaster bus as it
drove at speed down the steepest hill on the route. His second
misdemeanour was getting busted for selling tickets that he had
recycled from the rubbish bin and off the floor of the bus. This
was a good second income-stream for him and bad for the coffers of London Transport. Dad was a rubbish petty thief. He
didn't attempt to con travellers, he merely offered them a choice –
did they want to buy a full-price new ticket or a half-price

nearly-new one? Many passengers were very happy with his renegade discounted-fares scheme, and over forty of his regulars took the trouble to organise a petition to have Dad reinstated after London Transport gave him the chop.

Selfridges in London, the department store where he worked for many years as a petrol-pump attendant, took a while to discover Dad's dodgy driving, to their cost, but sacked him on the spot as soon as they did. Wealthy and well-known shoppers would arrive on the petrol station forecourt in their Daimlers, Rollers and Bentleys and press the keys into Dad's hand, wrapped in a £10 or sometimes even a £20 note, with the demand, 'Park it!' Left in sole charge of Max Bygraves' Rolls Royce, Dad said he often parked it, had a smoke and a snooze in the back seat before heading back to work.

The rich and famous would head off to shop leaving my dad, Mr Dodgem, to negotiate the corkscrew turns on the ramp to the multi-storey parking areas in their luxury cars. Mostly the cars were bigger than our front room at home. Inevitably, one day he had a prang, reversing a classic Bentley into a Mercedes convertible that wasn't even a week old. The amazing thing was it happened after he'd been working at Selfridges, and parking top-of-the-range cars, for over eight years. His manager asked to see his driving licence to complete the insurance claim. 'I haven't got one,' my dad answered. 'Why didn't you say so?' demanded his incredulous boss. 'You never asked,' Dad answered.

Mum and Peggy had worked as casual silver-service waitresses at every hotel in London. They could serve a single pea with a fork and a spoon they were so dextrous. It was tiring split-shift work. Breakfast was from 6 to 9.30am, lunch from 11.30 to 2.30pm and dinner 6.30 to 10.30pm. The front door opening or closing softly at dawn or after dark meant Mum was on her way to or from work. They swapped the life of a casual for a permanent job in the directors' dining room at the National Freight Corporation in London. As well as being waitresses, they were handed the keys to the chairman's grace and 'flavour' flat (as Peggy used to call it) in Central London, where they were appointed as joint housekeepers.

'This is no flat, it's a country,' was my mum's verdict on the palatial mansion flat when she first saw it. It was equipped with every mod con, many of which the goggle-eyed pair had never seen before, including a pressure cooker, which they were terrified of because they were convinced it was going to blow up, even when it was not in use, and a toaster. 'Funny place to keep an electric fire,' said Peggy every day as she moved the toaster from the worktop to the floor. The two had their elevenses as they warmed their feet over it.

They both loved the waitressing. Mostly for the spoils. They took empty shopping trollies on wheels to work and returned with wine, cigars, cutlery and crockery – all the very best quality. I would arrive home after school hoping it would be fish fingers or tinned ravioli for tea, only to discover it was halibut or porterhouse steak, yet again. Cabinet pudding or Eton mess for afters was some compensation. All courtesy of National Freight. Mum softened the blow of the epicurean meal that nobody wanted because it was so rich and heavy by making her own chips as an accompaniment. These were champion chips. My husband claims my mum's chips were a big part of the reason he married me. 'Chips big enough to suck on' is his drooling description. Glazed golden on the outside and hot, soft and fluffy on the inside, they were, and still are, unmatched.

Mum and Peggy would hotfoot it from the flat dressed as

housekeepers and arrive in the directors' dining room in wait-
ress uniform just in time to serve pre-lunch drinks. Lunch was
silver-served at 1pm on the dot by my mum, Peggy and a merry
band of Irish waitresses – one specially reserved for wine pouring and pass-the-port-and-brandy duties. The diners were
captains of industry but on the occasions I helped out in university holidays I was amazed at how thick some of these
intellectual giants could be. One was convinced that the buttered runner beans referred to on the menu were stored up my
skirt. 'Do you have any more beans?' he asked as his hand travelled up the back of my thigh. Another wanted to know, 'Are
there any more peas, Miss?' as his sweaty palm made a circular
motion on my black-skirted buttock.

The directors' dining room had no windows, floor-to-ceiling
drapes on three sides and, along the fourth wall, an ornate
mahogany spot-lit bar, the drinks altar. Nicely pissed and full to
the throat, the directors would meander back to their desks any
time after 3pm. Increasing productivity amongst the lower
orders was often discussed over their lunch table.

When I started at sixth form college to do my A levels, Dad had
just started another new job. This time he was a milkman and
was presented with the keys to a milk float. He drove it like a
dodgem at top speed, ten miles per hour. Some of the neighbours called him the Milk-shake-man because of the way he
wobbled up and down the road. That milk float was the closest we ever got to a family car. Between the hours of 6am and
4pm (after that, like Cinderella, it had to be back on dairy
grounds), and as long as it wasn't raining or snowing, he would
cheerfully and proudly drop us to the bus stop and to our
friends' houses, and wait outside shops and libraries or school

to bring us home. There was room for three people including the driver up front and ten on the platform at the back. Mum was the only member of the family too grand to travel by milk float, although she would graciously allow him to fetch home her heavy grocery shopping for her. Her excuse for not climbing aboard was, 'I don't care much for milk.'

Dad got stripped of his wheels after just ten weeks. They said they couldn't afford him because since he'd taken over the milk round revenues had dropped – dramatically. Although he was brilliant at delivering the milk with a smile and on time, Dad just couldn't bring himself to collect payment from his customers at the end of the week. He was a complete sucker and believed every doorstep sob story he heard about hard times, so much so that he even lent customers money from his own pocket. My mum went off like a firework when she heard about that, and chased him down the street waving her wicker shopping basket on wheels overhead as a weapon, demanding to know who had their money so she could bloody well get it back.

Dad told me that when he was an eight-year-old-boy, his parish priest in Ireland bestowed on him an unpaid job, which Father described as a singular act of devotion to God and a divine honour. The task was to knock on the door of every house in the village six times a year and collect the priest's 'dues'. This was distinct from the weekly church plate collection, which was for parish coffers. The dues were logged, ranked and read out – biggest amount first and then the rest in descending order – from the pulpit the Sunday after they had been collected. Dad says that collecting the dues in the bitter winter months was especially hard because from the doorstep he saw families of ten people and more sat around a table sharing food that was barely enough to feed two. Fires would be weak in their grates and he heard babies mewling with hunger. Nevertheless these families, petrified of denying the all-powerful parish priest his wants, would find something to offer. 'I was stood burning with the shame of it,' was how my dad remembered his duty. 'And then I'd arrive at the priest's house with a bag full of coins. Big belly first, he'd answer the door stinking of whisky with his hand already out to take it. The blast of heat from his fire would nearly knock me over and any day bar Friday there'd be the grand smell of meats roasting coming from the kitchen . . .' Dad swore he'd never again go door to door to ask for money from those who didn't have it. And that's why people in Paddington on his round got free milk for ten weeks.

Soon after that, Dad began work as a petrol-pump attendant at a garage in Chalk Farm. It was a few doors away from the famous Marine Ices, a luxury ice cream parlour. Dad would stop in there every night after work and buy us ice cream. He paid the owner in petrol and carried home our nightly treat on two long bus rides. When he arrived home, my brother and sister and I would decant what was left of the ice cream into glasses and drink it through straws.

I was having a romance with a boy called Todd at the time, who had ambitions to be an anthropologist. I think it was his association with my family that inspired him. The son of a serving Cabinet minister, he was boho posh. I thought his house was a block of flats when I first saw it because it was so big in comparison to mine. It had a library, one that you didn't need tickets for. When his mother met me her first question was whether I was a Catholic, asked in a tone of voice that suggested she thought it was a disease. She wanted me out of her son's life in a hurry, before my immigrant genes had any chance to scale her family tree. So we did a lot of courting at my house, where he was welcome.

By courting, I mean we sat side by side. Sex was just a word to giggle to. At school when I was aged fourteen a moist-faced nun, almost faint with embarrassment, tackled the matter of the birds and the bees in seconds. She stood at the front of the class and raised an A4-sized picture above her head. It showed two rabbits sitting together and eating the same carrot from different ends. By way of a helpful commentary she gabbled, 'And that's how babies get here! Class dismissed.'

My mum was no more informative. She had part-broached the subject of periods with me by explaining that when I became a woman, at around fourteen years old, I would start to bleed from my lily (vagina) and after that I could get a baby right up to when I was fifty years old. She showed me a Dr Whites sanitary towel with giant loops swinging from an elastic suspender kit and told me these were to be used when my 'friend' came to visit. Oh, and I wasn't to tell any of this to my little sister because it was a secret. I was mortified by this revelation and wailed, 'But I don't want to be bleeding every day for the next forty years!' Red-faced, Mum told me to shut up and not be so stupid. Sex education over.

One summer afternoon, Todd came home with me after college to find the hot-water taps in our kitchen, bathroom sink and bath all full on. There was a row of electric fires in the kitchen all turned to the highest setting. One was our own, the others borrowed. Fan heaters were running on maximum in every room It was mid-July and 81 degrees outside.

I guessed immediately what was going on. A month earlier, Dad and one of his brothers had tinkered with our coin-slot electricity meter and made it run backwards. I'm not sure how the pair of them managed it, but I know that a screwdriver, a magnet and a roll of thin wire were their toolkit-essentials for the job. The meter-reader had been spotted in the area doing his rounds and Dad had to get us out of credit in a hurry before the electricity board found out he had been tampering with their property. It was an offence serious enough to warrant a prison sentence.

Normally, because of the high cost of hot water, we were allowed only one bath a week. That day we all had nonstop baths, including a bemused Todd, who was ordered by my mum to strip off and do some meter-spinning duty. They could just have let it run away, but they simply couldn't bear to see good hot water going to waste.

Uncles, aunts and cousins came and bathed, too, and a few neighbours who could be trusted with the meter-fixing secret. A hose was attached to the hot tap in the first-floor kitchen and left hanging out the window to spray steaming hot water into the little yard below. 'Give the yard a hot wash,' said my grim-faced mother. Lights, electric blankets, TVs, radios and hairdryers were plugged in and left running in all the rooms. Double and triple adaptors were jammed into every socket and glowed red with electrical overload. The wheel inside the meter was spinning so fast it made a high-pitched sound that caused our dog Scampy to run around in circles until my mum gave him a tranquilliser she'd got from our downstairs neighbour. Stuck into a piece of black pudding, he gobbled it and fell over sideways within minutes and slept for eighteen hours.

Our house was clock city but we never knew the right time. If we wanted to know that we had to listen to the radio or dial 123 on the phone. Wall clocks, carriage clocks, alarm clocks and novelty clocks all ticked together but to a slightly different beat.

Clock Soup

Clocks were my dad's hobby and he believed one day he would unearth a priceless treasure and make us all rich. 'This one is worth towsunds,' he would declare after each Portobello market junk purchase.

One April the first, a posh-voiced radio presenter claimed that faulty clocks could be restored to working order by giving them a good boiling. I think my dad was the only person in the Commonwealth who heard that broadcast and didn't 'clock' immediately that it was an April fool's joke.

He went in deep beneath the sink and hauled out the pot my mum used for boiling tea towels and underwear – a stainless-steel tub big enough to sit on all four gas rings at once. Once the water had reached a rolling boil, one by one in went all his wooden-cased clocks, glass carriage clocks and a few pocket watches for good measure. The glass timepieces shattered instantly they hit the water, but undeterred, and as instructed by the man on the radio with the authoritative voice, he gave them one good stir and then boiled them all for an hour. Clock soup. *Almost* an hour, because my mum came home from work before the sixty minutes was up and flew into a rage when she saw what he was doing. She hated his clock collection with a vengeance so wasn't at all bothered that he had boiled them, but she was livid that he'd been duped. 'How could I have married such a total feckin' eejit?' she screamed. Fury made her strong and she swung the pot from the cooker and dumped all of its contents out of the kitchen window and down into the yard below.

The neighbour below us in our council maisonette was a single English lady, a retired civil servant called Miss Thomas. She once told my sister and me that during her thirty-year career in

Whitehall she had been a 'stamper', and made it sound like national security had been dependant on her actions alone.

Her flat was a temple to soft furnishing. Every object had a bespoke knitted or quilted cover. Ornaments, toilet rolls, cruets, tea and sugar caddies, even her HP sauce bottle had a knitted sock it lived in when not in use with the word 'sorce' misspelt in hand embroidery on the front.

Whatever we ate, Miss Thomas ate it too, from a plate double-wrapped in a clean tea towel delivered downstairs by my sister or me. Empty plates were handed back, unwashed, without a single word of thanks or even a smile. 'Poor auld ting all on her own,' my mother would say about our taciturn neighbour.

No matter what you brought Miss Thomas, or what you told her, she would never talk other than to issue instructions to turn off the light, close the door or move this and bring that from the mini Manhattan of pill bottles that rose from her bed-side table. I don't believe she saw my mum and dad's kindness and generosity for what it was. In her deluded mind, the frail and elderly woman was living the life of a lady in her London town 'hice', and Mum and Dad were her housekeeper and gardener. *Upstairs Downstairs* was being played out in Miss Thomas's head.

Dad was in the thrall of a clock that Miss Thomas hung in pride of place on her sitting-room wall. It chimed on the hour all day, and if any of us had been light sleepers we would have heard it all through the night, too. A wooden-cased clock, two feet high and a foot wide, it had a hand-painted country scene on its glass door, which opened to reveal a velvet-lined compartment for the weighty, ornate brass pendulum. Unlike anything Dad owned, this was a genuine antique, and it called out to him every waking hour from the flat below. He coveted

that clock, and swore Miss Thomas had promised that if anything ever happened to her it would be his. Something did
happen to her, but the clock never came his way.

One morning, as usual, my mum let herself into Miss
Thomas's flat carrying a frothy thick coffee made with boiled
Jersey gold-top milk — always milk, never water, because Mum
was trying to build the old woman up — and a currant bun for
elevenses. Lights in the flat were still switched on from the night
before and Mum's instincts were yelling at her that all was not
well.

She turned and ran out onto the street, slopping coffee as she
went, and begged the first passer-by, a train driver on his way
to work, to go into the flat and investigate. He stumbled back
from the curtain-drawn darkness into the daylight and in a
strangulated voice instructed my mum to call an ambulance, and
the police.

'She meant business,' was what the ambulance man said in a
weary 'all in a day's work' tone to my mum, who was white-
washed with shock. She had to use the landing walls to get
herself back upstairs for a steadying cup of tea and a cigarette.
The lonely old woman downstairs had said cheers to life with
a bottle of bleach and a few dozen aspirin.

Later that evening, after the police had informed him of his
aunt's suicide, her only relative, a nephew hammered on the
front door of our flat, instead of using the outside bell. My
mother answered the door and leant in to embrace him in his
time of loss. He had other plans. He seized her by the shoulders
and shook her, hard. 'Where is it?' he shouted. 'I'll call the
bloody police! You thieving Irish!' He went on about the wall
clock with the country scene. It was missing, but he had a
queue of other accusations, too: that my mum and dad had

been bleeding his aunt dry by forcing her to pay for food she didn't need, charging her for chores she didn't want done and stealing her valuable ornaments.

But the whereabouts of the clock remained a mystery. My mum watched my dad for several months from the side of her eye and even threatened she would leave home and get a live-in job somewhere if he had stolen from a dead woman and secreted his spoils away. But he always protested his innocence with passion, and knowing he was a tell-all-and-show-all kind of man, she believed him. Any secret would have fast burnt its way out of his mouth.

13

The Grateful and the Dead

My extended family swung in and out of one another's houses whenever it suited, and even when it didn't. It was as if there was no front door. They lived and socialised like they were still living in rural Ireland. And no matter what you were doing, you stopped to welcome them in. Tea was the law. Plus visitors had to be force-fed with everything you had in the house, and the whole family would gather round to watch them eat. The first rule of visiting was that 'no' spoken by any guest really meant 'yes'.

The 'no means yes' rule wasn't exclusively for tea and sandwiches. It applied to money, too. Children of the house would regularly be handed cash by visitors as they were leaving for home. The protocol was complicated. When money was offered we had to say 'no thank you', and if we valued our hides we had better make it sound convincing.

My mother's ears and eyes were at their laser-beam best when her children's manners were on public show. To say no three times and yes on the fourth time around was very rude indeed. The minimum number of times I had to say 'no thank you' was seven in my house.

'Ah go on, go on, take it, would ye?' or 'Take it out of my hand before I get annoyed' were the cues from the aunts and uncles that after a lot of no-ing it was getting closer to the time I could, at long last, say yes and stretch my hand out. When it got to the stage where an aunt or uncle was threatening to throw the money out onto the street if I didn't take it, or heading towards the rubbish bin to toss it in there, or even, God forbid, approaching the lit coal fire, then it was deemed mannerly to finally accept it. But even that wasn't straightforward. I couldn't snatch or seize the gift but had to move my hands in slow motion to take it.

I had to show no enthusiasm for the proffered cash, but still demonstrate the appropriate amount of gratitude for it. To get this right was the penultimate hurdle before pocketing it. Last of all was to say thank you – clearly enough and at the correct volume, and at the same time making eye-contact with the gift-giver. This ritual was proof positive to gift-bearing relatives that the children in our family were not greedy savages.

Getting it wrong had dire consequences. My mother would get me by the ear and twist it sharply as if she were winding a clock at speed if I failed any element of the Accepting Cash Gifts Code of Conduct.

'Put your money away!' was the communal shout from all of my relatives whenever there was anything to be paid for. It was bellowed by every one of them simultaneously as they speed-rummaged through bags, purses and pockets to try and be the first to pay for everyone else as well as themselves. 'I'm warning you now – put your money away or I'll be very offended!'

was sung out in different keys by a choir of impoverished men and women waving pound notes in shops, pubs or one another's houses. Splitting a bill was too peaceful and sensible an option for my family. They would sooner roll around on the floor battling it out to be the most generous. And it didn't end there either. Whoever it was that won and got to pay was then entitled to call the other mean. 'Did you see that tightarse letting me pay? No wonder they do still have their communion money!'

Our house was regularly teeming with visitors who came so often they weren't. The demon dropper-inner was, without doubt, Agnes. Cue lightning noises and the sound of creaking doors and banshees howling. Agnes came from the west of Ireland and married my first cousin Thomas, known as Tom.

Whatever the season, Agnes wore too-small sandals without tights or stockings and the underside of her toes rested on the ground, displaying dark, mussel-shell toenails. Incredibly it was not her sense of style that was Agnes's distinguishing feature. It was the fact that she must have been born talking. My dad once commented, 'That one must've been vaccinated with a feckin' gramophone needle.'

When Agnes arrived she was already speaking from the other side of the closed front door. Even when she went to the toilet the woman did not take a pause, but simply racked up the volume to make herself heard. She had the skill of being able to talk and listen simultaneously. She would switch the subject of her conversation to answer you if you dared to parallel-chat on a different theme, and then she was able to swerve back at speed to her original topic. 'Me mammy ...', 'Me auntie ...', 'Me cousin ...', 'Me daddy ...' were typical openers, followed by a

191

detailed verbal post-mortem of whatever illness had led to their long, agony-loaded and drawn-out deaths – along with every twitch and sniff they suffered whilst alive. Deathbed utterings were Agnes's specialist subject.

For all the years she visited our house, her son, known as TomTom, always sat on her lap. This was sweet until he grew taller, wider and heavier than his mother. Aged nine, and a good fifteen inches taller and four stone heavier than his mum, he still plonked himself on her lap and blotted out the stubby Agnes. Face unseen, she regaled us all with tales of rectal examinations, tumours the size and shape of watermelons and fungus feet that smelt of kippers gone bad. And gangrene. Always gangrene. Gangrene was the punchline of every story in Agnes's repertoire. 'Do you know you can get gangrene in your tongue? It happened to me mammy's cousin Grainne. A big lump of her tongue dropped into her cup of tea and she swallowed it by accident.' We sat listening, appalled, and hoping that gangrene of the tongue was hereditary.

But the visitor who lived longest, strongest and smelliest in my family was my great-aunt Winifred. When we were little we called her Aunt Win-afraid, because she had a face like a gargoyle and hair like a stack of black twigs.

I am not even certain where Winifred fitted into the family because nobody ever claimed her as their own. All my aunts and uncles refused to answer my questions about exactly whose mother, aunt, sister or grandmother she was. I have wondered if she was a stray who inveigled herself into the family for tea, cake and hot-stew-and-dumplings benefits.

Her disposition mirrored her facial expression. Gloom and doom on bandy legs. Death was her only topic of conversation and if anyone dared to recoil from the subject she would warn in a preacher's loud and sing-song tone of voice, 'Every single one of us is going to die. Oh yes. That's the one thing we can all be sure of. You won't be spared and that's a fact.'

'That's a fact' would be accompanied by three firm wags of her knarled forefinger for emphasis. A finger so twisted by arthritis that when she moved it through the air she looked just like a witch casting a spell with a crooked wand.

Aunt Winifred visited regularly, scuttling past whoever opened the front door straight to the best seat in the house. 'Guess who died?' was always the first thing she said, always with glee. And the more excruciating their demise, the better her mood. Someone elderly who had died peacefully in their sleep was a real disappointment to Aunt Winifred.

'I wish somebody would hurry up and die!' Aunt Winifred would regularly grumble. 'I haven't been to a good Benefit Dance in ages.' By ages she meant weeks because the social calendar of any Irish immigrant family in the 1960s and 1970s was peppered with Benefit Dances. These were high-kicking, heavy-drinking ceilis held in the name of a recently dead man, woman or child. All profits from Benefit Dance ticket sales went straight to the immediate family of the deceased, and were commonly used to pay funeral expenses. Behind closed doors my dad described Benefit Dances as 'ceilis for corpses'.

A squeaky bingo pen was wielded by Winifred to mark up the death announcements in the Irish county papers. She liked to keep abreast of who was dead at home and abroad.

Urine infections and 'diaree' were the two complaints that regularly indisposed her and could keep Winifred away from a funeral. That and the outer limit of her free bus pass. Otherwise, the priest, the undertaker, a casket, a dead body and Winifred were the essential funeral quintet.

A relative, a friend or a complete stranger, it made no difference. If it stated in the parish newsletter 'Private funeral to be attended by close family only', she turned up anyway because only she could see the line printed in invisible ink beneath that read: 'with the exception of Winifred, of course'.

Winifred hoarded all the memorial cards and Orders of Service for every funeral she'd ever been to. They were arranged in tall stacks that leant on one another on the shelf above her fireplace. At random she would pluck one from the pile and insist on reading out the sad and sentimental poems inside to any visitors to her home. This gave her immense pleasure.

Her all-time favourite sad memorial poem was one she thought she knew by heart, but actually didn't. We heard an infinite number of variations. Ladders and golden chains were somewhere in the original, but Winifred regularly mixed them up.

'If grief was a ladder I would climb it to heaven in golden chains and it will be very sadder still, till we meet again ... agains?'

She would recite these incomprehensible rhymes aloud to my sister, brother and me every time we saw her. Momentarily she would struggle with the words but after a brief stumble always managed to convince herself she had it right after all. Confident then, she would repeat it louder.

'If grief had me in chains on my ladder I would climb it to heaven where God would be waiting, never hating ...' A pause. 'No, wait a minute! Let me think now. He is waiting at the foot of the ladder getting sadder but out of pain because of the golden chain ... hang on there ...' And she would rewrite the whole verse in her head as she stared at the ceiling lights for a couple of minutes, her head nodding to a silent beat as she did so, before beginning again with gusto.

The woman wept with intense enjoyment after each performance and would demand of us, with menace, 'Now. Wasn't
that beeeyoooootiful?' Narrowed eyes, grey set in yellow, dared
us to say no. But we just weren't brave enough. So she would
recite it again, with yet more variations. If my brother and sister
and I were home alone, we prayed for our mum and dad to
return quickly and get the sherry bottle out from the side-
board – it was the only distraction that had any staying power
for Winifred.

Her actual age was a bit of a mystery, but if you used your
nose and not your common sense to age her she was already
dead. Winifred had stopped bathing in her early seventies after
a team from her local council had to break down her front door
and rescue her from her bath where she was well and truly
stuck, her generous dimply hips suckered onto the porcelain.

Cream sherry and cheese-and-onion-flavour Tayto crisps
were Winifred's staple diet. She put her longevity down to good
living and also to the fact that her husband, Malachy, had died
in his early thirties. He fell down a hole in the road walking
back from the pub and broke his neck. Malachy was discovered
dead in the hole the following day, his body facing down but his
face looking up. 'I am very thankful, really. I had no man to sap
me,' declared the jolly widow on what would have been their
silver wedding anniversary.

Winifred's funeral 'rig-out' was glossy with age. A pleated
skirt, ruffle-neck blouse, ankle-length black coat with a moth-
eaten velvet collar and a fez-shaped pillbox hat with ripped
netting hung ever ready on the outside of her wardrobe. Her
shoes were from Clarks, black men's brogues with a compass in
the heel.

Winifred could strip off her floral housecoat, which she wore indoors day and night over her shrimp-coloured underwear, slide into her 'blacks', as she called them, and be out the door and on her way to a funeral in minutes.

Immediately after a service, the burial or cremation and the refreshments, Winifred of the Dead would hotfoot it to the nearest relatives for a debrief. We lived close to Kensal Green Cemetery, the apex of Winifred's social life, so too often she chose our house.

First item to be judged was the Order of Service. The quality of its paper, the size of the print and its style and how many there were. Two per person was Winifred's required minimum number, one to make notes on and one to file. A shortage of Orders of Service meant the nearest and dearest 'couldn't be arsed', according to Winifred's Bumper Book of Funeral Etiquette, which she stored inside her head. A copperplate typeface was essential in every Order of Service. Anything less signalled indifference on the part of the chief mourners. 'No copperplate? The scuts! It's like sticking two fingers up to the dead!' decreed Winifred.

The photograph in the Order of Service had to be a good and true recent likeness of the deceased. If they dared to look too well, too thin or too young, Winifred would tut loudly and wave the page around above her head and attempt to make eye-contact with someone else, anyone at all in the congregation, who might share her disdain. If she couldn't establish a connection from a distance, she would leave her pew and wander the central aisle stabbing the offending photograph with her curly finger. 'Look! Look! Be honest, now. Sure isn't that just cheating?' Her loud voice was heaped with disgust.

Other Winifredisms: pale wood coffins? 'Cheap and disrespectful.' Chrome handles? 'Would you credit it? Sure why didn't they just open up the casket and spit in his eye?' Elaborately carved dark-wood coffins featuring Jesus and his disciples at the Last Supper were an abomination, according to the doyenne of all things deceased. 'Talk about showing off! And that lot don't even have the price of a whole chicken on a Sunday. It's only drumsticks you'll see on their dinner plates! The Last Supper indeed! Who do they think they are fooling, at all?'

At one burial the coffin was brought to the church in a glass coach that was drawn along the streets by four black horses accessorised with tall feathered plumes. 'Horses now, is it?' snorted Winifred. 'And why not – considering every penny that bastard ever had went on the racing. They should have tethered up a few greyhounds as well to get him to the church on time. You never saw his kids with full bellies or right-fitting shoes and now he's stone dead it's still all about the horses. They have no shame!'

The scripture readers at the service, their clothes, the sincerity of the emotional wobble in their voice, the hymns, the flowers, the depth of the grave and the number of black cars supplied by the undertaker – all these merited a score according to Winifred's unfathomable points system.

The standard of the food and drinks served after a funeral could resurrect a chance for the occasion to be top-ranked by Winifred. A hot, sit-down meal usually got full marks, especially if they served beef and not chicken. Finger food served with napkins by waitresses on the move was deemed borderline disrespectful, and if just drinks and nibbles were offered, Winifred would actually approach and berate the chief mourners. 'I'm sorry' was her opener, which got their attention because they believed, quite reasonably, that she was about to offer her sympathies. 'No one, no matter how bad they were in life, deserves Hula Hoops as a send-off!'

Other miscellaneous items that came under the general heading of disrespectful at a funeral according to Winifred were cheerful hymns, red lipstick, too much rouge, too many curls of a certain height or length, strong perfume, sheer tights, men with hands in their pockets, stubble, anyone chewing gum or fidgeting and shoes with worn-down heels. Also the entire congregation had to be one move ahead of the priest when it came to kneeling, sitting, standing and thumping of the chest. She could spot a lone non-Catholic in a packed church, and if she did would declare afterwards, 'The place was *full* of heathens!'

My mother glowed with love and pride for her grandchildren and at one family gathering remarked to Winifred about my babies, 'Aren't the four of them just grand?'

Winifred gurned at her and drew her warty neck in before she answered. 'Now. There was a woman at home in Cavan and she was always praising her grandchildren and children. Saying they were this and they were that ... Good-looking and clever and all nicey, nicey special. You'd swear she had knitted them herself the way she was carrying on. Oh, a right wicked auld brag that one was for sure.'

Fearful of where the story might be going, Mum tried to get Winifred on a different tack, butting in with, 'A bottle of Guinness for you, Winifred?'

'I will, of course. Three sugars,' she answered, waiting for her drink to arrive before continuing her tale of the woman from Cavan. 'And do you know what happened to them?'

She stopped in her tracks and in a dramatic pause drew each of us in with her eyes until she had our full attention. Then she finally spoke ...

'And they all died!' she declared triumphantly, and then raised her Guinness, which was foaming over the sides because of the sugar.

Aunt Winifred herself died at ninety-three and got a happy-clappy send-off. 'A funeral lite' was how one of her great-great-nieces described the express service, and the only one in the family that she'd missed in almost a century.

14
False Teeth and Fairies

My mum and dad and aunts and uncles regularly spoke of how their hearts were in Ireland but their lives were in London. Even though they lived in England from their teenage years to their deaths, my parents and aunts and uncles always spoke with an Irish accent so broad it sounded like they had just stepped off the boat. My mum told me that as she travelled on the train from Holyhead to London, she heard the rhythmic wheels clacking beneath her and was convinced they were saying, 'Never going back, never going back, never going back . . .' and the idea thrilled and appalled her in equal measure.

One aspect of their appearance changed for ever when they came to live and work in London. Their teeth. Within months they were all toothless. Taking out was cheaper than taking care of them. Without the help of dentists or an orthodontist, or even the application of toothbrushes and toothpaste, every one of them started out in Ireland with pearly white, beautifully proportioned, ramrod-straight and perfectly spaced teeth. The secret of the whiteness of their teeth was apparently the regular application of soot taken from the chimney walls of their cottages. 'Before a dance we'd rub soot in, mostly on the front ones, and then rinse it out with a gargle of tea!' my uncle Bren told me when he heard me wailing about the toothpaste tube being empty one time I was desperate to brush my teeth before a teenage night out.

My mum was a teeth fanatic in later life. She blamed her formative years and the enduring memory of what having teeth pliered out from deep in her gum did to her. At random times in the day she would herd her eight grandchildren into the bathroom of her little flat and issue them with a toothbrush apiece loaded with paste. Using an egg timer she would make them all brush simultaneously for three full minutes. Under her tutelage they would do tops, bottoms and tongue. When the timer had drained of sand, she would turn it over and get the children to change brushing arms, like soldiers on rifle drill, and demand, 'Again!' A rap on the bottom was dispensed for any tot who didn't show sufficient enthusiasm for getting his or her teeth sparkling clean.

Aunt Katsie said, 'I only married Mick for his teeth! They were so lovely and *all* his own!' She was sorely disappointed when her husband arrived home a month after their wedding without a tooth in his head. A dentist in London removed all thirty-two teeth in one visit. Mick had sat into the dentist's chair complaining of toothache and had been expecting a filling. 'Cheaper for you in the long run to have them out!' the dentist decided rolling up his sleeves and setting to work.

They tried a few homespun cures before arriving at the dentist's door. They had a special prayer for toothache that was the first resort and had to be repeated nine times for it to work:

'Peter sat upon a marble stone, Jesus came to him alone and said, "What ails thee, Peter?" Peter said, "O Lord, my tooth doth ache." Our Lord said, "Arise, Peter and come with me – King of Nazareth and King of the Jews."'

My poor uncle Patrick spoke only that prayer for months on end. He was plagued by toothache and a fear of the dentist's chair. The postmistress from his home village in Ireland took pity on him and sent a cure for toothache in a letter to his address in London. My mum kept the letter for years because re-reading it always made her laugh until she cried. She'd fold it up carefully when she was finished and say 'Moooooo!' and laugh all over again. The letter read: Go to a graveyard and kneel upon any grave and say three Paters and three Aves for the souls of the dead lying beneath. Then taking a handful of the grass from the grave, chew it well, casting out each bite without swallowing a portion. After this the sufferer, though were they to live for one hundred years, will never have toothache any more.

Dentures were currency. They were expensive and highly sought after. My mother told me that an uncle of hers had stolen a pair from the deceased at the wake by sticking his hand into the dead man's mouth and helping himself when no one was looking. Unashamed, he'd declared, 'He won't be needing them where he's going!'

Dad told me that it was common practice for drinking men in London pubs to help themselves to another man's pint if it was left unattended. Dad wasn't all that interested in beer, but on the principle of he'd paid for it, he wanted to drink it. As an insurance policy, when he went to the toilet he dropped his dentures into his glass to deter thirsty thieves. One night someone with a strong stomach downed Dad's beer and stole his dentures leaving Dad just an empty glass.

My dad's brother Joseph died at home and Martin, his son, decided that his father shouldn't be laid out without his false teeth, so he cleaned his dentures and tried to put them back into the dead man's mouth. Poor Joseph had been ill for some time and lost a lot of weight and his dentures were too big for his shrunken mouth. Martin employed the assistance of his wife and, watched closely by his seven-year-old daughter Maria, he managed to get the dentures in and kept them in position by wrapping a scarf under his father's chin and tying it tightly on top of his head. Shortly afterwards, the parish priest arrived at the house to offer prayers and condolences and discuss funeral arrangements. 'And how did he die?' he asked sympathetically. 'Daddy strangled him, Father,' came the little-voiced answer from Maria.

Aunt Peggy bought a pair of second-hand dentures from the dentist who took out the last of her own teeth. He offered them at a big discount if she bought them then and there. Peggy arrived home in agony, dentures jammed into position over her open wounds. But bargain happy, she was wearing a huge blood-soaked smile. 'Two shillings I saved on these falsies!'

The Timer visited a dentist who turned out to be an impostor. He was, in fact, a vet's assistant in a white coat trying to make a quick buck from the Irish who at the time were desperate for cheap dental treatment. The charlatan used a pair of pliers to break off the Timer's teeth just above the gums, saying it was cheaper and quicker than a full set of extractions. Serious infection set in and the Timer ended up in an ambulance heading for hospital roaring in agony. 'Turn the bells on, mate, and put your foot down, this bloke's in trouble!' the paramedic called to the driver. The reply was cool and his foot stayed steady on the accelerator. 'He's Irish. There's plenty more where he came from.'

My family swapped dentures all the time if they hurt or if the wearer just liked the look of someone else's pair. 'Take these, they're nicer,' one sister who was staying at home would say to another heading out to a dance. Dentures were communal property.

My aunt Mary went to her grave convinced she had swallowed a set of dentures. Always a night bird, she would relax into her bed at 2am and have a final settling-down smoke as she lay on her back and studied her special patch on the wall above the bed – the corner where it met the ceiling. It was there that she believed her stillborn babies had gone after they had been taken from her, unseen. When her only living child, Declan, was born safe, her torment abated but she refused to paper over the spot where she had hunted for what she had lost. She said she liked to lie back each night knowing that her treasured son Declan was safe sleeping in the bed next door – whilst she lay and loved the brothers and sisters that might have been.

Noisy nights in Mary's house had previously meant that she was searching and suffering. When she let out a roar in the middle of the night years after Declan's safe arrival, her husband was fearful that she had lost her mind again and that she would be taken away in the white van to the county mental hospital, as she had so many times before. 'Gone, they're gone,' she yelled, clawing at her husband. 'Help me find them, will you?' But this time, to his great relief, she was talking teeth, not babies. 'They're gone, me teeth are gone! I've swallowed them and they'll bite me arse coming out!' She was hysterical and a fingertip search of the bed and the entire bedroom didn't turn the dentures up. Neither did prayers to the always reliable St Anthony, Patron Saint of Lost Things. They had vanished. 'I definitely swallowed them,' Mary would tell anyone who wanted to listen, near boasting about her advanced digestive capabilities. 'It was the fairies who had them away,' her husband Niall contradicted.

The unseen fairies were as much a part of my family as the flesh and blood members. Their houses in Ireland were surrounded by a criss-cross of fairy paths whose inhabitants governed much of our family fortunes. There was a pale patch of grass about sixteen feet square at the back of the garden in Dad's cottage that was known as the Fairy Fort. The fairies met there weekly to dance and sing and chat. Their dedicated space was always carefully walked around, never over or through, by humans and even animals.

My nan's cottage in the country had been known as a rambling house when her husband was alive. This meant that the front door had a latch, not a lock, and was open at all times to visitors. No one was turned away because, in her own words, 'Sure they could have been Jesus himself . . .'

In the evening, men from the village would gather around the fire. Granddad would cut a piece of tobacco from his block, place it into a pipe and thumb it down. He lit and passed around the pipe for all to share, along with plenty of hot tea and fruitcake. Truths, lies and fairy tales were exchanged. 'Those big brutes of men liked talking about the fairies best of all!' Nan would laugh. The fairies would warn of an impending death by sending something heavy in the house crashing to the floor, or sending a bat or bird inside a room to swoop around and terrorise everyone in it. The fairies, they claimed, had the power to choose someone to become an immortal. An immortal crumbled and rotted physically but never died and would wander the country lanes, unhappy and alone, into perpetuity, and the worst part was that if a mere mortal was unlucky enough to encounter an immortal they would die instantly of pure fright.

It wasn't only the men who were fairy-wary. The ashes from the fire were always kept inside the house on a Monday because it wasn't lucky to put them out on the day the fairies pegged their clean washing out.

My own dad claimed he had been walking home alone after a dance in a town seven miles away, on a night bright with moonlight, when he heard a horse approaching from behind. It was galloping and he stepped closer to the ditch to let it pass safely. Glancing over his shoulder as he did so, he saw the horse and its rider were shifting, like a smoke sculpture, expanding and contracting as the horse pushed forward. Dad said his legs gave way with fright and he lay bundled in the ditch with his head in his coat so as not to see any more of the rider's face. From one glimpse he said he saw it was 'dripping skin'.

Death was at the epicentre of all their tales. My nan told me that when she was six, her mother fell ill and she was sent away to be looked after by an aunt. She walked the ten-mile journey there alone, arrived late and went straight to bed with a sputtering candle. Several times during the night her irritated aunt came to the room to ask why she was disturbing the whole house with her crying, and each time my nan replied that she wasn't. Finally her aunt got cross and said, 'Lizzine, it's midnight and you are waking us all with your crying. Stop it and go to sleep.' My nan said then she felt tears welling up, because she was being accused of something she wasn't doing. By then too anxious to go back to sleep, she stayed awake for the rest of the night. And she realised she wasn't alone. All through the early hours she heard a constant and insistent rapping of fingers on her windowpane, a sound she was too terrified either to go and investigate or to report. First thing in the morning, news arrived from home. Her mother had died at midnight, calling out her daughter's name. My grandmother said she knew then that the knocking on the window had been her dead mother coming to fetch her and take her where she was going . . .

The story that was reworked a hundred times over during my childhood was about someone deceased coming back to claim someone alive. These peripheral ghosts-on-a-mission would be spotted from the corner of an eye, or through a window at dusk, a few days before a death. Slippery spirits, they melted away on any close inspection. The idea of a mother, father, brother or sister who was dead returning to accompany a loved one to their dark world – as a child this idea spooked me so much that I wouldn't dare to look sideways or through a window in case there was someone there waiting to escort me or one of mine to eternity.

I once complained of being cold in my father's cottage and my grandmother said, 'Everyone who sits there feels the cold. That's where the roads used to meet on the way to the burial ground. There's been a hundred thousand tears cried right there on that very spot.' My mum refused to take any talk of fairies seriously and declared that all the ghosts and fairies in the village disappeared on the day the electric light bulbs were switched on.

The superstitions my parents and their extended families imported to London were a source of mystery to the locals. I didn't know any English families who did Operation Thunder and Lightning, for example. During a thunderstorm, day or night, my mother would hurl herself around the house, covering mirrors with towels and blankets as if it was a matter of life and death. She said she had to stop the lightning from bouncing off the mirrors and straight into our souls. Should that happen, we would detonate and go straight to hell. She insisted she knew of a lot of people who had been that unlucky. Once the mirror blackout was complete, she would douse everyone and everything in the house with copious amounts of holy water. The holy water had to go inside our vests, and she used her thumb to make the sign of the cross on our chests, as well as on our heads and over all the furniture. In one torrential storm my brother, who was hiding behind the sofa with me and got the full force of a slosh of holy water, hissed, 'We'd be drier outside in the rain.'

15
Cancer and Confetti

My nan's death knocked the stuffing out of all my aunts and uncles. From my child's perspective it felt like Nan had taken all the fun away with her, wherever it was she had gone. I was scared for them, the way they all missed her. After her funeral the women in my family drooped; their posture and the width of their smiles tightened. The chat around the table became subdued and sometimes they even fell silent with one another as they sat smoking and brooding and searching for something in the middle distance. After that, one by one they toppled, and each of their illnesses took a chunk out of the others. It was immediately after I'd graduated, and been to all my aunts' funerals, that it was my mum's turn to discover she had breast cancer. I became her full-time cancer chum.

She had a radical mastectomy, and the word 'radical' was an understatement. Her surgery was a slash fest and it took her almost a year to fully heal. The first time I saw her wound uncovered was in the hospital and the ward floor came up to meet me. Mum needed company and care and an escort to her various appointments, and that became my job for almost a year. Radiotherapy sessions, in those days called cobalt treatments, took place in a basement in the Middlesex Hospital behind and below the busy, buzzy world of Oxford Street. We travelled there on the bus and home in a black cab because she would be legless afterwards, and all sway. In the back of the taxi she was floppy. I can still feel her sad shape as she leant against me and how she generated no warmth. Her irradiated body was cool and her teeth would chatter all day after a treatment. Only her teeth chattered. She would be quiet and brooding, silenced by the giant crab-like x-ray machines.

Her confidence caved in. That was the beginning of a fifteen-year sedative dependency. Cancer had piggy-backed her and her mum and her sisters for too long and she finally buckled. The tranquillisers worked on everything but her shame of having to take them, and she tried hard to keep her addiction a secret. Elbow-deep in her handbag, Mum could flip the lid of the tablet bottle and get a 'soother', as she liked to call them, into her hand and then to her mouth in one smooth movement. Cross words, contrariness, callers to the house, Christmas, Easter, bills to be paid – an Ativan muffled all those things nicely, and once removed her from life in general. She was still my mum, but Ativan-diluted.

My nan's ovarian cancer and my aunts' breast cancers were as double diseases at the time. The very word 'cancer' was a death sentence. And to have it somewhere private, like breasts or ovaries, was pure shameful. Those women couldn't even speak the name and location of their attacker aloud, not even to one another. Once they knew for certain what they had, they would just point to the affected body parts and whisper or mime information about their illnesses. Shame definitely added to their suffering. Aunt Peggy confided she couldn't even bring herself to tell God about her breast cancer in prayer, in case she embarrassed him.

With four of her sisters dead to cancer by the time of her own diagnosis, Mum had no reason to be optimistic about her odds of surviving, no matter what the doctors told her. Her family's illnesses had all started softly with an unremarkable complaint or symptom that fast bloomed into terminal disease.

Theresa had a constant hacking cough and declared she was going to make herself better by giving up the fags for a fortnight to see if she could get on top of it. A lump the size and shape of a hard-boiled egg appeared under her arm at that time and she and her sisters spent hours sat around the table taking turns to massage the swelling, trying to press it back into her body. She'd ask them, 'Do you think it's a ball of phlegm? My lungs cleaning themselves now I'm off the smokes?' Her sisters all murmured yes in agreement, that that was most likely the cause of the lump. They were all wrong. Her GP told her, 'You have a malignancy in your breast.' Theresa was highly relieved when she heard that news and replied, 'Well, thank the Lord above! At least it's not you know what ...' She couldn't even bring herself to utter the word.

They stopped swapping shoes when the cancers took hold. Like many of their generation, they believed that cancer was contagious, no matter what doctors insisted to the contrary. I heard Auntie Peggy wonder aloud if a library book could have been the cause of her disease. She also sighed to my broken-hearted mum, 'I managed to get this, but not to have a child.'

When Theresa's husband Con first heard, from a neighbour,

that his wife had cancer, he warned her to be sure and sterilise the cutlery with boiling water when she was washing up in future. She didn't get a lot more time to do washing-up. Her cancer had already invaded her lungs and her liver by the time it was diagnosed, and she deteriorated quickly. Within a month, Theresa was admitted to hospital, never to return home, and Con burnt all her clothes and shoes in the week before she died. Tony One and Tony Two visited her twice in hospital. One borrowed a fiver from her handbag in the bedside locker, and the other brought her some uncooked sausages as a get-well gift.

Mary's disease was discreet, and she died, cat-like, by going off quietly into her bed one afternoon and never waking up. Breast cancer had been her secret and she refused all treatment. She had handled Theresa's lump, and when she found her own she was fully expecting bad news, so she simply surrendered. Mary was convinced that cancer was a hunter. One that never missed its prey and there was no point resisting.

The disease at least spared her sight of her son's decline. For all the tender loving care she gave Declan, the boy grew into a wild man. In freefall after his mother's funeral, he dropped into the perfumed, bosom of Bernadette, a female property-hunter. Locals said Bernadette was born with a frown. The pair married so fast that a few desiccated petals from the funeral flowers were still blowing across the floor of the church when their confetti fell.

Declan was, as his wife had fully anticipated, a massive disappointment as a husband and father. But the comfortable house bought with his mother's money consoled them. The man simply couldn't switch from being looked after to looking after – even four lovely children of his own didn't inspire change. Declan proved un-trainable. Bernadette eventually changed the

locks on the house and sent him back to live with his widowed
father.

A routine medical check revealed that it was Peggy's husband,
the Timer, who had the face of a contrary owl and the sensi-
bility of a tomcat and regularly called her 'useless', who was
sterile, not her. He immersed that fact in whisky and took to
beating Peggy even harder, stopping only when she was diagnosed with advanced cancer of the breast. The kitchen-table
talk was that Peggy's lump was the size of a grapefruit when she
finally went to her GP, and she was dead, untreated, within
three weeks of the visit. She was almost sixty when she died,
and doctors believed she'd had the disease for ten years or more.

Peggy died of shame, although her death certificate said car-
cinoma. She lost the ability to swallow and went to the doctor,
who insisted on giving her a full examination. Peggy tried to
hide her left breast as he used his stethoscope, but even with her
fingers spread wide she couldn't hide the swelling there. The
doctor asked her why she hadn't come to see him sooner, and
said that if it was a cancer early surgery might have saved her.
Naturally she repeated what he said to the tableful of sisters.
They poo-pooed his observations – it was a well-known 'fact'
amongst their generation that cutting into a cancer was guaranteed to spread it.

I visited her every day she was in hospital. The Timer never
went. He said he hated hospitals. On the day of her death it was
unbearably hot and she lay still beneath a grey sheet printed
with the words 'property of London County Council'. It was
stuck to her skin in places with sweat. If she could have
extended her thin, weak limbs, it would have been possible for
her to hold hands with the patients in the beds either side of

her, they were so horribly close. There was nowhere for Peggy to look without seeing the sickness, pain and distress of strangers staring right back, so she mostly lay there, unmoving, with her eyes tight closed.

That August afternoon, I stood helpless at the foot of the bed, contorting over the iron frame to reach forward and hold her hand – it was shockingly cool and unresponsive. Peggy had once shyly told me that her own mother had marvelled at those hands when she was born and proudly declared to the midwife, 'Would you look at this? This one has the hands of a lady.' When I left her lying there later that evening, her breathing was shallow and her eyes closed but I had no idea that her time was so close. If I had I would never have left her side. Yet – did she try and tell me? Those alabaster hands gave me a small tug as mine slid away from them. Was it a message? Did she know death was near? Was she scared? Was it my imagination? I'm not sure, but the sensation of that feeble pull-back has stayed at the forefront of my heart for almost thirty years. Crammed into that hospital ward she apparently died shortly after I left her, with her head flopped to her left and the breath of another patient on her face.

The Timer was in the pub, as usual, on the evening his wife died. The hospital called my mum with the news of Peggy's death because they had never seen him and didn't even know she was married. My dad went to tell the terrible news, and when the Timer saw my teetotal dad walking through the pub doors, he knew it meant only one thing. Fixing his stubborn gaze on the bar optics, the Timer wouldn't turn to look my dad in the eye, so the sad report was delivered to the back of his head.

Katsie was next to take ill. 'It's the change,' was Mum's confident diagnosis of her sister's symptoms: forgetfulness, weight

214

loss and the disappearance of her smile. She spent her days hair awry, make-up and nail-varnish free, out on the balcony of her council flat, brooding and smoking. Hauled to the doctor by my mum, when he asked what the problem was, Katsie replied that her body just wasn't working properly any more. 'Show him,' my mum ordered, and Katsie demonstrated by trying to walk across his consulting-room floor in a straight line but travelling sideways. She was swiftly diagnosed with a secondary cancer in her brain; the primary was in her breast and she died a couple of months later. She had hospice care at the end and Mum sat by Katsie's bed curling her hair and painting her finger- and toenails even after she became too weak for words.

Dad never lost his love for dancing. When we were small and light enough, he was ever ready to invite my sister and me to climb aboard his feet for a whirl around the kitchen. With the lightest touch of his elegantly extended hand in the small of our backs, he would steer us around the Formica-topped table and into another dimension. As we spun around, behind my closed eyes I could see the crystal chandeliers sparkling in my personal ballroom. Our brown lino became golden oak parquet, sprung from beneath just as dance floors should be. As I grew taller he would circle me away from any worries I had. And he always made sure he danced with me the day after a funeral.

These were pits of misery. Out came the same hateful black coats and serious shoes, time and again. My mum was unreachable after each one. Grim-faced and so, so angry, a wipe of crimson lipstick exaggerated the downturn of her mouth. Graveside she would take the scoop offered by the priest to drop some earth down onto the coffin – everyone else was gentle – and pelted it so hard that some bounced back. I would stare up at the sisters arranged around the newly dug plot and saw that, separated, they were a fading force. They never hugged one another in consolation in public, just exchanged nods and looks that had an immediate effect on their stoop. And between them they cried a waterfall of tears. Wet silver streaks criss-crossed their faces and rounded their chins and soaked the nylon scarves knotted at their throats.

The husbands and sons carried domes of tears in their eyes that they never allowed to fall. Later it was difficult to tell what they were thinking because their eyes were always latched onto their pint glasses. After the burials, Mum would sit sideways at the corner of the kitchen table smoking, for weeks on end. She held that taut pose of despair and stared ahead, as if by sitting exactly so she could reach them all again in another dimension.

But they were unreachable. Just as she was to us. As she mourned, we all lived in the same house but were alone in spirit. Finally, as if a fever had broken, Mum would emerge. She would cook and clean and shop and go to work again almost as before, but she carried with her something that needed a lot of her strength and concentration to manage.

With four sisters already lost to breast cancer, Mum believed after her diagnosis that no matter what treatment she had she was still on a fast-track to the cemetery. Whilst she was in hospital recovering from her mastectomy, George, my first ever boyfriend, turned up out of the blue to visit her. He and my mum had always got on well and he was a lovely, kind bloke. We had been to primary school together; he was in the school year above me. At fifteen he and I had an innocent lip-brushing-only sort of romance that petered out after a year because there were so many other social distractions for both of us.

And suddenly there he was again. My first proper boyfriend,

George. In the flesh, sat beside my mum's sick bed and with a gorgeous blonde clamped on. Two years after we had split up I could see that George was now taller, broader-shouldered, smart and hilariously funny – he was all-round gorgeous.

Post-mastectomy my mother was sedated and sore but she turned her eyes first to George, then to his new girlfriend, and finally to me. She raised her eyebrows in a 'do you see what I see?' gesture and laughed out loud. It was a gurgly, chesty, post-anaesthetic laugh that made a nurse dash forward bearing a steel kidney bowl. I told the nurse not to be concerned and that Mum didn't feel sick. But I did.

It wasn't easy levering George's girlfriend out of the way. Unlike me first time around, she knew a good thing when she saw it and dug her long-painted nails in – but ultimately I put up the better fight. My strategy was to turn up everywhere they went until I wore her down and out of his life. I had an insider in his camp, a friend of George's keen to see us reunited who tipped me off about where they would be and when. I was a stalker with freshly washed hair, tasteful make-up and a convincing line in amazement. It wasn't long before George and I were a couple again and we still are – almost forty years after we first met.

I have no proposal story. It was just obvious to us and everyone else that we had to get married and so we did. I was twenty-two and he was twenty-three. George did the traditional thing and asked my dad for his permission. Trouble was he called unannounced on a night that my dad had a 4am start at work the following morning. So when my prospective groom entered the room, formally dressed in his work suit, shirt and tie, my dad was sat in his vest and Y-fronts all ready for bed and winding and setting his alarm clock. When I told my mum we were getting married, she rolled her eyes and said, 'Wind or water can't be stopped!'

An Irish wedding flushes all the living relatives out into the daylight, and ours was no different. One of my husband's maternal aunts, who had never been outside her tiny village in Kerry even though she was almost eighty years old, took the monumental decision to travel to London for our nuptials. 'The boy has no father,' was her reason for coming. George had been just thirteen years old when his father died in a building-site accident and his tears and torment at that time had never been forgotten by his aunt. At Killarney train station, Evelyn told the clerk as she handed over her money, 'I'm going to England to see my nephew settled.'

All the way from Euston in the cab, Evelyn prayed the rosary over and again – because through the taxi window she saw that the shops were open at an ungodly hour, the women wore too much make-up, and there were tables outside pubs with men drinking in public. Everything about London appalled her, until she arrived at her sister's house and uncorked the holy water bottle in her sack. Then her mood softened. The bottle was in the shape of the Virgin Mary, to fool Customs at Holyhead, and contained poteen.

I was introduced to Evelyn for the first time that evening. She was less than five feet tall; I am five feet ten. 'Jesus! You're huge altogether!' were the first words she ever spoke to me. I had bought her a welcoming gift. It was a large tub of posh talcum powder from Selfridges. She unwrapped it and eased the circular lid from the box. Sweet-smelling dust burst forth as the fancy powder puff was revealed. Evelyn, mystified, gingerly lifted it using the peach silk bow to reveal the golden pressed talc beneath. She studied it as we all waited patiently for her to speak. Then, before anyone could stop her, she bent her head and stuck her long pointy tongue into the talc and scooped up a good mouthful. She swallowed, grimaced and shook her head before announcing, 'Too sweet!'

George confessed too late that he didn't think his aunt would appreciate the talc. He told me that at home she shared her sitting-room turf fire with a giant sow for company, and it snored so loudly you couldn't hear the battery-powered radio that was permanently tuned to the local radio station. He'd spent many nights in Auntie Evelyn's company straining to listen to the tinny transistor, and all it broadcast were prayers, knitting patterns and the names of the recently dead.

'Did you sleep well, Auntie Evelyn?' George asked his aunt on the morning of our wedding. 'The bed is too soft,' said Evelyn, grimacing and rubbing the small of her back. At home, Evelyn's mattress was rock hard because it was stuffed to bursting with decades of uncashed cheques. Sent monthly by the creameries in Ireland in payment for the milk from her cows, Evelyn stuffed them, still in their envelopes, into her mattress to keep them safe 'for later'. Extended family urged Evelyn to open a bank account and pay in her cheques, but her only son – forty years old but neither man nor child – agreed with her that all banks were 'crooked' and she was better off minding the money herself.

On our wedding morning Evelyn didn't join the queue for the bathroom. She got ready in the tiny kitchen. 'Ye all carry on!' she said to George, his mother and his sister. 'I'll just have a quick wash here.' She tipped the breakfast crockery from the washing-up bowl into the sink, filled the bowl with warm water and added a squirt of washing-up liquid before lifting it and placing it on the floor.

No modesty was needed as, elbows out and raised, a fully dressed Evelyn marched in and out of the bowl once and then reached for the string dishcloth on the drainer. She wrung it out, leant forward and rubbed vigorously beneath her paisley print skirt. A couple of leaves, several blades of grass and a dead bluebottle dropped down into the bowl. Underarms came next, with the same cloth. To complete her ablutions she took the bowl from the floor to the drainer and splashed her face with the grey water before siphoning up a mouthful, gargling and spitting it back. Then she put all the crockery from the sink back into the bowl without emptying the used water. 'All yours,' she said to the small audience, who had watched in silent wonder.

Evelyn did look memorable at our wedding in her patterned skirt, a thick Aran cardigan perfumed with assorted fish oils and her signature black wellingtons. She insisted one of her nieces backcomb her perm. 'Because it's a very special occasion,' she declared, and she virtually ate a deep red lipstick. The look was a frizzy Marie Antoinette from the neck up and Wurzel Gummidge from the neck down.

My husband-to-be wore a green mohair suit with a matching velvet collar and tie. He asked the local dry cleaner, Pedro, to make him his wedding suit. He had been a master tailor until he became an alcoholic. Then his hands, drunk or sober, became too shaky for stitching.

On the night before the wedding the suit was on the floor in Pedro's dry cleaners in eighteen different pieces and we had to pray hard to the Patron Saint of Suitmakers and Perchlorethylene that it would at least be tacked together on the day. Pedro threw an all-nighter and, fuelled by various illicit substances, he saw to it that the ensemble was all hanging together nicely and delivered with ten minutes to spare before the start of the ceremony.

I went with big dreams and a small budget to Pronuptia on Oxford Street. After a session when I tried on several dresses and rejected every one of them, I rebelled. I declared I would design my own and find someone to make it. I wondered if Pedro had a sober sister.

I got one compliment on my wedding day that touched me more than all the others put together. It was from Uncle Jem, my dad's brother, and a big surprise coming from the man who usually only grunted about potatoes or greyhounds. As my dad and I climbed the church steps, Jem was standing in the porch at the back ready for the service to begin. He never missed Mass in seventy years, but he had never actually entered a church since he was a boy.

When he was nine years old, Jem and my dad tried to sneak out of church whilst Mass was in progress. The priest spotted the two escapees from the altar and made the whole congregation wait whilst he followed them outside and gave chase. Dad and Jem knew they were in for a terrible beating and judged it would probably be better if he caught them, so they stopped by a tree to allow the fat and furious parish priest to catch up. As he puffed around the corner into sight, Jem pushed Dad's head towards the grass and started to thump him on the back, saying over and again, 'Cough it up! Good man you are! Cough it up and ye'll be fine and we can go straight back into Mass so we won't miss much at all!' The priest wasn't fooled by their performance and hauled the terrified twosome back to church by their ears. After Mass he punched and kicked the pair around his garden until his housekeeper called him in for his roast lunch with all the trimmings.

Jem never went back into church after that day. Instead, like so many Irishmen of his generation, he stood in the doorway or on the pavement outside for the duration of the service. A new white shirt tightly buttoned to the neck was on display for my special occasion, and it heightened the ruddiness of his skin. Clearing his throat nervously, Jem mumbled, 'You're a fine girl, Anna May, and that's one fecker of a dress!' The poor man blushed red on purple because he couldn't find the right words to say what he really wanted to – that he thought I looked nice. I was so touched but didn't dare thank him or kiss him because that would have been an embarrassment too far for him. I half smiled and he half nodded, enough to show we each knew what the other meant.

My bridal car was a white Mercedes on loan – without the permission of its owner – and driven at high speed by my uncle Bren. He was a part-time chauffeur and had to have the Mercedes back outside his boss's garage straight after the service before it was discovered to be missing. 'No car, no job!' he kept muttering to himself under his breath as he drove with his foot punishing the accelerator.

Time in the car was tight. I got a one-way ride only. George and I walked from the church to our reception. Even though the kindly Bren was clock-watching, I was still late getting to the church because Dad instructed him to pull over to the side of the road so the pair of them could concentrate on the radio broadcast of the 3.15 horse race at Leopardstown. It was over the jumps and a long one so I fiddled with my veil and played 'he loves me he loves me not' with the petals of my flowers for nine minutes whilst the two of them made the bridal car rock as they cheered their horses on.

Ours wasn't the first wedding in my family. We'd had snap nuptials three years before mine when, with just a month's notice, my compliant brother married his long-time live-in girlfriend Una. The couple were presented with a Christmas Eve fait accompli after Mum decided they had been 'living over the brush' for long enough and besides, she and Dad had their sights firmly set on grandchildren. The reception hall, the photographer were all express-booked and paid for within a matter of hours.

Catholicism was Una's father's weapon of choice for driving first her and then all three of his other daughters away. When my brother made the journey North to ask for Una's hand in marriage, her father was in a fury about the sin they had committed by living together and answered, 'Take her, she's scum.' So Michael did – that same night she left her family home for ever and came to live with us in London. Una's father drew up the emotional drawbridge and didn't lower it back down in his lifetime, despite her best efforts. 'She flew into the face of God!' was the only explanation he ever offered for casting her out. I have often heard the saying, 'You can't give what you haven't been given' but an hour in the company of Una and her children proves that she needed no lesson in how to love. The night her dad said to my brother, 'Take her' it wasn't just my brother who did. We all did, and to this day are proud to have her. Her three sisters begged their parents to let them travel to London for the wedding. 'Just the church part, Daddy, we'll come home the same day, please ...' His dogged reply every time was, 'Whose wedding?'

In one respect Una's sisters had a lucky escape. No wedding meant they were exempt from bridesmaid duties. My sister and I were conscripted, and featured as giant, moody Bo-Peeps in their wedding album. Stuffed into cornflower blue dresses, with stitched-on broderie anglaise aprons matched with high-heeled sandals made from diamante-studded cheese wire, we towered over the bride and groom. The final indignity was a single over-sized white carnation that had to be positioned behind our preferred ear. That was the only choice about anything we were offered on that day. I suggested it went behind one of my dad's enormous ears, but the bride insisted it had to be behind one of mine.

Their wedding reception was held in the local headquarters of the Knight's of St Columbus. It was a venue that the London Irish considered very grand. Mum got it on the cheap because she dared to ask for a discount and promised that the bar tak-ings would be astronomical. The cost of hire plus a buffet that turned out to be burnt black was £1.75 a head and they threw in a toastmaster who would announce guests as they arrived.

An entrance hall with ornate plasterwork and a family-car-sized sparkling chandelier hanging above the sweeping staircase led down one level to the reception hall, buffet and dance floor. Stationed at the top of the stairs was the liveried toastmaster. This haughty chap caused much confusion amongst my relatives by insisting that they each needed to be 'announced' before they were permitted to walk down the stairs to the drinking and dancing action below.

His hand was raised in a very definite *Stop* sign as they stam-peded in like buffalo and rushed towards the stairs and the bar below. One by one they screeched to an emergency halt and teetered on the edge of the staircase, then fell in and formed a puzzled and impatient queue.

'What's all this then?' asked my aunt Delia of her first cousin Frank. His beer belly was in the tight grip of a black satin shirt and draped with a red tie, and the man was slavering to get bar-side. He rebuked Delia. 'Announced, of course. Sure don't we have to be announced! Where were you reared that you don't know that?' he answered her as if he had been announced umpteen times before. 'Announced is it? My arse,' she grumbled before joining the back of the queue.

The liveried toastmaster had clearly decided that my family was rabble and had no intention of trying to explain protocol to them. He should have asked each guest who they were and called out their names to those below in the ballroom. Instead he just went through the motions and repeated in a loud sing-song voice their replies to his standard top-of-the-stairs question, which was, 'And you are . . .?'

'Auntie Betty and Uncle Tom.'

'Very well thanks, and yourself?'

'Dying for a pint.'

The Knights of St Columbus had a ballroom-size sprung dance floor and my aunts and uncles and cousins had every inch of it covered with ceili dancing, rock and roll moves and a bit of ballroom bunged in. Uncle Joseph came over to fetch me for a jive, both arms extended and said, 'Are ye coming out for a slide or what?'

A life-size crib was set up for Christmas in one corner of the room. It was a shanty-style cardboard stable featuring papier-mâché animals that dwarfed the human figures. The Three Kings were wearing women's brocade dressing gowns and baby Jesus was swaddled in a blanket and lay in a milk crate trimmed with tinsel. Real hay was artfully arranged on the manger floor, which the barmaid said would come in handy for the New Year's barn dance.

My auntie Molly, who had arthritic knees and declared her dancing days well and truly over, had positioned her chair in front of the Christmas manger to get a good view of the floor.

She particularly enjoyed watching her sister-in-law Margy, whose party piece was to groove along to whatever the band was playing, whilst still managing to sing along loudly to another song entirely. Molly drank large gin and tonics without pause all night. Each was served with a fresh glass and a mini bottle of tonic. She was tossing her empties into the nearby manger and by 9pm you couldn't see the baby Jesus beneath her mixer bottles.

Sometime after 10pm her husband Paddy, boss-eyed from several pints of Guinness, climbed into the crib and tried to jive with the Virgin Mary. His wife reprimanded him, saying in a slurred voice, 'Jesus Christ, Paddy, would you leave her alone? The woman has just had a feckin' baby!'

16

Lonely Hearts and Leukaemia

My mum and dad and all their brothers and sisters came to this country with no sense of self-importance. They well knew their place as the Invisibles, always grateful for the opportunities to work and for healthcare and education for their children. 'This country has given us a good living and we want no trouble,' was Dad's refrain in the face of all the Anglo-Irish political unrest that rumbled through the 1970s and 1980s. There was nothing militant about them, even though they were daily misjudged as terrorists because of their accents by the English. 'All we did wrong was to be from somewhere else,' my mum once said, her eyes bright with tears, after a neighbour had refused to take in a parcel for her. Her reason was that 'it might contain bomb-making ingredients'. Mum took a bus ride to the Post Office depot to collect it herself – it was a shoebox from Mary that contained black pudding and three dozen Kimberley biscuits.

By providing England with educated, useful children, they felt they had in part redeemed themselves for turning up uninvited – but it was through their grandchildren that my parents felt entitled to raise their chins. Eight in total, each one of them a little offshoot of Mum and Dad's stock, and who made them believe, after forty years living and working in England, that they finally belonged.

Other people had grandchildren too, and Mum and Dad considered them nice enough – but there was no one like their own. They had five granddaughters and three grandsons and my mum claimed that every one of them looked like her side of the family. Mum was a busybody extraordinaire when it came to her grandchildren. There is a piece of family video that shows her and my husband's mother each holding one of my twin girls on the day of their christening. Mum's is cradling May in one arm, and her other is reaching across to tuck and fiddle with Amy who lay in my mother-in-law's capable arms.

My dad was a grandchild magnet. They couldn't leave him alone. I often saw him gardening with a spade or hoe in one hand and with the other clasping the hand of one of my children, who would move companionably with him up and down the flower-beds. He never lost patience with one of them or shortened his smile, not for an instant.

Always there without fail, they appeared in the ward soon after the births of my babies and made me feel they came to see me first, not their new grandchild. Each of them studied my face for a long time to be certain I was well and happy before they ever switched their attention to the swaddled superstar in the cot.

When my twin daughters were born in the early hours, Mum and Dad arrived at the hospital at dawn. 'Visitors. You have visitors outside,' the nurse told me. I knew immediately it must be them and my heart did a little back-flip of love and gratitude. 'I hope they're in no hurry,' she said.

'What do you mean?' I asked.

'Visiting's not till 1pm. I've told them. They said they'd wait.'

I was unsteady on my feet. Having delivered two babies just a few hours earlier, there was a lot of sway in my walk. I had a scooped-out sensation in my lower half, and was under attack from extreme fatigue and excitement. I leant on the Perspex hospital cot-on-wheels containing my twin babies, who were sleeping cheek to cheek, and, ignoring the nurse's shouted protests, steered it slowly and painstakingly through the security doors of the maternity unit and into the lift lobby of the hospital's third floor.

My frail parents were sat dozing on a wooden slatted bench by the silent lifts, leaning part on the wall behind them, and part against one another. Dad, his mouth hanging slack, was wearing a checked sports cap, and Mum a yellow floral headscarf that had slipped sideways to reveal a few rows of her tight white perm.

'Hello, you two,' I said through tears that sprang hot and happy and sudden. My mum turned to me and opened her eyes and smiled a smile that was all joy. She levered herself with some difficulty up from the bench. She put both her arms around my waist and I bent low to press my forehead to her left shoulder. It was an embrace that could have been awkward but wasn't because it was so perfect. My dad put one arm around both of us and pulled the Perspex cot bearing his two granddaughters closer and said, 'God bless all the girls . . .'

It is that memory of them being there, of being embraced and of being so completely understood, that makes me ache for them still, even a decade after their deaths. When as a family we are sick or troubled I feel glad now they aren't here to be burdened or worried, one small bonus of grief. But in the many moments of fun and happiness and pride family life has brought, I am just as devastated that they are gone as I was on the day I buried them. They have left empty spaces that no one else can fill.

They scooped up a granddaughter apiece and sat back down onto the bench, me in the middle. The five of us sat warming one another, silently contemplating how kind life could be. Since my daughters arrived I hadn't closed my eyes, even for just a few minutes. In that corridor, tucked between my parents and the two columns of love they provided, I slept deep and safe.

'Grand!' chuckled my dad. 'This is grand!' as he stroked May's baby cheek with his work-worn but tender fingers.

Mum and Dad bought and sold their two-bedroom first-floor council maisonette and moved out to the north-west London suburbs, an uneventful residential location where my mum didn't have to stash her shopping money in her bra for fear of being mugged. Their ground-floor flat was a minute's walk from my house in one direction and from my sister's home in the other. After working hard for so long, and for so little, to see my parents proudly hold the keys to their own property was one of life's shining moments.

The two of them were like good fairies in those first happy years when we all lived so close. One enormous lucky leprechaun key ring that held their own house keys, mine and my sister's. They would let themselves in and out of our houses and poodle around tidying, pegging out laundry, cooking and gardening. I would open my front door to an instant high created by their liberal use of Lemon Pledge furniture polish. I wanted to tap dance, even though I can't, when I saw an empty laundry basket because they had washed, dried, ironed and put away the clothes, and a delicious meal all prepared and ready just to reheat was sitting on top of the oven.

My mum was general works manager in spite of being disabled after radiotherapy treatment for her breast cancer. She had one wasted arm, her left, which looked like just bone hanging in a loose sheath of skin. Her right side, where she had the mastectomy, was elephantine because of complications with post-surgery lymphoma. It was a puffy mutton-leg shape, creased and dimpled and constantly painful. She had a method of using her right arm as a prop and moving the other in order to get household tasks done.

Dad did the gardening and smiled so hard at the bushes and flowers they would grow especially for him. He loved it, and had a transforming touch. It wasn't all work though. They managed to get an awful lot done between snoozes, watching daytime TV and filling betting slips to the brim with complicated accumulator bets.

For those first two years in their new home they were the most content I had ever seen them. I believe that the regular contact with their adored grandchildren eclipsed some of the constant grief for their lost brothers and sisters. The saddest things they ever said began with 'If only ...' and it was followed by a name of their brother or sister and a wish that they could have seen and shared the grandchildren.

My mum was a sterling sorter-outer. That's a nice way of saying she was Captain Bossy, or 'Mrs Right' as my dad often called her, and it wasn't always a compliment. Her no-nonsense, bullshit-dozing approach to woes often made people very cross before they eventually got around to being grateful. 'Lose the fat bum', 'Get a job' or 'Bless your face for what you have' were her standards. Family, in-laws, neighbours and people she worked with always seemed to want to confide their troubles to her. She had a flair for cutting through them instantly and straightening out the sad, the lonely and the guilty.

But she had one unsolved fret of her own. The fact that my sister, who was approaching her thirties, hadn't bagged a man. 'Don't you worry about it. Remember it's the old birds that make the best broth,' was her breezy reply to any family questions about Julie's boyfriend status.

Mum was very proud of Julie's career, especially when she was discussing it with friends, neighbours and extended family, and was always curious about what went on at her office in town. Daily Mum would dial Julie's work number, which connected first to her secretary. 'Has she had her lunch?' Mum would ask, and if the answer was yes would want to know exactly what she had eaten. Or if it was too early to be discussing lunch, Mum wanted to know what Julie was wearing that day. If the answers were detailed enough, she would hang up the telephone without actually speaking to Julie.

Mum believed that her youngest daughter outclassed any Miss World and struggled to come to terms with career-girl Julie's not-at-all-busy love life. Another reason she wanted her married was that she was eager to add to her grandchildren count. Every week, with fresh hope in her heart, Mum would ask Julie the same questions. 'Have you met a nice fella?' And when she got no for an answer came the follow-up query. 'Are you a les-bean? You can tell me if you are . . .'

Confident that she could make the maybe problem of an old-maid daughter go away, Mum took matters into her own hands. Masquerading as Julie, she answered some of the lonely-hearts ads placed in the London Irish press. Mum used a magnifying glass to scour their tiny print. She thought that the abbreviation 'gsoh' (for good sense of humour) meant gas central heating and she put a big tick in a bingo marker pen next to any ads that specifically mentioned that. A car owner was also an essential for her daughter. 'And should the auld mammy be dead, all the better!'

In just over a week she got a mini mountain of replies. In her letters, Mum had described her Julie as a blonde (she was mid-brown), size 10 (yes, when she was nine years old), a Guinness heiress (substitute the word drinker for heiress) and a Rose of Tralee winner (she once backed a horse with that name – it came in third). Or rather I did. Mum had emotionally blackmailed me into writing the letters, loading on guilt about my sister suffering a lonely old age and it being all my fault if I didn't help her.

'It's easy to get a fella, see . . .' Mum crowed at Julie, proudly waving her list of love-hungry Celtic beefcake. Some of the respondents had included photographs, not of themselves but of people they had been told – probably by their mothers – that they looked like. These included Elvis, Johnny Weissmuller as Tarzan and Prince Charles. The only letter Mum tore up was the letter from the royal looky-likey.

There was a lengthy chill in the air between them when Julie refused to read any of Mum's lonely-heart reply letters. It was me who reunited them, in concern, when I kept falling asleep all the time. In spite of the help with the house and children I was getting from my parents, I was constantly tired. I kept nodding off in unexpected places. On Christmas Day 1996, I fell asleep eating Christmas dinner and went face down into my plate before I'd even had a sip of wine. My mum and sister stopped thinking my tiredness was funny and jointly diagnosed me as anaemic. I was ordered to the doctor for a blood test.

Seven hours after I had that blood test, I was tucked up in a hospital bed. I was placed in an isolation room so I assumed I must be infectious and wondered what sort of tropical disease I could have picked up in northern Brittany, which was our last family holiday destination six months earlier.

My hospital room was sealed from the outside world by an anteroom that had a sink and enough dressing-up space for staff and visitors to change into plastic gowns, hats and masks before being allowed into my company. My mum drowned in the giant hospital gowns and reminded me of the woman from the Krankies when she visited. She sat on the edge of my bed, wrapped in plastic, and railed at the NHS for being stupid and wasting my time. 'Keeping you in for nothing when there must be a queue of people who really need to be in that bed!'

I found out what was wrong with me by being rebellious and breaking the ban on entering the anteroom, imposed by doctors who warned infections were lurking out there. I fiddled with the blinds on the door glass to get a look through into the hall outside. What I saw shocked me senseless. Some of the other patients, who I had heard through the walls but never actually seen, were wandering around aimlessly. There were maybe a dozen of them, men and women, in nightclothes or T-shirts and tracksuit bottoms, pushing or pulling drip stands. They all had one striking thing in common. They were all bald. This was no Star Trek convention. I knew before anyone had to tell me that what I saw meant only one thing. These people had cancer – and that must be what I had, too.

Blood tests told that I had an advanced malignancy somewhere, but that after a week's worth of tests the medics still didn't have a clue where. My cancer was playing hide and seek with the doctors. Because there were no obvious lumps or bumps, they had no pointers as to where it had set up camp in my body. My baby-faced doctor tossed me one small consolatory bone. 'One thing we do know for certain is that we are not dealing with a leukaemia.' My husband and I toasted this goodish news with hospital-issue styrofoam cups of tea. Three days later it was confirmed that I did have leukaemia.

Finally we were dealing in facts. My test results showed I had a very rare variety of leukaemia, a first cousin to non-Hodgkin's lymphoma, which typically affects men over sixty. I was a medical freak. A mathematical friend with a beautiful mind mashed the statistics – I had more chance of winning the lottery than getting my particular type of the disease.

My leukaemia was of a hairy cell variety. Thanks to my mutant hormones I already had a hairy chin and hairy legs, and now hairy blood cells, too.

So it turned out that my tiredness hadn't been normal for a busy mum of four – it was actually a primary symptom of a potentially deadly disease. My blood counts were dangerously low, making my heart work overtime and my body super-susceptible to infection. The disease had infiltrated 100 per cent of my bone marrow. I was in trouble.

I was permitted home for a couple of days to sort my life out before starting chemotherapy, on the promise that I stayed indoors and welcomed no visitors. Anything with a heartbeat, human or animal, was a dire threat. I had been worried about being a risk to my family's health when I was in isolation waiting for a diagnosis. But I'd got that wrong; it was all of them who were a constant threat to me.

My mum and dad were broken by the news that I was sick.

I told Mum with the lightest possible touch over tea and cake, 'It's very treatable. They said it's the best kind of cancer to have! Really!' She was paralysed with despair. Telling someone who has lost four sisters to a killer disease not to worry when their daughter is diagnosed with it is an insult. My dad left his mug and Chelsea bun untouched on the table and went into the garden muttering, 'It's a punch to the heart, so it is.'

My mum and I couldn't look one another in the eye for the couple of days before I returned to the hospital for my treatment. We fixated on housework like it was the cure for blood cancer. My dad gardened for England and Ireland, keeping an anxious eye through the downstairs windows on what was going on indoors.

George stayed close. He said very little other than, 'It's all going to be good, believe me, Anna May,' again and again. I wanted to shout at him and demand how he could possibly know. But I really, really wanted him to be right because I adored him and never wanted to leave him – so I said nothing and silently begged God to agree with him.

In those few days after diagnosis, it was like we had turned to stone trying to protect ourselves and one another from the truth that cancer had booted its way into our lives – again. In my mother's generation it had kicked its way into their world when they were in their early forties. I was only thirty-five. Was cancer getting greedier for us?

My chemotherapy took place over a fourteen-day period in an isolation room. I was moulded to the mattress, viewing the world side-on. Being alone in that room was the pure definition of loneliness. In there, it was just me and my mortality. I lay with my eyes closed and thought of my children for most of the time, concentrating on what they sounded like and how their faces looked when they laughed. I tried to remember their rapt expressions when they heard stories like 'Chicken Licken' and 'Dr Dog' or the day when they came home from school and saw their beloved cat had delivered nine kittens. These images would console me but brought tears so hot that I feared they'd burn channels in my cheeks. Memories of my lovely aunts who had all died from cancer kaleidoscoped in front of my half-opened eyes.

I fretted a lot whether I was 'battling' hard enough, especially on my worst days when I couldn't even sit up and had to be washed and spoon-fed. My aunts were gutsy ladies who 'battled' the disease but died anyway. Sometimes cancer undercuts you so swiftly and with so much force that no matter how fight-willing you are, and no matter how much you long for life, you end up having to make peace with your enemy. I didn't want to have to try and be that brave. I wanted to live and see my children grow up. But I didn't get to do the choosing. God did? Cancer did? That was my crisis of faith.

George had a lot to attend to at home. He was coping with four children under seven years old and trying to work full-time as a teacher. Reports from my mum, dad and sister, all of whom had been drafted in as emergency aid, reached me. Robert was wearing the girls' underwear and vice versa, there was a dirty-washing mountain, dawn bedtimes and toffee popcorn and crisps sometimes acted as meal substitutes. I was completely thrilled to hear all of this because I knew if I ever got out of the isolation room and hospital alive, he would never again breeze in from a day at work and ask, 'And what have you been doing all day?'

237

Visiting inside my isolation room was limited to two named people. After much debate it was agreed that would be George and my mum. The room was one of eight in a row on the ground floor of the hospital and general visiting took place in a corridor that ran alongside them. There was a wall of glass between patients' rooms and the corridor. Friends and family could sit out there on a bench and use the intercom phone to chat to me. The arrangement made me sympathise with animals in a zoo. When my children came to visit, questions spilled out of them from the other side of the glass.

'What are you doing in bed in the daytime, Mummy?'

'Are you living here because you don't love us any more?'

'Jack in my class told me his auntie at school died from what you have. I told him you weren't ... you won't do that, will you? Promise?'

'Daddy's mash potato is too lumpy, Mummy.'

'Kitty [the cat] can't sleep without you in your bed; she is getting very tired and might get run over if you don't come home. So come. Nooooow.'

'Don't be lazy in bed, Mummy, come home.'

Their pleading wide, wet eyes were heart-rending. That visit and departure was so traumatic for all of us that it was a one-off. Neither my husband nor I had enough emotional courage to repeat it. On that day, as the children left they put sticky kisses onto the glass wall between us. The four of them put their whole hearts into those kisses and there were at least ten, at lip height on their side of the glass and at knee height on mine. I guarded those precious lip prints from the cleaners and their cloths and sprays. But when I became too ill to get out of bed and the usual cleaner was on a day's leave, they got wiped away as I slept. When I woke and saw the kisses were gone, I was distraught and wanted to scream, but my mouth was too dry and scabby to let me.

Nin, an older relative on my dad's side, came to visit halfway through my treatment. She banged on the glass to wake me up and then sat in silence staring at me for twenty minutes. I pointed to the intercom telephone on her side which would allow us to chat but she resolutely shook her head. Smiling a closed-mouth smile, Nin waved periodically. I attempted a bit of Marcel Marceau-style chat through the glass, asking her how she was, had she won at bingo lately? She didn't even attempt to answer. Exhausted and self-conscious, I lay down on the bed and stared right back at her. I must have fallen asleep and when I woke Chatty Cathy had gone. She left me some back copies of *Ireland's Own* on the bench outside where I couldn't reach them, and a packet of half-eaten Rolos.

Everything was out to get me, and that wasn't paranoia, it was a fact. Bacteria, from any source, were my number-one enemy. Specially for me, water had to be ionised, food nuked to extreme temperatures to kill any potential bugs and my room thoroughly cleaned and disinfected twice a day. I was even breathing filtered air. For the first time in my life I was high maintenance.

On my first day home after the chemotherapy, I hid behind the kitchen door to surprise the children as they trooped in from school. When they saw me they were like a moving wall of excitement and joy. I was overwhelmed by their life force in seconds and had to find a seat from which to hug them and hug them and hug them.

I tried not to look at myself in the mirror because when I did I got very scared. I saw falling hair and grey skin and no light

239

in my eyes. I was diminished and didn't know how to begin to put that right, or even if there would be any time for me to do so. Worst of all, George was nice to me all the time, and I wondered if this was it. Had I come home to die?

17

Arteeyay

I knew I was on the road to recovery when my husband and mother both told me, 'Belt up, would you?' about something I was going on about within an hour of one another. I was ordinary again – and it felt fantastic.

Being able to walk to my children's primary school and stand and wait for them in the playground at the end of their day made me pure fizz with excitement. I would wear bright, eye-catching colours so my four children would spot me instantly the school doors were thrown open. In my head I was cartwheeling with joy just to be there and upright. By always being early, and colourful enough to stand out from the crowd, I was trying to cancel out the fear and worry they must have felt in all the times when I wasn't there. To all the other mums, the school pick-up was a chore. To me it was a divine gift, and to my children it was a promise that I'd never leave them again.

Six months after my treatment I was still having weekly

blood tests that showed my blood counts were slowly improving. When, about nine months after chemotherapy, I heard the words, 'Your bloods are normal, and stable, and we don't need to see you for three months', I felt like I'd been released from prison. I ran to the hospital payphone and phoned home. My mother answered. My damp, sweaty forehead was pressed against the wall above the phone, and when the moment came to tell her my news I could only weep. She answered me back with her own happy tears. No words were exchanged.

My hospital visits were whittled down to three-monthly blood checks and a monthly outpatient appointment. Always escorted by Mum, who was fearful I might explode, be kidnapped or run amok if left unattended. Bar the toilet, at that time she took me everywhere. She developed a habit of approaching strangers in shops, or in church or wherever we were and asking, 'Do you think she looks well?' pointing at me. Too polite to say anything else, they always said yes and then she would say, 'Leukaemia. She had it. Nearly died. Would you credit it?'

It's odd that when terrible things happen you can't always remember the date, the month or the year but the day of the week sticks in your mind. It was a Friday. Mum was having a snooze in the back sitting room and Dad was in the bookies. He'd left an hour or so earlier, convinced after my good news that this was surely a super-lucky day. His pockets had been bulging with instant-win scratch cards, lottery slips and betting papers. The gambling that had been like a demolition ball to high days and holidays when we were young was now just a benign hobby. He lost some, he won some and we all laughed about it. When he was in the bookies and the children wanted to know where Granddad was, we would answer, 'In his office in town.'

The knock that came to the door was actually a bell tolling, although I didn't know it at the time. Through the stained-glass panel I could see a flashing siren. For one daft and selfish moment, I thought the hospital had made a mistake, got my results horribly wrong and sent an ambulance to come and bring me back into their clutches. A silver balloon with the word 'Celebrate!' was tied to the door knocker and bobbed about in the space between me and the policeman. He said my dad's name and asked if he lived at this address. He said he needed to speak to my mum. 'It's very urgent' were his exact words.

There was a nurse waiting for us inside accident and emergency who led us to the 'family room'. Painted crimson, it had a row of open tissue boxes on a low coffee table. She told us that Dad was the victim of an RTA. 'Arteeyay?' replied my mum. 'How did he catch that? Where did he get that? What is it? Does he need an operation? Where is he?'

The nurse stopped speaking in letters. 'An RTA is a road traffic accident. He was hit by a van as he crossed the road –' she checked her watch – 'approximately two hours ago.'

'Two hours ago?' Mum shook her head in disbelief. 'But I was asleep.'

The accident was catastrophic, although he was unmarked other than a graze on his knee. My dad wasn't dead but he wasn't alive either. A small van had hit him as he crossed the road to the betting shop. It had been travelling at less than ten miles an hour but carrying ladders that weren't properly secured to the roof rack. They sped forward when the driver hit the brakes and struck Dad in the right temple area of his skull. His brain ricocheted around his skull, bled and swelled up. This left him in limbo between life and death for ten lost weeks.

Comas don't suddenly stop, they lighten. And day in day out, night after night, we studied his face and milked his fingers for the smallest signs of normal life and we talked to him incessantly.

The doctors gave Dad a less than ten per cent chance of survival. For two and a half months he lay in his hospital bed deflating – face, tummy and limbs – as we waited in a nervy ring around him for any signs of life.

When he finally regained consciousness it was a huge letdown. We had been hoping for a reunion, recognition and rejoicing. But it was obvious from his startled expression that he didn't know any of us. We reached for him and he drew away. My dad couldn't talk, walk, use the toilet or eat and drink unaided. Doctors judged he had the mental age of a toddler. Younger than any of his eight grandchildren.

It was a body blow. My illness and recovery were forgotten as my mum, my brother, sister, all the children and I poured our energies into getting him back. We taught Dad all our names using a roll of wallpaper with our photos glued to it. This went everywhere he did in the hospital and one of us would follow him around chanting, 'Annie is your wife, Michael is your son, look at them, they're here, look! Look again! Anna May and Julie are your daughters, see their pictures. Curly hair, two daughters ...'

We brainwashed him into first knowing us, then bludgeoned him into loving us again. We organised shifts so he was never alone and during one of mine I was sat next to his hospital bed reading the *Longford Leader* to him when I felt a flick on my forearm. I dropped the newspaper in surprise and he fumbled for my hand and squeezed it with as much might as he could muster. Looking into his eyes I saw that he recognised me. Not as the harridan with the roll of wallpaper who spent days shouting into his face, but as his daughter. It was a look of true recognition, and was lit from behind by love.

The hospital telephoned my mother at home with the news that after three months Dad was ready to be discharged. She was mortified. 'He can't talk, or walk, or use the toilet. He's not sure who I am. I'm not sure who he is. He's not better yet.'

The devastating answer came: 'We've done as much as we can for him. And we need the bed. I'm sure you understand. He'll be ready at 3pm for collection.' Like a parcel.

The unspoken truth was that he was never going to get better. We had been kidding ourselves that in time he would be restored to his former self. So we decided that if he couldn't get better, he could definitely *be* better.

Getting him to remember who we were and what our names were had been our first challenge, and an even bigger one was getting him toilet trained. We bribed him to pee in a bucket using Jelly Babies. He was brain-damaged and didn't know who he was – but he remembered that he *loved* Jelly Babies.

Dad had been home from hospital for a week when he awoke with a shout in the middle of the night. '*Who* the feckin' hell are you?' he wanted to know of my mum.

Raging that he had forgotten nearly forty years of marriage, she was short on patience. 'Shaddup. Go back to sleep. You know bloody well who I am.'

'No I don't. And my advice to you, you hussy you, is to clear off out of this bed because when my wife gets here she'll make short work of you, so she will!'

245

There were just two things he could still do without prompting. One was to roll up his fags, and the other was to write out long and complicated horseracing bets. It took him almost all of his waking hours to complete these tasks, but he did them just the same with the tip of his tongue pressed in concentration against the corner of his lip. My mum was incensed that he could remember those two passions – smoking and gambling – but not her. 'Who am I?' she would ask again and again as he looked blankly at her.

My dad had worked for Westminster Council in their parks and gardens, many of which were very beautiful. He had been an intuitive gardener, but after the accident he would sit staring out the back window without a flicker of interest about what was growing out there. We tried talking to him about the plants and flowers he had nurtured in his garden and mine, but he would either fall asleep mid-conversation or demand a Jelly Baby.

Looking after Dad was, put simply, tall-toddler watch. Only he was less obedient than our children had been. Under our noses he would embark on crazy or dangerous DIY activity. Mum could be napping in her armchair just feet away or I'd be pottering in the kitchen and he would seize his opportunity to get started. Once he painted an antique mahogany side table, a gift to my mum from one of the women she cleaned for, with a blue eggshell paint. Another time he washed down the electrical fuseboard with a bucket of hot water and Flash. 'You're a naughty man!' my mum would cry and Dad would beam back at her, 'Thank you very much.'

He developed Houdini elements to his character after the accident, and liked nothing better than to disappear and turn up somewhere completely unexpected. Any open front door in any street was, in his head, an invitation to drop by. Once we had to collect him from the local police station where he was taken after wandering into a stranger's house. Their door was open because the lady owner was chatting to a neighbour nearby and Dad slipped in unnoticed. He headed upstairs and took a little nap in the master bedroom. When he was discovered the houseowner dialled 999 and sat in the front garden holding a breadknife in self-defence until the police arrived. When they burst into the bedroom and woke him up, Dad beamed at them and said, 'Four sugars, please.' We called the police to report Dad lost and the officer who answered the phone said drily, 'You looking for Rip Van O'Winkle by any chance?'

Two summers after his accident, we left my dad alone for the first time. He was dozing in the chair at my house and we were confident that he would be there for at least a couple of hours – plenty of time for us to get back from Mum's GP appointment.

Wrong. When we quietly let ourselves back into the house, tiptoeing and whispering so as not to wake him suddenly, we were stunned by what we saw through the kitchen window. Dad, hardwired to help out, had let himself into my husband's shed. I think he might have been searching for his pre-accident self in there. He discovered instead cutting shears, a pruner and an axe, and he had gone busy, berserk in the garden with them.

Every single shrub and bush had been pruned vertically. Yes, right down the middle. In less than an hour he had destroyed every plant. He lay on the grass, arms and legs spread wide like he was doing a horizontal star jump. Untroubled by the rain that was falling, he slept like a baby with a wide, satisfied smile on his face.

Worst of all, he had cut the heads off the four giant sunflowers my children were growing for their hotly contested, annual tallest sunflower race. For months they had watered their individual sunflowers, massaged and whispered secrets to them, and even shared their sweet treats by pushing Maltesers and Milk Buttons into the earth close to the flowers' roots. The four much kissed, stroked and talked about, tenderly nurtured sunflowers had just reached seven feet tall when Dad cut them down to bald stubs just six inches high. And after he did that, he tossed their big, bright sunny heads over the fence into next door's garden.

It was a credit to my children that they wept about the demise of the treasured sunflowers on the lap of the man they knew had lopped them off, their beloved Granddad. One said at the time, through her tearful sniffles, 'Granddad can't help it that he's sick in the head,' as the other three rubbed his bald scalp in a futile effort to try and make it better.

18
Jelly Babies and Angels

I think my dad's accident, and how he left the house a man and returned a little boy, deeply traumatised my mother and sparked her breast cancer, which had been dormant for a decade, back into bright life. On the way into the hospital for her annual check-up, she saw a sign above the entrance that read 'Oncology Department'. 'What's Oncol?' she asked me. I didn't understand what she meant. 'What have you got if you suffer from Oncol?' she wanted to know. Mum had been a cancer patient for sixteen years and had just discovered the word 'oncology'. 'Cancer. It means when you've got cancer.' She was very disgruntled by that news and kept glancing back at the sign and muttering, 'Who do they think they're kidding? If it's cancer they should say so. Oncoooology, my arse!'

Mum's appointment was a quick in-and-out affair. A young doctor, who looked like she was on the run from the hospital crèche, played with her plaits and advised my mum to double up on the multivitamins from Tesco and said she'd see her again in a year. In the same week she got a chest infection and her attentive GP sent her for an X-ray. This revealed that her lungs resembled a dalmatian's coat: spotted all over with malignant lesions. Further investigations showed the cancer had spread to her liver and brain too.

When Mum heard the dreadful news that her brain was affected, she said, 'Oh well. At least that explains why I've been walking like a turkey.' It was as if the diagnosis accelerated her disease. Life went into fast-forward mode and her cancer was outpacing me, ravaging her faster than I could take care of her.

Whatever time I arrived, she would be in her dressing gown, propped upright in the corner of the sofa with her head tilted backwards. This pose was best to try and ease the pain caused by overnight swelling of the tumours in her brain. From that position she tried to manage my dad, who was at his most mischievous when she was too weak to chivvy him using touch, look or voice. Like a child who wanted to play, he would tug at her dressing-gown sleeve and beseech her to take a walk with him or come out into the garden or make him a sandwich to eat. For those last few months their marriage was an unbearable-to-watch union of the sick.

A Macmillan nurse was sent in by the GP, but she didn't last long enough in Mum's company even to finish the hot drink I made for her. Compassionate and friendly, the nurse, called Wendy, checked on all aspects of Mum's care and how it was progressing. Then she pulled half-a-dozen claim forms from her bag – was Mum claiming all the benefits she was entitled to?, the nurse wanted to know. My mum jumped up, the best she could in her weakened and light-headed state. Poor Nurse Wendy hadn't realised she was dealing with Ireland's proudest and most independent woman. One who was violently opposed to state handouts. 'I have never spent a penny I didn't earn myself and I'm not starting now I am on the way out!' declared my outraged mum before snatching the cup of tea back and bundling the poor woman out onto the street. After she'd slammed the door behind Nurse Wendy, my mum sat on the stairs and cried.

Dad was easier to help than Mum. He was a willing patient, and even when he wasn't, a handful of Jelly Babies could usually be traded for some cooperation. Mum was different: she was fiercely self-reliant and it was a constant battle to assist her with anything. When it came to her personal care, if we touched her she behaved as though she had been stung. Too frail to help herself and too proud to allow my sister and me to do it, she shocked us when she announced that she had booked herself into a cancer hospice for some respite care. It was a done deal. All she needed from me was a lift there and for Dad to be taken care of whilst she was away.

None of us knew on the morning she left home that it would be for the last time. On the way out the door, she turned back down the hall and into her bedroom to look at her favourite photograph of her and Dad together with all their children and grandchildren. She'd had the photo enlarged and fancy-framed and kept it in pride of place on her dressing table. It was the last thing she saw at night and the first thing she saw in the morning. That day she kissed it with her eyes closed as if she were pasting it into her memory. I asked her did she want me to wrap it and put it in her bag to bring with her. 'I'll come back to it,' she said, without conviction.

My mum's last days there, six in total, were very happy. One visiting time she was very excited and had urgent news to share. Words tumbled out as she told us she had seen angels playing trumpets in the ward during the night, and that they had thrown sweet-scented flower petals over a woman in the opposite bed. According to my mum, these angels were each eight feet tall, wearing white robes, and had enormous wings when they were extended but which were mostly triple-folded down by their sides. They had approached her too with their trumpets and petals but she had told them to clear off. To go and do whatever it was they had to do with the woman across the way because she was very sick and needed them – but no way should they include her in their carry-on. 'I told them I was only in here for respite,' she said, and after scanning my face she anxiously added, 'I was right to do that, wasn't I? I wouldn't dream of offending an angel, usually.' This account of heavenly visions was totally out of character for my down-to-earth, no-nonsense mum. Did she see angels? Or was it her diseased brain playing last-minute games with her?

The night before my mum died, we sat together on a bench in the hospice garden so she could have a feeble smoke. I noticed she had very little power in her lungs to draw the nicotine in and she had to prop her hand up by her elbow to steer the cigarette towards her lilac lips. We were not a touchy-feely combination, my mum and I. Close and tight, we meshed with words and looks, not hugs and kisses. That evening my right arm was extended across the back of the bench and I was surprised when she nestled and leant into my side. 'I don't want to die but I know I have to and it's close,' she told me suddenly. And when she spoke she sounded so uncharacteristically shy. A fountain of denial welled in my throat but she sensed it and shushed it with a feather-light press of her fingers on my arm. 'There was nobody as dear as my own mother to me ... and when she went I made myself ill. I don't want any of that nonsense, do you hear me?' Undercut by dread, I could only mew in reply. 'Look after them all and remember ...' She couldn't carry on, and I didn't want her to. For ten, maybe twenty seconds, we were welded together. In spirit, she had handed over to me and then we were separate again. I wanted her to live for ever.

The end came hours afterwards. It was swift and peaceful. Her death was a doze that turned into a sleep that turned into unconsciousness that turned into for ever. My brother did a motorway dash from the north-east and she held on just long enough to speak with him. Her last words were to him. 'See you tomorrow.' We all had a private moment with her, and she died softly surrounded by her three children who adored her.

My dad had been at the hospital earlier in the evening but couldn't comprehend what was happening. We explained over and again how sick she was, and close to death, which momentarily made him very upset. Then he would forget and try to rouse her asking, 'What's for dinner tonight, Annie?' Dad became exhausted and overwrought and my sister, George and I took the difficult decision to send him home and allow him to sleep, even though we knew her time was very near.

Losing Mum felt like a huge hole had been blown through the centre of my body. I didn't dare to be me because I was frightened of life and everything about it without her backing me up. My grief was a physical pain that locked me out of the wider world.

It was about three months after she died when I took stock of myself in the bathroom mirror. I saw a wide white stripe down the centre of my head. The white roots of my hair.

Illness and bereavement had written all over my face and body. My mum was gone, my dad was brain-damaged and fully dependent on me and I was recovering from cancer. But even though I had a jelly belly, grey hair and worry wrinkles – I was above ground and able to make peace with my imperfect self. My grey hair represented a new beginning.

19

Lollipop Feet

Bereaved and still recovering from leukaemia, I became my dad's full-time carer overnight. My brother and sister sighed with relief, and my husband? Well, he just sighed. I was appalled by my runaway life. Could I cope ? The worry about what taking responsibility for my severely brain-damaged dad would do to my own family life and health kept me awake at night. I tried to count sheep to get back to sleep but all I could count was calamities.

We moved house to give him space and comfort at ground-floor level. His room turned out to be the heart of the house. Its door was open day and night and the children spent hours in there, either playing with him or by themselves close to him when he was napping during the day. One afternoon as he slept they 'pimped' his Zimmer frame with ribbons and charms and teddies and balloons. I laughed hard when I saw it. Their sweet, simple action somehow lightened my load, and I believed for the first time that I could and would manage. I just needed to pimp my attitude and all would be well.

My husband shamed me with the kindness and patience he showed his father-in-law. 'It's an honour to help such a lovely man,' he repeated over and again when I thanked him for being jollier than I could always manage. There were times when I was too tired or too frazzled to be nice and I remember them with shame. Perversely, the nicer George was to my dad, the worse I felt. He made so much effort, and my persistent worry was that me and my crisis-heavy family had spoiled the potentially lovely life George could have had elsewhere. There was no arguing that he would have had truckloads less trouble if he hadn't married me, Cancer Lil, and into my tumour-ridden family.

Being a carer meant that overnight I became invisible to the wider world. At social gatherings I would see the disappearing backs of the employed, the important and the interesting. When they heard I was a carer, they immediately judged me too dull to talk to. I did care about that, but refused to show it, and consoled myself with Dad's disabled parking badge. I may not have been popular at parties, but I could park with the bonnet of my car touching the entrance of John Lewis and Marks and Spencer.

Dad's health was fragile, and he frequently had what I called 'seven dwarf' days when he was dizzy or sleepy or grumpy and would refuse to get out of the car when we went shopping together. Then I would reluctantly leave him in the front passenger seat to snooze. This never worked well. Sick or tired, he just couldn't resist fiddling with the car controls. Once, after a supermarket trolley dash, I huffed and puffed and perspired back to the car park to find another car in the space where I had parked mine. Dad had released the handbrake and the car had rolled back to the space behind, which was thankfully next to a brick wall that stopped the driverless car travelling any further.

I can't remember if anyone told me, or if being of Irish descent I just always knew, that the seventh son of a seventh son was born with the gift of healing through the laying on of his hands. Dad was a fully dependent man-child and as a family we were desperate and impatient for improvement in his condition. Finbarr Nolan, the seventh son of a seventh son, and a well-known healer, was our next port of call for a cure. He had a huge following in Ireland and did regular healing tours overseas. His laying on of hands began when he was aged just two.

Dad and I met with Finbarr in a hotel lounge near Paddington Station. Dad had no clue where he was but kept saying, 'Are we going to play bingo, Anna May? I feel lucky today.' We were invited to sit in a huge inward-facing circle and wait for Finbarr to arrive. The scarred, the lame and the sorely afflicted made up the silent ring. And hundreds more of them formed a queue that snaked through the hotel and out into the street beyond. Without fanfare, Finbarr entered the room, carrying a suitcase. I thought that must be his bag of healing tricks, but it transpired to be his toothbrush and underwear as he had come straight from the airport. A bright and confident presence, Finbarr went straight into the money talk. 'You can pay me with money or you can pay me with a smile!' he said, which shut up the cynic part in me. 'I have a gift and I don't sell it for money, but I have to live too, and if you offer me a donation I won't refuse it. You'll find a collection plate by the exit door over there. Now down to the real business.' Then Finbarr stepped inside the circle and led a group prayer before approaching every person individually and asking them what their ailment was and whether he might lay his hands on their affected parts. My dad was watching what was going on and chortling away at what he saw. 'Who's the quare fella?' he wanted to know. 'Is he the bingo caller?'

When it came to our turn I explained to Finbarr that my dad was there for healing and that his name was Andy. Standing in front of us, his presence seemed to cancel out all the other people and voices in the room. 'Andy, thank you for coming today. I am Finbarr Nolan the seventh son of a seventh son from Cavan, and if you give me permission I will try to help you feel better today.' Finbarr smiled down at Dad. 'And what is the nature of your illness?'

Dad replied in a crystal clear and indignant voice, 'There's nothing at all wrong with me,' and waving his arm at the seated circle added, 'It's these poor feckers you should be worried about.' I looked at Finbarr and tapped my own skull, mouthing 'Brain damage – it's his head.' Finbarr nodded and lowered both his hands down onto Dad's bald head. He met no resistance. Dad closed his eyes as soon as Finbarr made contact and sat completely still, clearly liking his touch. The encounter lasted less than two minutes in total. As we left I made a donation to the collection dish by the door and had to wrestle Dad away because he was trying to help himself to some cash out of it.

The weeks after Dad had visited Finbarr were some of the best we had with him after the accident. He seemed to try harder and there were several small but significant improvements. He put his jumpers on the right way around and remembered the dog's name and stopped putting his cutlery and crockery into the dustbin after every meal.

Dad was dysphasic and couldn't match his words to his thoughts. If it wasn't so tragic, dysphasia has the makings of a side-splitting parlour game. For example, he called our GP a

Dalek, his sister a giraffe and the dog a sausage. There was a howler in every sentence he spoke, and after a while you could usually discern the thread of a connection between his choice and the correct word. A lifelong Labour supporter, Dad shouted the word 'Prick!' every time David Mellor's face appeared on his TV screen or in a newspaper. Whether this was attributable to his condition or rooted in his long-standing political beliefs, I couldn't be sure.

Ever keen to help around the house, Dad watered my plants with undiluted bleach and used a hammer to knock out a light bulb that wasn't working from a table lamp. Once he constructed a neat pyramid of sticks, paper and coal on the end of his bed. We were lucky to discover his fire just before he set light to it. Unusually for him, he got quite sulky when I said I wouldn't allow him to set fire to his bed and possibly the entire house. He called me 'a right miserable old banana' and said he'd only done it because his feet were 'lollipops' in bed at night.

The general hierarchy of care was that the children shadowed Granddad, I watched over all of them, and when George came home from work, he took care of me with a cup of tea and time to listen. We were a mini care-giving corporation.

One bright summer morning my dad soiled his bed in the early hours, and then attempted a solo clean-up job. Using the washing-up cloth and tea towels. In his brain-damaged confusion he had managed to get excrement in his eyes, mouth, nostrils and ears. He'd daubed everything he'd touched. When I saw the mess, and Dad smiling and drinking tea in the middle of it all, I wanted to murder him. The children would be up for school at any moment and I didn't want them to see anything of their Granddad's accidental dirty protest.

George was hot on my heels and like Dad, but in a different

way, he had it covered. He calmly called work to explain he would be coming in late that morning and set about running a bath for Dad and scrubbing and sterilising the house for several hours to restore order. All the time he worked he chatted and laughed with my freshly dipped dad.

In his usual jumbled way, Dad kept asking why George was at home cleaning when he should have been at work. After I'd dropped the children to school I came home and every door and window in the house was open to try and disperse the smell, but it hadn't worked. I headed for the kitchen and closed the door and put my forehead down on the kitchen table and sobbed as I listened to my father and husband, both of them talking absolute nonsense and enjoying it. Shuffling in on his Zimmer frame to join me, Dad caught my moment of abject misery. With some difficulty he wobbled down to kiss me on the back of the head and then levered himself back up, using his hand on my head to push himself off. Without realising he was even doing it, he pressed my face with force into the table. I thought he'd broken my nose. 'Tired looking you are, Anna May. More care taking here wanted so there is. Always go, go, go, yes.' It was the first almost coherent sentence he'd said from start to finish in nearly a year. Head crooked to one side, he examined my face with gentle concern all over his and pointed at my red nose. The lovely man had absolutely no idea that he was the cause of my exhaustion, distress and nose pain. I was glad about that. My dad was essentially 'missing in action'. There but not there. His dirty protest was testing, but little did we know it was pure Disney compared to what happened next . . .

You can rely on me in a crisis. Rely on me to be the scream-ing, hysterical panicker. Only once have I defied the odds and stayed calm in the face of shocking provocation. It began as a typical weekday evening for me . . .

It was just a couple of weeks after Dad's early morning poo party and around eight in the evening. The children were bathed and in bed and Dad was chest-deep in a bubbly bath and enjoying his nightly soak. It was close to his bedtime and I was letting him linger a bit as I sorted laundry in the upstairs hall. I could hear him splashing about through the open bathroom door. Laundry all put away, I took his warm towel from the hall radiator and stepped into the bathroom to heave him out of the water. What I saw in there made the room pitch from side to side. The soap bubbles had flattened out and Dad appeared to be sitting in a bathful of blood. Several floating clots, like jagged crimson water-lilies, were bobbing around him, and a few had even stuck to his skin like livery leeches.

Head down, he was scooping up handfuls of water and bringing it to his face to look more closely at it. He was aware that something he couldn't articulate was very wrong. He turned his face to me and I could see blood pouring from his nostrils, accompanied by clots that made him snort and landed in the red water with a heavy plop. His eyes were two huge question marks. 'Lookit, I've got a mouse!' Dad said and he laughed. I think he meant a moustache, referring to the blood clots clinging to his top lip.

Doctors quickly established that Dad had a massive head and neck tumour. Radical surgery was Dad's only option, but his ear, nose and throat surgeon had probing questions to ask about the value of such a complicated and life-threatening procedure. He didn't try to spare our feelings and was brutally frank. Was Dad worth the effort ? Without any intervention the surgeon judged that Dad would die within days of a fatal haemorrhage because the tumour was growing dangerously close to a main artery and was en route to rupture it fatally.

My brother and sister and I were in complete agreement about what we wanted the doctor to do. We were unashamed miracle-seekers and we wanted Dad to have a chance at least. Mum was dead and he was all we had. To outsiders he was diminished and dependent, but to all of us, although he was not perfect, he was all the more precious for that. We pleaded with the surgery team to take him to the operating theatre. I went to the hospital chapel to pray for Dad, and found his surgeon already in there kneeling close to the altar. I am certain we both had the same person on our minds that morning.

My husband, sister and I sat vigil in the intensive care waiting room after Dad's surgery. There had been complications and we were warned to prepare for a shock. 'There is extensive disfigurement to his face. You may not recognise him immediately. My advice is to look at his hands first, then move your eyes to his face,' said the nurse in a calm voice. After all the anxiety and waiting, you would think that my sister and I would have run to our dad's bedside without caring what he looked like. We didn't. We were cowards and bailed. We sent George in ahead. An advance party of one.

'He's OK, really. Have you ever seen those old Hammer horror films?' he began unhelpfully when he stepped back out of the room to where we waited, terror-struck, outside. We had been listening at the door for a gasp of shock or the sound of him keeling over because the sight of Dad was so gruesome. There was none of that. What we heard George say was, 'Hey there, Granddad! Welcome back.'

My dad was a crash-test dummy, trailing tubes and pipes and a wee bag, and we were struck dumb by the sight of what we had begged the doctors to do to him. A trio of guilt, we just stood and stared at his helpless body. With perfect timing and immense effort, he stiffly moved his right hand away from his torso in an incy-wincy-spider movement, got it just a few inches across the white sheet and painstakingly rolled it over and stuck up one thumb. He was telling us all he was good. Three-quarters dead already, but good. That first night in intensive care we asked the doctor what Dad's chance of survival was out of ten. 'Nought and a half,' he said grimly.

The tennis-ball-sized tumour they removed needed its own suitcase. It did a lot of travelling. Because the histology was inconclusive, it went to various specialist centres around the UK and was even prepared for dispatch to Australia, where an international tumour panel was convening in the hope that they might declare exactly what sort of cancerous mass it was. If the Australian panel couldn't categorise it – and the tumour was declared as an original – it could even have been named after Dad. The Mangan Tumour. What a poxy tribute to two afflicted generations that would have been.

Initially doctors said the tumour could possibly be a non-malignant growth, and that made my sister and I laugh so much we had to visit the ladies to pee, blow our noses and wipe our eyes to deal with a lot of mirth-induced mucous. If the tumour had a mouth it would have laughed along with us. Cancer was stalking us and, in Dad's racing parlance, the odds of it being non-malignant were millions to one.

It turned out to be an extremely rare T-cell non-Hodgkin's lymphoma and they threw everything at it: surgery, chemotherapy and radiotherapy. Chemotherapy and radiotherapy were to follow surgery, and the hospital took a 'treat and street' approach to administering chemotherapy. It was an in-and-out arrangement, no overnight stays, like a day spa with PICC lines and drip stands. Very economical for the NHS Trust, and the arrangement can work, if you are not elderly and already brain-damaged and clinging to life by a thread.

I was jubilant when he survived the chemotherapy and made it to radiotherapy. Just three short weeks' worth of that and he would belong to us again and not the hospital. The final hurdle, so I thought. 'Tiredness will be the most worrying side effect,' said some white-coated professional. After chemotherapy-induced septicaemia, pneumonia, double incontinence, vomiting and kidney and liver damage – just good old tiredness as a side effect was thrilling news and worthy of a celebration with party poppers.

Only it wasn't just tiredness. He checked out on us. The man became a zombie. For three months he slept in his bed in the front sitting room for twenty hours out of every twenty-four, rousing only for bodily functions.

So we shifted the axis of the house as much as possible so that almost everything happened in Dad's room. We brought life to him, even though he was asleep in bed. I chopped vegetables, made phone calls, ironed and sorted laundry next to his bed. The children read, played, dressed for school in there, and watched their afternoon programmes on his TV. We all ate dinner in there off our laps, hoping the smell of hot savoury food would get his taste buds going. I bought a huge cream cake every day and left it in his line of sight in case he opened his eyes, certain that a big oily slab of sweetness would prompt him to sit up and tuck in. It didn't. We hoped that our daily activities might rev him back into consciousness. When friends came we would sit chatting, laughing and drinking wine in his room. If our visitors were disturbed or surprised by the snoring, sometimes farting bundle in the bed, they never said so.

Those catatonic post-radiotherapy months were the beginning of his slow end. I begged the GP to investigate further so she sent in a psychiatrist to assess Dad in case his sleeping sickness was a form of depression. The psychiatrist, who did a rare home visit, was on fast-forward. 'Now leave this to me!' he demanded as he dashed into Dad's room, even though I had done or said nothing to suggest I wouldn't.

The psychiatrist used Dad's bony shoulders as handles, dragged him into a sitting position on the mattress and tried to shake him awake. That didn't ever work. I knew, because I tried it myself several times a day, only a whole lot more gently.

The psychiatrist pressed on, shouting, 'Did you have a good relationship with your mother?' and 'Who is the Prime Minister?' into Dad's slack, lemon-coloured face. He got no answers, of course, but persisted with, 'What's your earliest memory?' and 'Are you sexually active?' before finally giving up and letting Dad drop back onto the pillow. 'So, in your expert professional opinion, is he depressed?' I asked, and yes, I admit I was being a bit facetious.

'No' replied the psychiatrist, 'but you *must* be. What a life looking after him!'

A geriatrician came to visit Dad, too, and we consulted another oncologist for a second opinion on his cancer diagnosis and treatment. Their final general consensus was that the radiotherapy to Dad's head had adversely affected the part of his brain that controlled his sleep patterns. His sleep sensor had been zapped to destruction point and there was no cure for his catatonic state. He was moved to hospital, too severely ill and dependent to be cared for at home. I felt I had failed him.

In a bed that wasn't his own, Dad drifted away from this life under siege from heart failure and complications from his cancer treatment without ever enjoying life again. It was a peaceful, sleep-steeped death.

But that didn't mean I got a clean getaway from mourning. Instead, guilt took the place of grief, and leapt up and grabbed me by the throat. For months after he died I relived every conversation we had, every wash I gave him, each meal I cooked him, every egg I scrambled, the drug doses I doled out several times a day. I wondered if I could have or should have done better. Being a carer is the loneliest job in the world.

After Dad's funeral, my sister didn't want to walk away from his graveside. I can still see her swaying in the lightest wind at his graveside, tear-streaked and loose-necked. She tried to throw a white rose on top of his coffin as it was lowered into the grave, but she missed and it fell at her feet. I didn't know who to cry for that day.

Sinking deeper and deeper into the wet clay, she stared down into the burial plot and became highly distressed. She was convinced that our parents had been laid to rest facing in opposite directions, head to toe, and this appalled her. The undertakers and gravediggers at first did their polite best to reassure her that all was as it should be, but she became tearful and insistent and demanded that they prove their claims by raising Dad's coffin back up and digging down further to expose Mum's. Her face was tight, shiny with perspiration and bloodless – like the colour of milk. Beneath her bulky coat her knees were knocking with weakness and the scars from her surgery were livid and pulsing with pain. Cancer hadn't finished its malevolent work when it took my dad – it had already staked its claim on my 31-year-old sister, too.

20
Apple Therapy

If I was granted three wishes, like in all the best fairytales, I would use them for the promise that my three daughters will be spared a cancer diagnosis. Their great-grandmother, grandmother, great-aunts, mother and aunt have been dogged by the disease and, although there have been big changes over the decades in how the cancer is found and treated, the fear is timeless, and I don't want them to have to know it.

Cancer crept up on my nan and her daughters. For my sister and me it was different. We went looking for it in annual screening appointments. Our timebomb breasts gave us an annual jolly day out lunching and shopping near the Marsden Hospital – until the year radiologists found something suspicious on Julie's mammogram. She was thirty-one. A lumpectomy followed, and another one after that, and then she got the all-clear. But the words brought no joy. 'All clear', when delivered by a doctor to anyone in my family, translates into 'Hahaha! But not for long.'

Like Mum, she had bilateral breast cancer, and her only treatment option was a double mastectomy, but with reconstruction. Mum's falsies were foam bra inserts. She was never keen on wearing them, partly because they were scratchy against her scarred skin but mostly because they would work their way out of her bra and up towards her collarbone within the hour after she'd stuffed them into place. 'No hot-stone therapy or Reiki for Mum, was there?' Julie remarked sadly after visiting a complementary treatment centre for cancer patients.

On the morning of my sister's surgery, I crossed London at 4.30am to be with her at the hospital before she went into the operating theatre. The roads were deserted and I did the ten-mile journey without my foot ever touching the brakes. I drove into the sunrise, which was calming. When I got there Julie was already sat up in bed and strobing anxiety. She told me that, during the night, the air-conditioning vent in the ceiling had delivered comforting messages to her from our late mother, and she asked me if I thought she was going mad. It was the first time I had ever heard her say something that flaky. Had stress and sedatives sent her temporarily loopy? Or did that vent really send a loving message from my mum? I feared she had cracked under all the strain and I was about to join her. I was busy putting on a bright face but it struck me that morning that there are a lot of ways you can lose someone.

'They're not there!' Julie wailed before I had stepped through the door of her room the day after her surgery. She was staring down at her chest and shaking her head in disbelief. I rushed to her side and hugged her and said, 'They had to go, Julie, they were diseased ... you know that.' She tried to push me away but was too weak, so instead she shouted back at me as best she could with a low anaesthetic rasp. It's the one and only time I have ever heard her raise her voice. 'I know that, you silly cow, I'm a cancer patient not a psychiatric patient. I'm talking about the implants! Where the *fuck* are they?'

I wanted to jolly her along and talk her into a good mood but I took a long hard look at her chest and there was no denying she was right. With the outer bandages removed, which we had assumed were compressing the implants, there was very little to see. In fact, if I had been forced to describe the breast area I was staring at open-mouthed, I would have said flat, at best, and concave at worst.

I waved her back through the rubber swing doors to the operating theatre for her second major operation in three days. The surgeons had to revisit and rebuild. The last thing Julie said to me as she was wheeled in theatre was, 'How's Dad? Send him my love and tell him I'll see him soon.' It's a good job she was heavily medicated or she would instantly have spotted my smile was fake. I had a secret I was keeping from her. On the day of her second surgery, our dad had taken a turn for the worse and was fighting for his life in another hospital across London. I was darting between the two of them, willing them to get better and praying that they would see one another at least one time more.

Julie's new breasts were uglier than the old ones for sure. She had previously been the proud owner of a 36DD embonpoint – but the plastic ones were much more splendid because they were cancer-free. I photographed her breasts for posterity the night before her surgery, a suggestion that came from the plastic surgeon who was doing the reconstruction. It seemed a bit bonkers at the time. Now Julie says that, although she doesn't ever look at those photos, she's glad they are hers to ignore. We used a Polaroid camera. It was a silent photo session. Afterwards I asked Julie if she would miss her breasts, even though they were diseased. 'No,' she answered sadly. 'I've kind of gone off them now.'

Four days after Julie's second surgery, Dad's doctor told me he had less than 24 hours to live. My brother drove down from the north-east, and the big dilemma was whether to tell Julie whilst she was in hospital and could do nothing about it, or wait until we had to tell her after the worst had actually happened.

With her words from a few days before – 'Silly cow, I'm not a psychiatric patient!' – ringing in my ears, I decided to tell her what was going on. Or some of it. What I didn't tell her was that Dad asked for her every time he floated back into con-sciousness. I had told him she was having a lovely holiday in America. I had to lie. He would certainly have died sooner, from worry, if he had understood she was in hospital at the same time he was, and having life-saving surgery.

Julie made her choice instantly. Her discharge was accompa-nied by grim warnings about what she was doing and its possible impact on her recovery. Julie arrived at the hospital an hour after Dad died.

Something else worse always rolled in. We coined a family saying at that time. It was: 'Don't waste today worrying because tomorrow will be even worse.' And of course it was.

I was offered a free thirty-minute consultation with a grief counsellor by the hospice where Mum died. I'd just heard that my leukaemia was back for the second time and was furious with myself and my body for being such a pushover. For being so easy to defeat. I was more than ready to talk. No coaxing was needed.

'My mum died, my dad had brain damage and I looked after him and then he got cancer and died, my sister got cancer at thirty-one and I've got leukaemia again and I have four—'

'Whoa, whoa.' The young counsellor stopped me mid-flow and abruptly left the room. He was quickly replaced by another man, older, who apologised that his inexperienced colleague had been 'overwhelmed' by my account. 'It's not an account. It's my life,' I wailed. I repeated my saga of death and illness and despair and the counsellor explained that, in emotional terms, my problem was that I was trying to eat the whole apple at once. I needed to deconstruct events and cope with them singly and not lump them together, was his advice.

His comment was baffling to me but did remind me that my nan and all her sons and daughters and my dad and all his family did something with apples that I have seen few other people do. They ate every bit of them – including the core and the stalk – until they were completely gone. Because they had to scale walls, climb trees, run miles and dodge the Garda even to get an apple when they were young, once they had one in their grasp they wouldn't leave a single morsel of it uneaten. The apple memory energised me. I suddenly felt a huge charge of affection for and from them all and left the counsellor's office with the realisation that life was like that, too. If you were lucky enough to have it, enjoy every last bit of it.

Second time around in hospital, having my chemotherapy in an isolation unit, I slept a lot, and was having a recurring dream about my dad. Even though he didn't die alone and my brother

272

was there, I felt constantly guilty that I hadn't been with him at the end.

In my dream it is deep night and I wake up, suddenly certain that my dad has come home. I can hear him outside. He is back and working in the garden! I recognise that familiar sure and steady sound of his spade turning the earth. I rush downstairs and peer through the patio doors trying to find him in the unlit garden. And there he is. Wearing his old checked sports jacket, the one with patched elbows, and his tweed cap crooked on his head. Glowing in the darkness I can see a roll-up hanging from the side of his mouth. A well-read copy of the *Sporting Life* is jammed, folded, into his jacket pocket. He is bent over, tending a flower-bed. One he planted the year before.

My sad heart soars to see him again and I rush at the doors, fumbling with them, desperate to throw them open. I keep my eyes on him, not the door locks, because I am so fearful he will disappear if I look away. But he sees me and stops me with a hand gesture that means 'Wait', then approaches the doors. Dad places his big, square-palmed hand flat against the glass. I raise my hand, yellow and purple from the hospital chemotherapy cannulas, to meet his. We stand there, him in the grainy moonlight smiling, me sobbing and searching his face for something, I don't know what. We are together, but separate in the blue dark, until he slides his hand down and away from the glass and goes back to his work. I can see he is keeping well because the back of his neck is plump and his shoulders are straight. He part turns and gently waves me away. Silently he is telling me to go back to my family. Using no words, he has explained that he is happy where he is, doing what he is doing, and that I should be too. It is the first time his kind hands have ever refused me, but I know he is right.

There was no reason for me to feel guilty. My brother, his beloved son, had sat by Dad's hospital bed and held his hand on the night he made his peaceful way to rejoin his wife. I pictured him restored and back linking arms with her – and there was great beauty for me in the certainty that they are reunited.

It was a moment of clarity and everything changed after it. There was a generation of women missing from my life and my children's so I had to be more. I had to be brave and I had to be grateful. Anything else would have been a travesty and allowed cancer to be the winner. My viewpoint on life switched instantly from being black and white to being in full colour again. Just as he had so often in life, in death my dad had rescued me.

When they were all alive I was Mum's writer: letters, bills, Christmas, Easter and St Patrick's Day cards and Mass and sympathy cards. If she was sending money to a niece or nephew for their birthday, I would write the card and she would write her signature on the banknote she was enclosing. Aunt Peggy would often sit at the far end of the table blowing cigarette smoke over my efforts. She was clearly moved and impressed by my penmanship. 'Isn't she grand for the writing? Fast and everything,' she murmured to my mum. Peggy's soft, tired eyes swelled with tears of pride as she slowly traced her slender fingers on the tablecloth, practising her own signature. Even now Mum is gone, I feel like I am still her writer.

My lost generation smoked, danced, gambled and loved and loathed weak and angry men. Not all to be recommended but, oh, how they talked and laughed and lived with an avalanche of love and generosity for their children and nieces and nephews. Spectacularly flawed is how I measure them, and they were all the more special for that.

Apple Therapy

Combined, they are in the curl of my hair, the width of my hips and they each add a distinct note to my laughter. To the bitter end they were shot through with kindness and fun. Their spirits are my jumbly inheritance.

Acknowledgements

This book wouldn't exist without the stellar skills of my three graces: agent Judith Murray, editor Elise Dillsworth and my dear sister, Julie.

To all the kind people who gave me tea and chats about their experiences: Paddy and Mary Bates, The Bergins – Bridget, Dan Jnr, Dan Snr and Marjorie, Mary and Frank Gill, Kathleen Brennan, Paddy Hickey, Joanne Wade, Ros McHugh, John Spillane, Dave O'Grady, Gary and Moya Mangan, Eileen and Nora Nagle and Linda Conway. You made me laugh and cry with your memories, and helped me to trust my own. Thank you.

Robert, Amy, May and Roisin – I love you most in all the world.